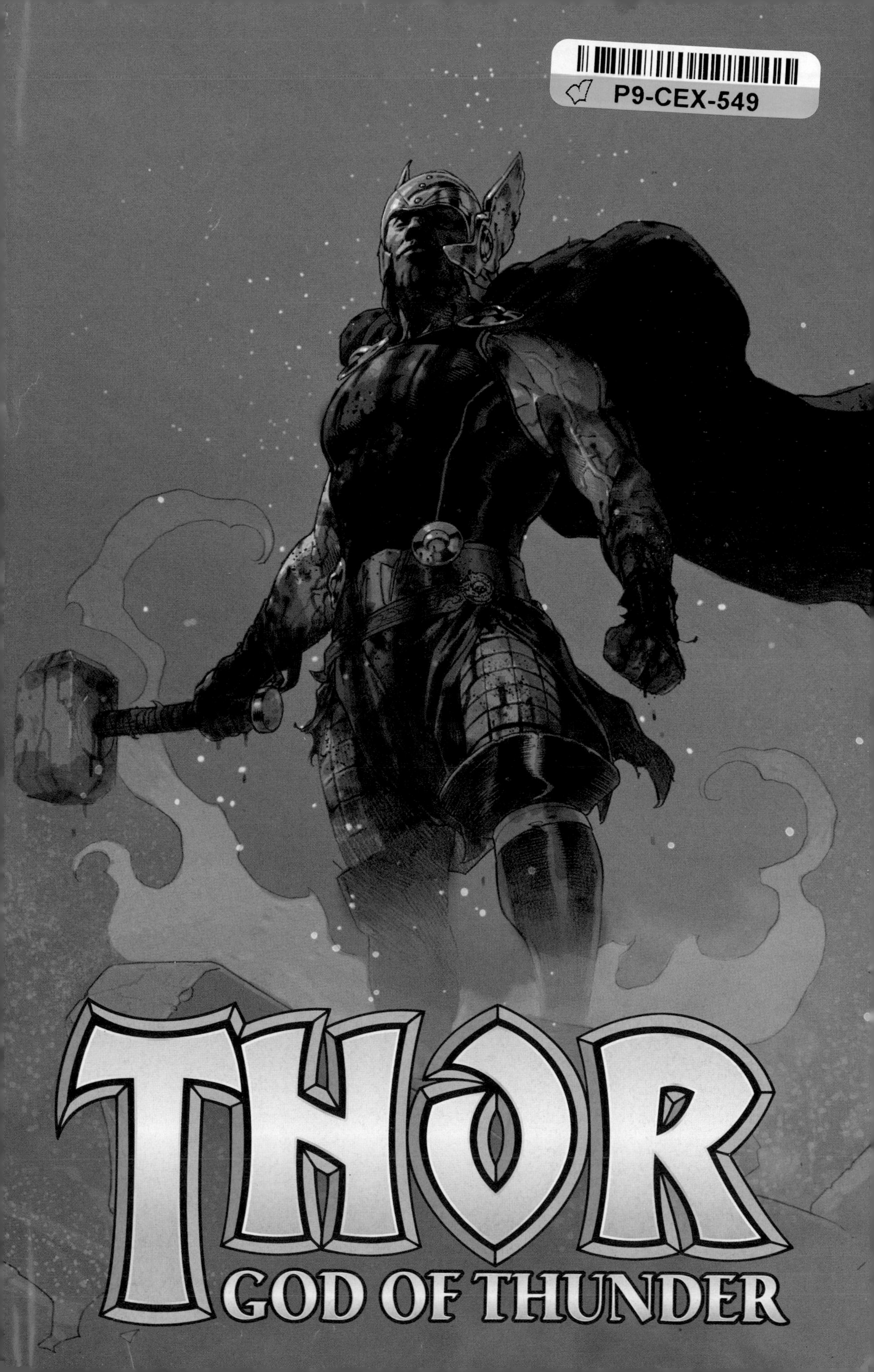
THOR
GOD OF THUNDER

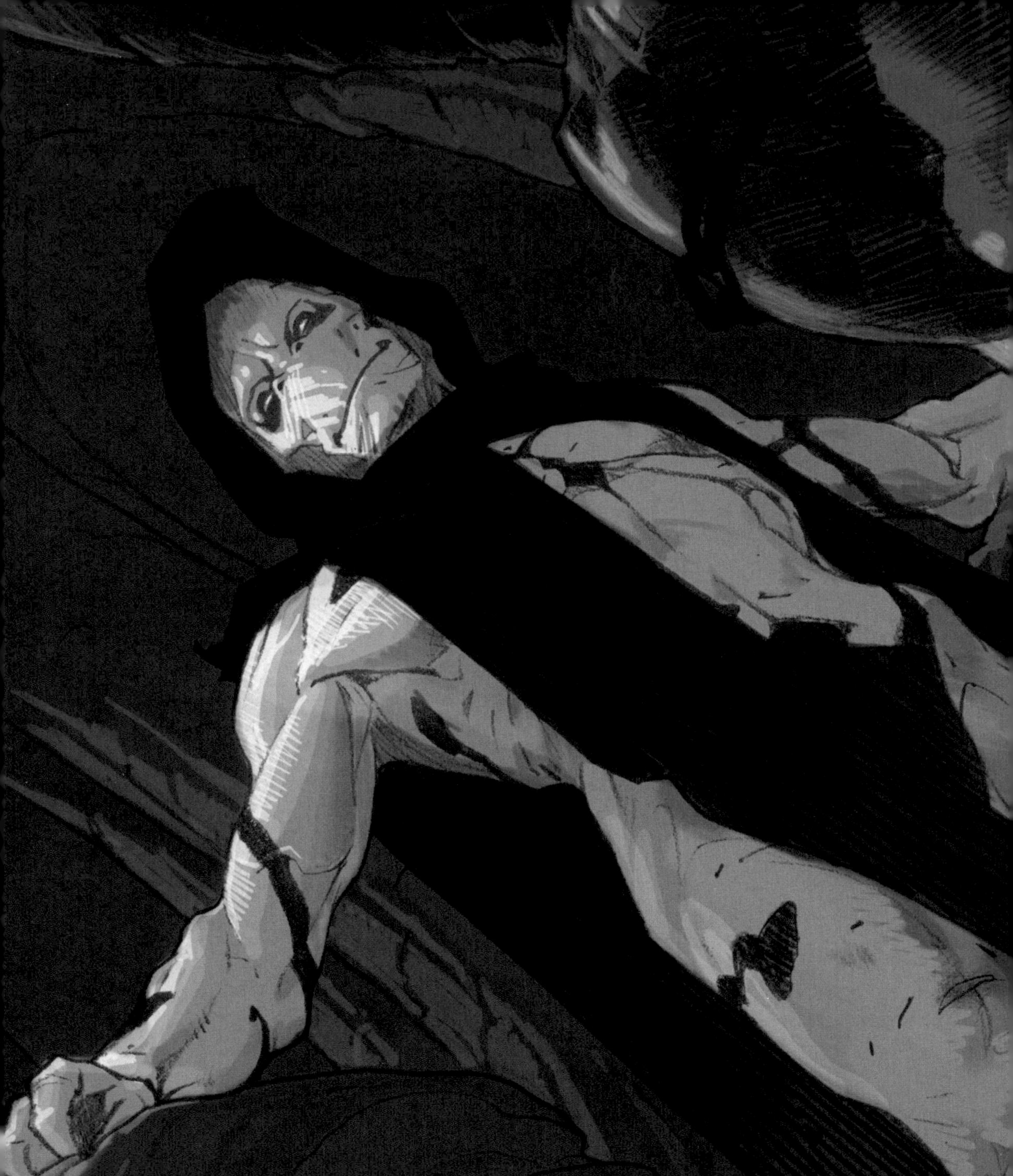

Collection Editor: **Jennifer Grünwald**

Assistant Editors: **Alex Starbuck & Nelson Ribeiro**

Editor, Special Projects: **Mark D. Beazley**

Senior Editor, Special Projects: **Jeff Youngquist**

SVP of Print & Digital Publishing Sales: **David Gabriel**

Book Design: **Jeff Powell**

Editor in Chief: **Axel Alonso**

Chief Creative Officer: **Joe Quesada**

Publisher: **Dan Buckley**

Executive Producer: **Alan Fine**

THOR: GOD OF THUNDER VOL. 1 — THE GOD BUTCHER. Contains material originally published in magazine form as THOR: GOD OF THUNDER #1-5. First printing 2014. ISBN# 978-0-7851-6697-9. Published by MARVEL WORLDWIDE, INC., a subsidiary of MARVEL ENTERTAINMENT, LLC. OFFICE OF PUBLICATION: 135 West 50th Street, New York, NY 10020.

Printed in the U.S.A. ALAN FINE, EVP - Office of the President, Marvel Worldwide, Inc. and EVP & CMO Marvel Characters B.V.; DAN BUCKLEY, Publisher & President - Print, Animation & Digital Divisions; JOE QUESADA, Chief Creative Officer; TOM BREVOORT, SVP of Publishing; DAVID BOGART, SVP of Operations & Procurement, Publishing; C.B. CEBULSKI, SVP of Creator & Content Development; DAVID GABRIEL, SVP of Print & Digital Publishing Sales; JIM O'KEEFE, VP of Operations & Logistics; DAN CARR, Executive Director of Publishing Technology; SUSAN CRESPI, Editorial Operations Manager; ALEX MORALES, Publishing Operations Manager; STAN LEE, Chairman Emeritus. For information regarding advertising in Marvel Comics or on Marvel.com, please contact Niza Disla, Director of Marvel Partnerships, at ndisla@marvel.com. For Marvel subscription inquiries, please call 800-217-9158. **Manufactured between 11/22/2013 and 12/30/2013 by R.R. DONNELLEY, INC., SALEM, VA, USA.**

10 9 8 7 6 5 4 3 2 1

THOR
GOD OF THUNDER

THE GOD BUTCHER

WRITER
JASON AARON

ARTIST
ESAD RIBIC

COLOR ARTISTS
DEAN WHITE (#1) **& IVE SVORCINA** (#2-5)

LETTERER
VC'S JOE SABINO

COVER ART
ESAD RIBIC

ASSISTANT EDITOR
JAKE THOMAS

EDITOR
LAUREN SANKOVITCH

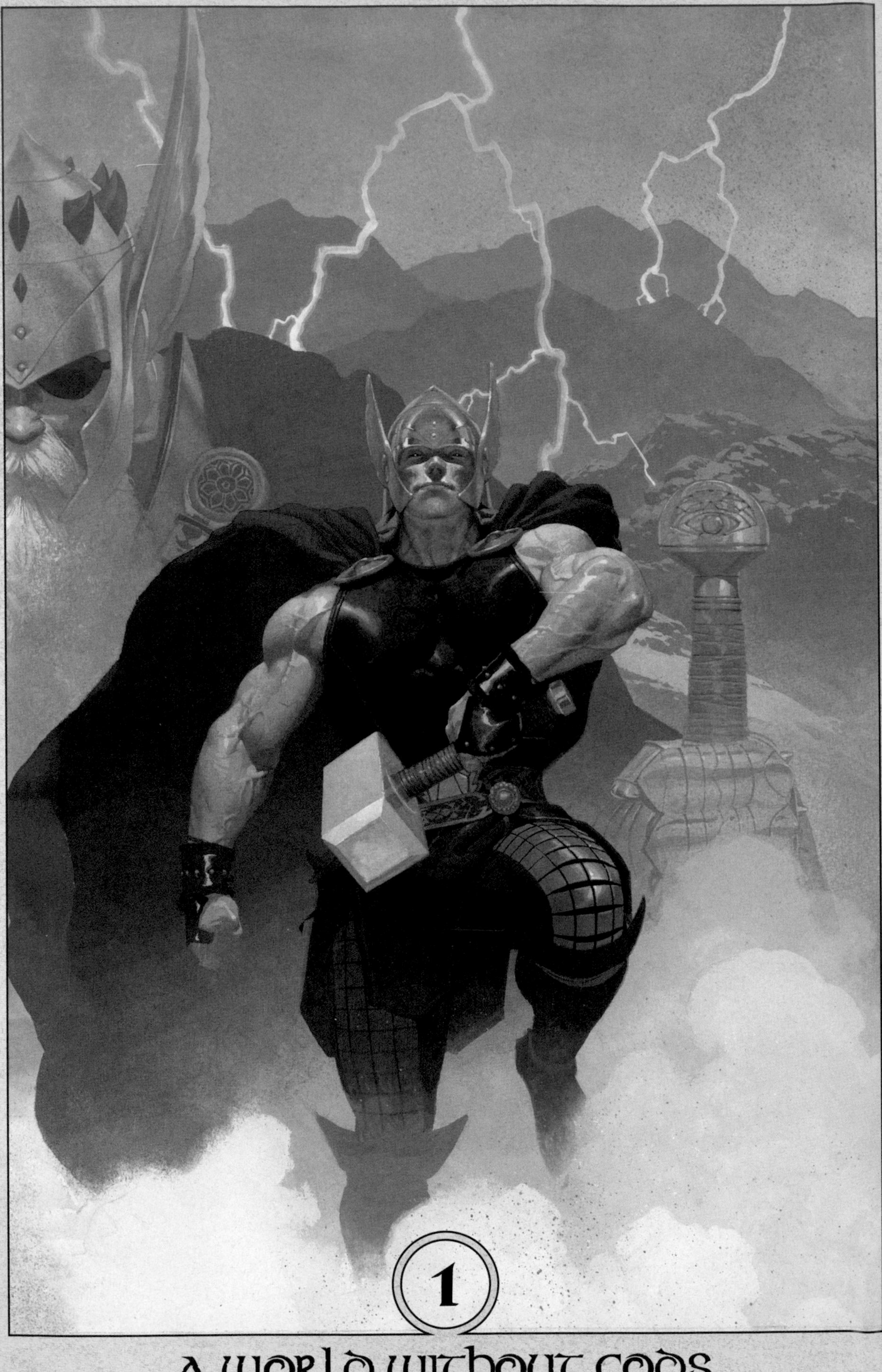

A WORLD WITHOUT GODS

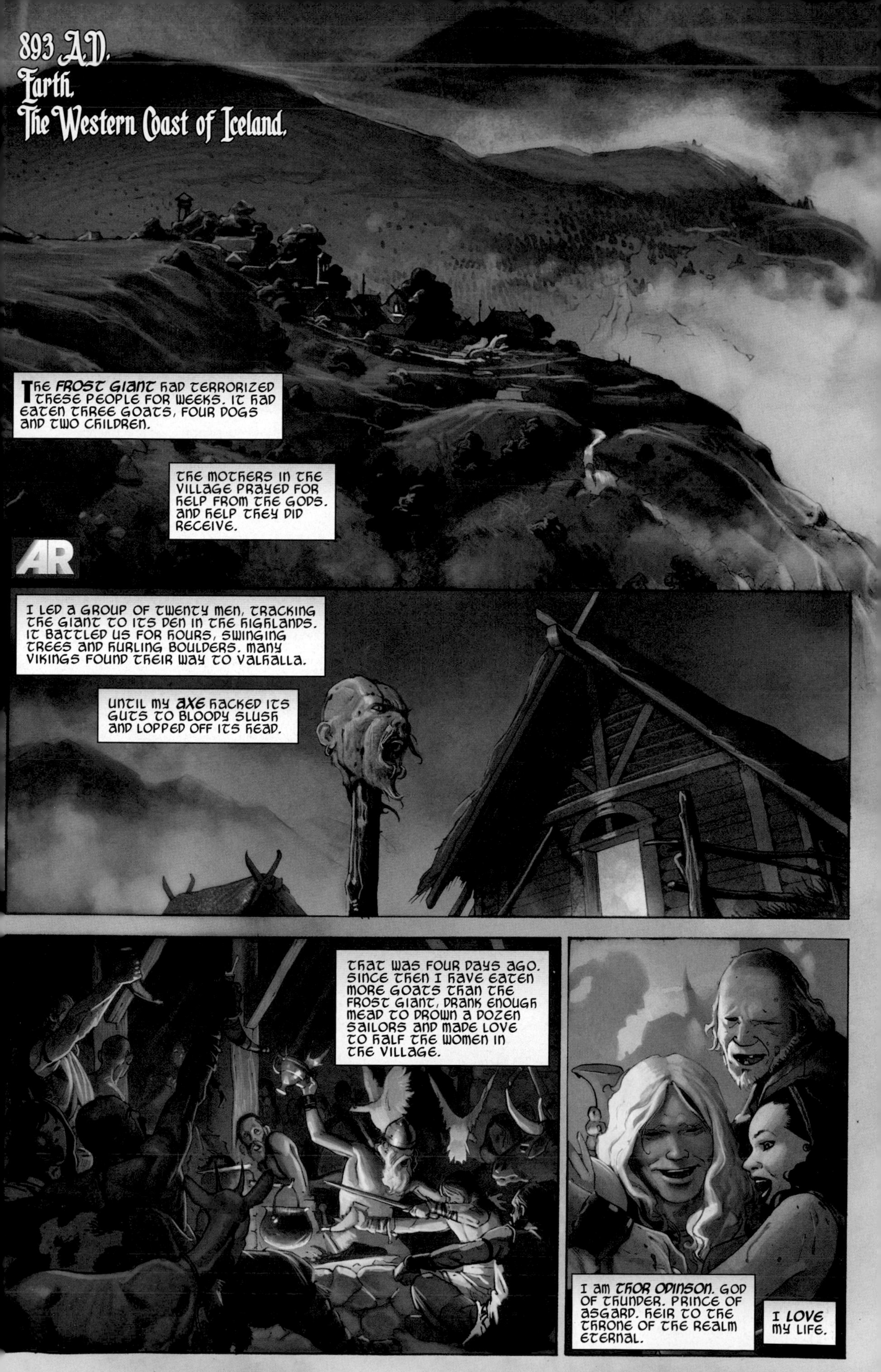
893 A.D.
Earth.
The Western Coast of Iceland.
THE FROST GIANT HAD TERRORIZED THESE PEOPLE FOR WEEKS. IT HAD EATEN THREE GOATS, FOUR DOGS AND TWO CHILDREN.
THE MOTHERS IN THE VILLAGE PRAYED FOR HELP FROM THE GODS. AND HELP THEY DID RECEIVE.
I LED A GROUP OF TWENTY MEN, TRACKING THE GIANT TO ITS DEN IN THE HIGHLANDS. IT BATTLED US FOR HOURS, SWINGING TREES AND HURLING BOULDERS. MANY VIKINGS FOUND THEIR WAY TO VALHALLA.
UNTIL MY AXE HACKED ITS GUTS TO BLOODY SLUSH AND LOPPED OFF ITS HEAD.
THAT WAS FOUR DAYS AGO. SINCE THEN I HAVE EATEN MORE GOATS THAN THE FROST GIANT, DRANK ENOUGH MEAD TO DROWN A DOZEN SAILORS AND MADE LOVE TO HALF THE WOMEN IN THE VILLAGE.
I AM THOR ODINSON. GOD OF THUNDER. PRINCE OF ASGARD. HEIR TO THE THRONE OF THE REALM ETERNAL.
I LOVE MY LIFE.

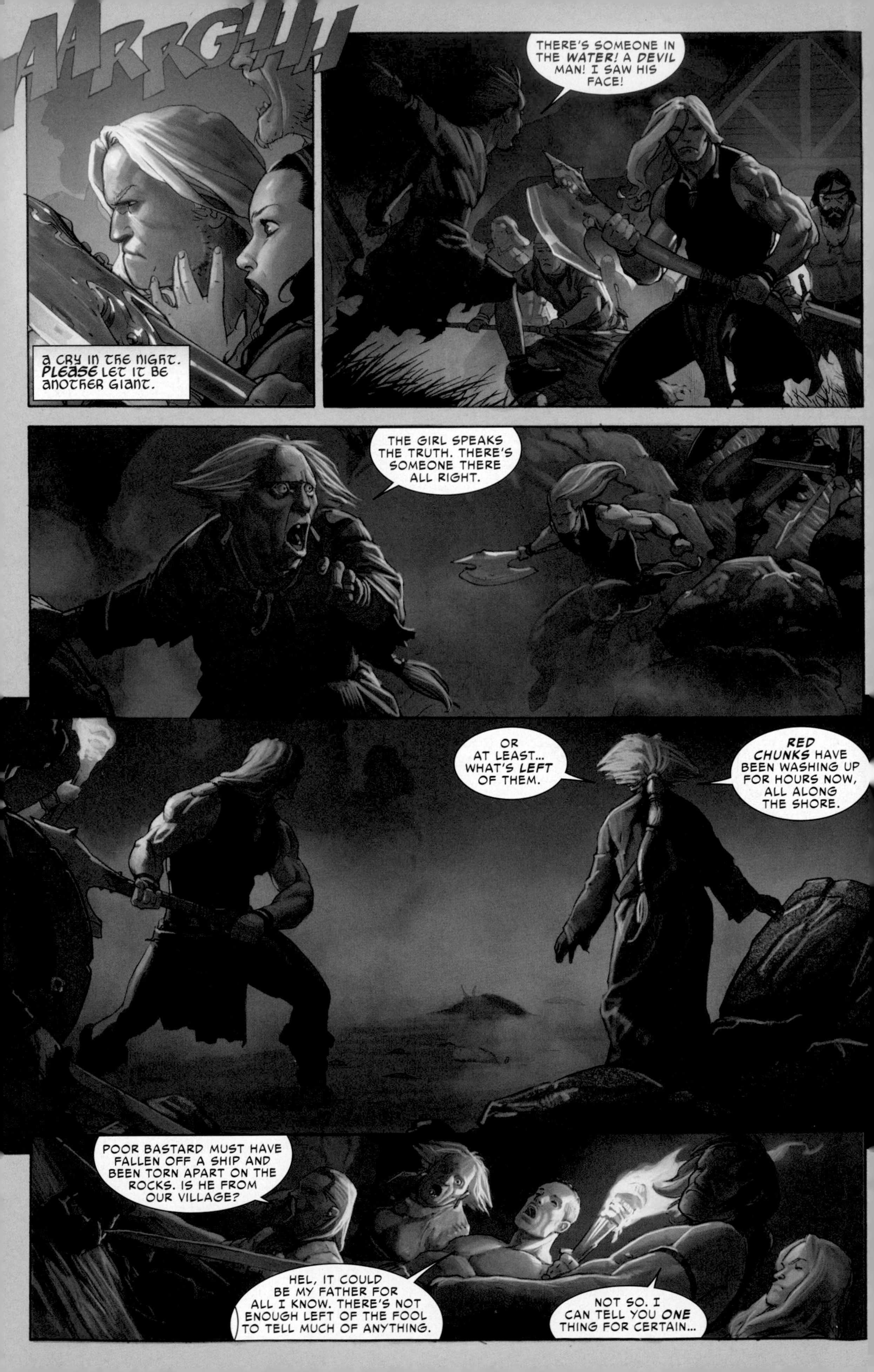
AARRGHH
A CRY IN THE NIGHT. PLEASE LET IT BE ANOTHER GIANT.
THERE'S SOMEONE IN THE WATER! A DEVIL MAN! I SAW HIS FACE!
THE GIRL SPEAKS THE TRUTH. THERE'S SOMEONE THERE ALL RIGHT.
OR AT LEAST... WHAT'S LEFT OF THEM.
RED CHUNKS HAVE BEEN WASHING UP FOR HOURS NOW, ALL ALONG THE SHORE.
POOR BASTARD MUST HAVE FALLEN OFF A SHIP AND BEEN TORN APART ON THE ROCKS. IS HE FROM OUR VILLAGE?
HEL, IT COULD BE MY FATHER FOR ALL I KNOW. THERE'S NOT ENOUGH LEFT OF THE FOOL TO TELL MUCH OF ANYTHING.
NOT SO. I CAN TELL YOU ONE THING FOR CERTAIN...

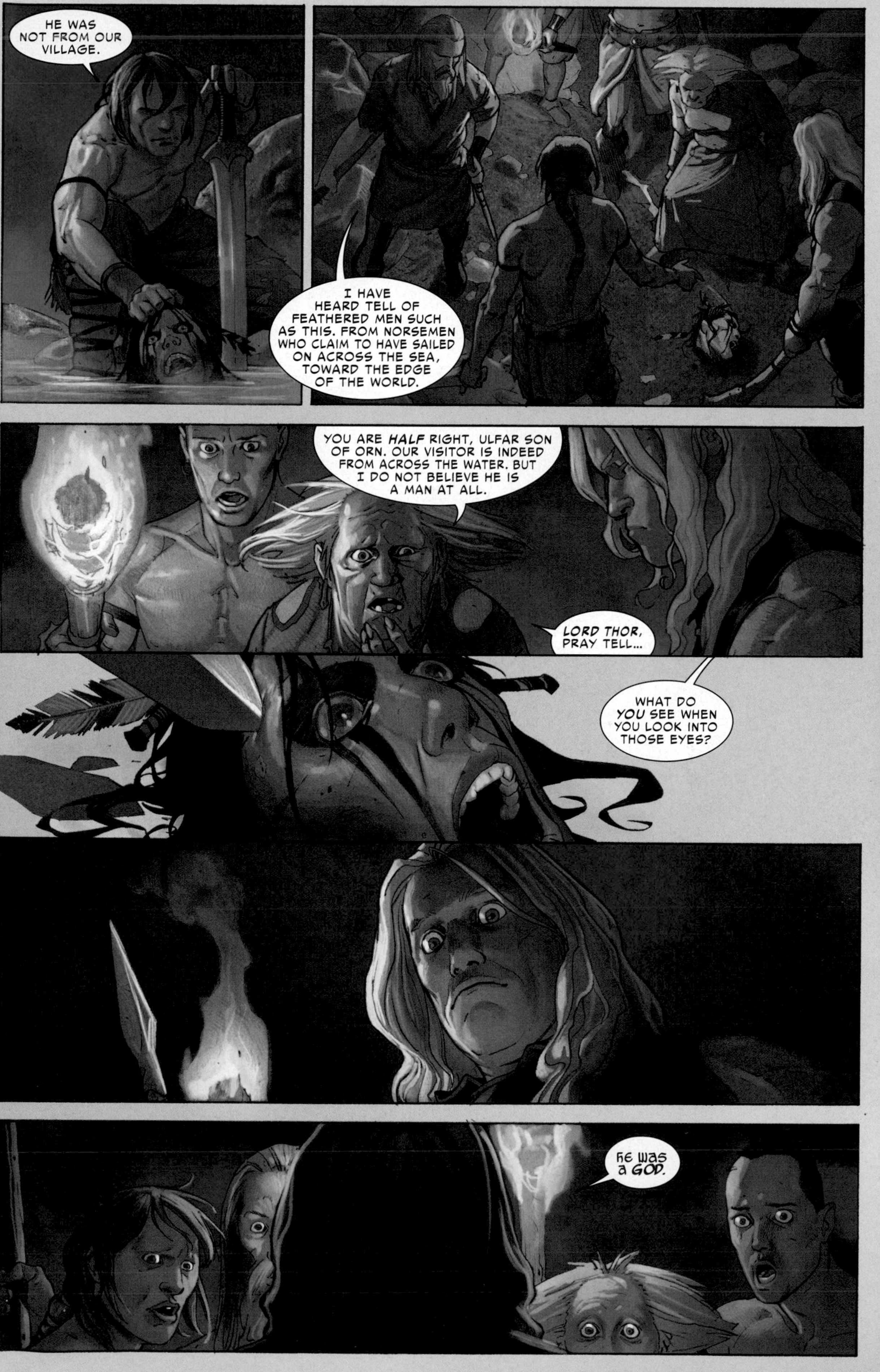
HE WAS NOT FROM OUR VILLAGE.
I HAVE HEARD TELL OF FEATHERED MEN SUCH AS THIS. FROM NORSEMEN WHO CLAIM TO HAVE SAILED ON ACROSS THE SEA, TOWARD THE EDGE OF THE WORLD.
YOU ARE *HALF* RIGHT, ULFAR SON OF ORN. OUR VISITOR IS INDEED FROM ACROSS THE WATER. BUT I DO NOT BELIEVE HE IS A MAN AT ALL.
LORD THOR, PRAY TELL...
WHAT DO *YOU* SEE WHEN YOU LOOK INTO THOSE EYES?
HE WAS A *GOD*.

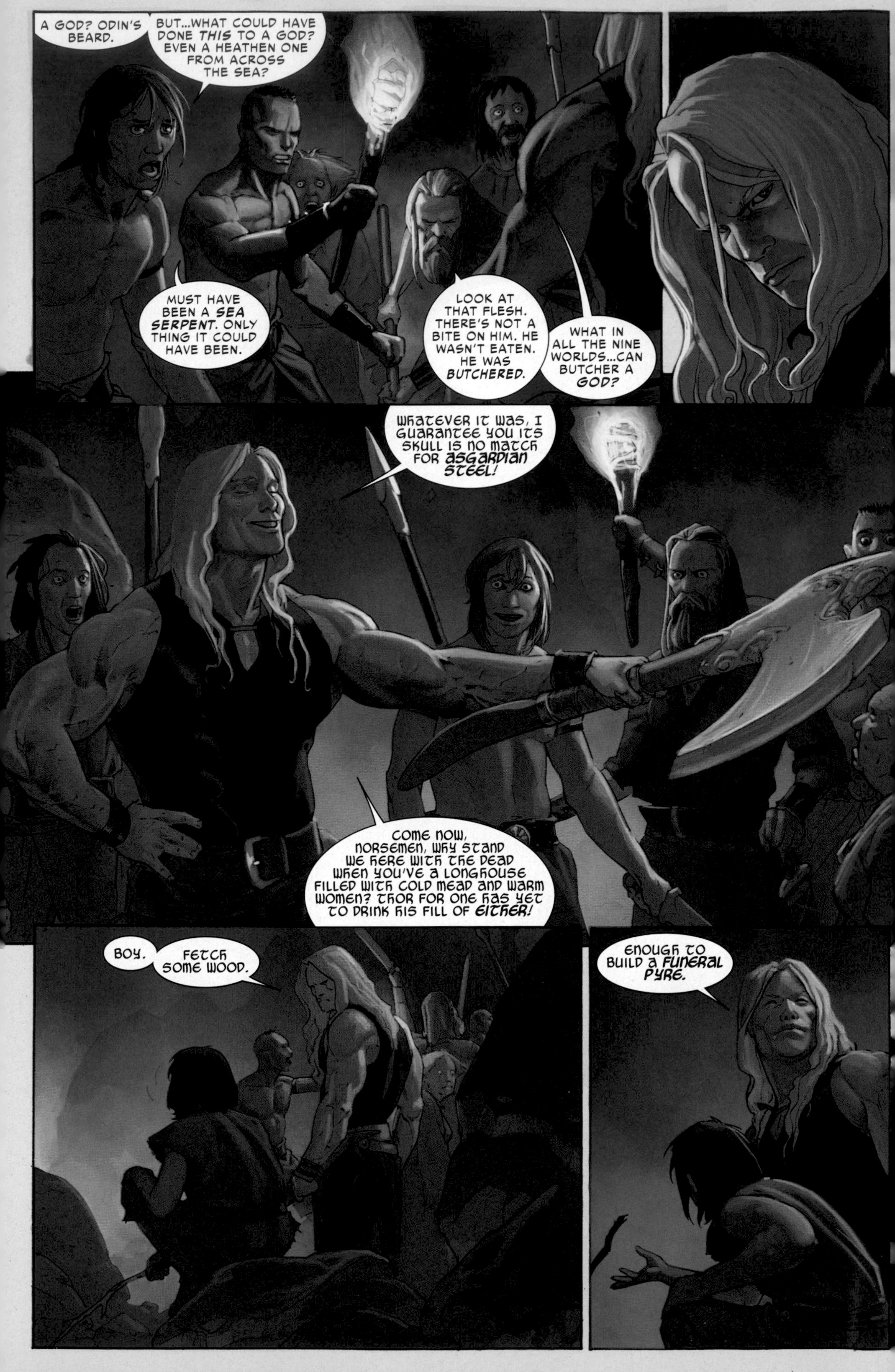
A GOD? ODIN'S BEARD.
BUT...WHAT COULD HAVE DONE THIS TO A GOD? EVEN A HEATHEN ONE FROM ACROSS THE SEA?
MUST HAVE BEEN A SEA SERPENT. ONLY THING IT COULD HAVE BEEN.
LOOK AT THAT FLESH. THERE'S NOT A BITE ON HIM. HE WASN'T EATEN. HE WAS BUTCHERED.
WHAT IN ALL THE NINE WORLDS...CAN BUTCHER A GOD?
WHATEVER IT WAS, I GUARANTEE YOU ITS SKULL IS NO MATCH FOR ASGARDIAN STEEL!
COME NOW, NORSEMEN, WHY STAND WE HERE WITH THE DEAD WHEN YOU'VE A LONGHOUSE FILLED WITH COLD MEAD AND WARM WOMEN? THOR FOR ONE HAS YET TO DRINK HIS FILL OF EITHER!
BOY.
FETCH SOME WOOD.
ENOUGH TO BUILD A FUNERAL PYRE.

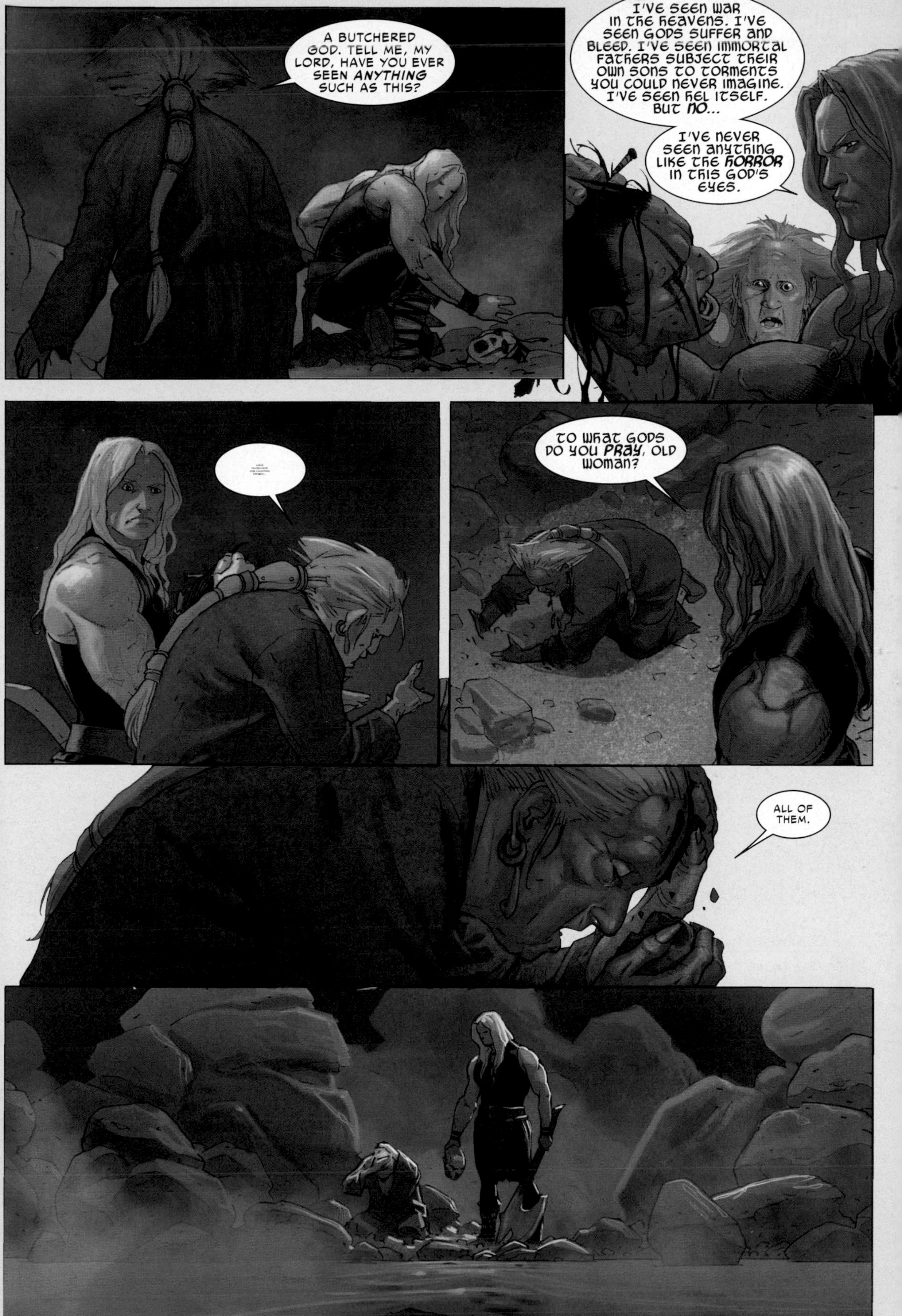
A BUTCHERED GOD. TELL ME, MY LORD, HAVE YOU EVER SEEN ANYTHING SUCH AS THIS?
I'VE SEEN WAR IN THE HEAVENS. I'VE SEEN GODS SUFFER AND BLEED. I'VE SEEN IMMORTAL FATHERS SUBJECT THEIR OWN SONS TO TORMENTS YOU COULD NEVER IMAGINE. I'VE SEEN HEL ITSELF. BUT NO...
I'VE NEVER SEEN ANYTHING LIKE THE HORROR IN THIS GOD'S EYES.
TO WHAT GODS DO YOU PRAY, OLD WOMAN?
ALL OF THEM.

The Present Day.
Deep Space.
The Planet Indigarr.

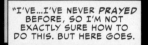

"I'VE...I'VE NEVER *PRAYED* BEFORE, SO I'M NOT EXACTLY SURE HOW TO DO THIS. BUT HERE GOES."

"DEAR *THOR*, MY PEOPLE NEED YOUR HELP."

"IT HASN'T RAINED ON MY PLANET FOR MANY YEARS. EVERYTHING HERE HAS DIED."

"SOON *WE* WILL DIE TOO."

"EVERYONE THROUGHOUT THE SPACEWAYS SAYS YOU'RE THE GREATEST GOD WHO'S EVER LIVED AND THAT YOU CAN DO ANYTHING. PLEASE, THOR..."

RRRRRR

KRUMMB

SAVE US.

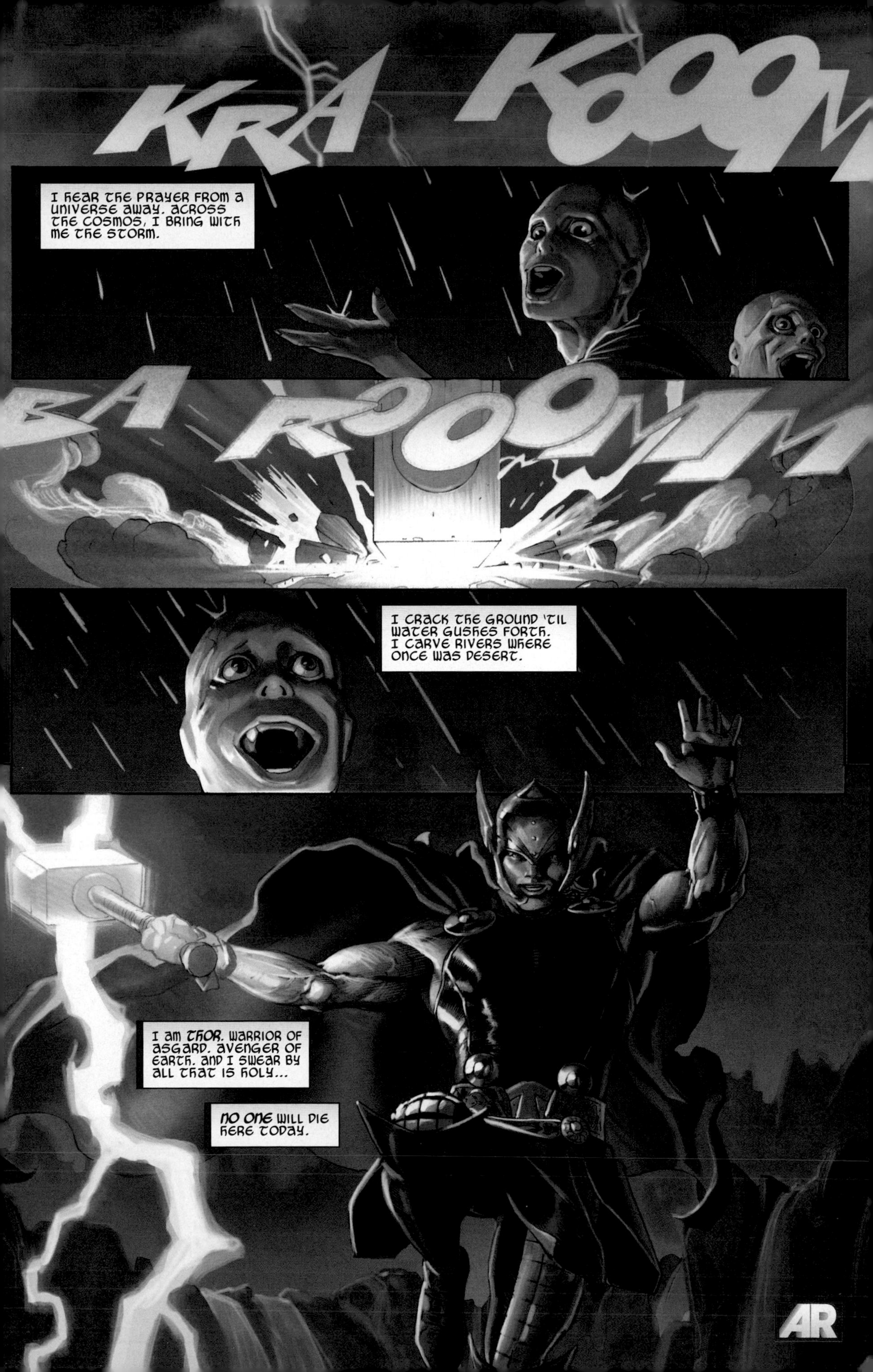
KRA KOOOM
I HEAR THE PRAYER FROM A UNIVERSE AWAY. ACROSS THE COSMOS, I BRING WITH ME THE STORM.
BA ROOOMM
I CRACK THE GROUND 'TIL WATER GUSHES FORTH. I CARVE RIVERS WHERE ONCE WAS DESERT.
I AM THOR. WARRIOR OF ASGARD. AVENGER OF EARTH. AND I SWEAR BY ALL THAT IS HOLY...
NO ONE WILL DIE HERE TODAY.

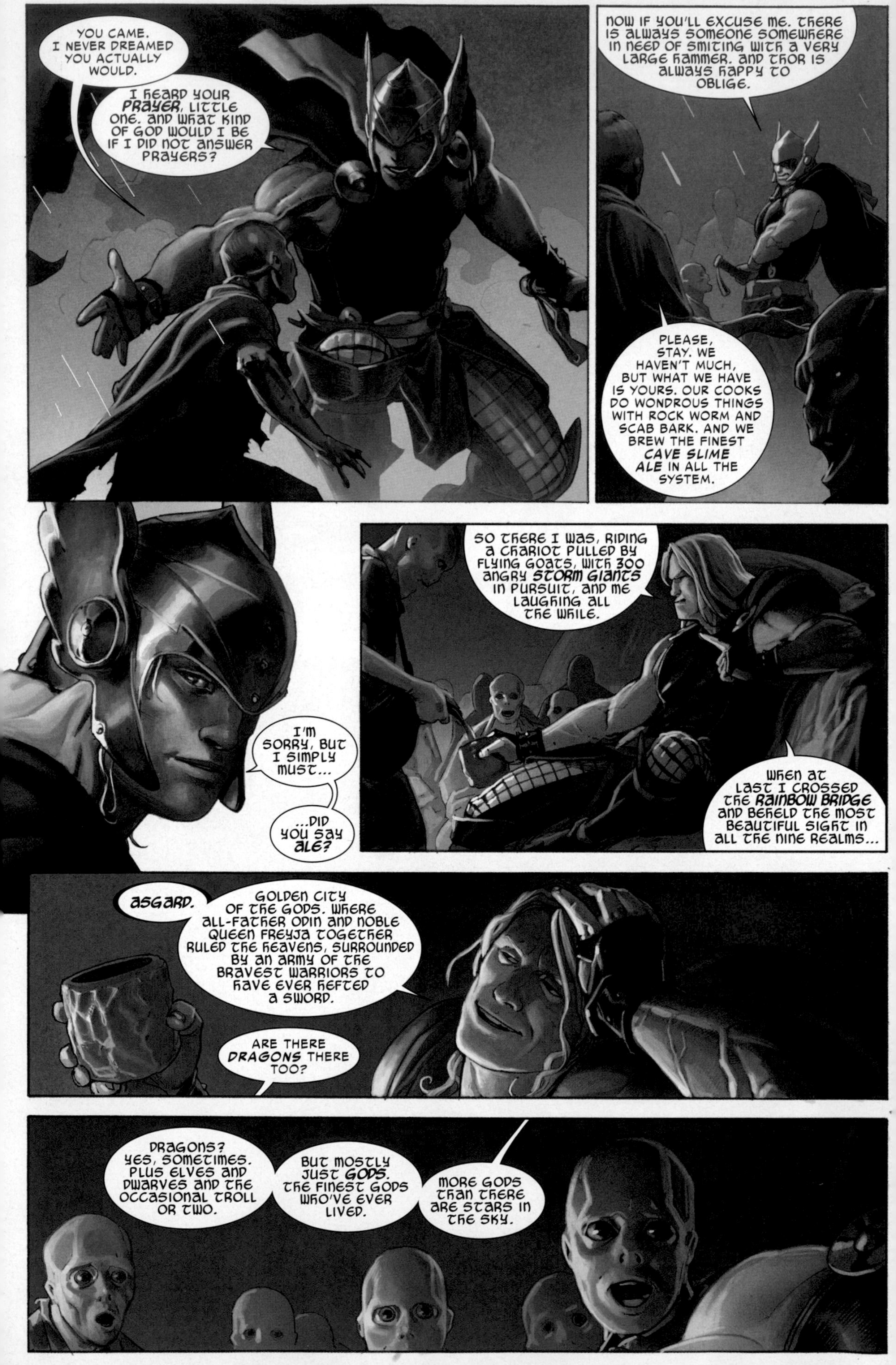
YOU CAME. I NEVER DREAMED YOU ACTUALLY WOULD.
I HEARD YOUR PRAYER, LITTLE ONE. AND WHAT KIND OF GOD WOULD I BE IF I DID NOT ANSWER PRAYERS?
NOW IF YOU'LL EXCUSE ME. THERE IS ALWAYS SOMEONE SOMEWHERE IN NEED OF SMITING WITH A VERY LARGE HAMMER. AND THOR IS ALWAYS HAPPY TO OBLIGE.
PLEASE, STAY. WE HAVEN'T MUCH, BUT WHAT WE HAVE IS YOURS. OUR COOKS DO WONDROUS THINGS WITH ROCK WORM AND SCAB BARK. AND WE BREW THE FINEST CAVE SLIME ALE IN ALL THE SYSTEM.
I'M SORRY, BUT I SIMPLY MUST...
...DID YOU SAY ALE?
SO THERE I WAS, RIDING A CHARIOT PULLED BY FLYING GOATS, WITH 300 ANGRY STORM GIANTS IN PURSUIT, AND ME LAUGHING ALL THE WHILE.
WHEN AT LAST I CROSSED THE RAINBOW BRIDGE AND BEHELD THE MOST BEAUTIFUL SIGHT IN ALL THE NINE REALMS...
ASGARD.
GOLDEN CITY OF THE GODS. WHERE ALL-FATHER ODIN AND NOBLE QUEEN FREYJA TOGETHER RULED THE HEAVENS, SURROUNDED BY AN ARMY OF THE BRAVEST WARRIORS TO HAVE EVER HEFTED A SWORD.
ARE THERE DRAGONS THERE TOO?
DRAGONS? YES, SOMETIMES. PLUS ELVES AND DWARVES AND THE OCCASIONAL TROLL OR TWO.
BUT MOSTLY JUST GODS. THE FINEST GODS WHO'VE EVER LIVED.
MORE GODS THAN THERE ARE STARS IN THE SKY.

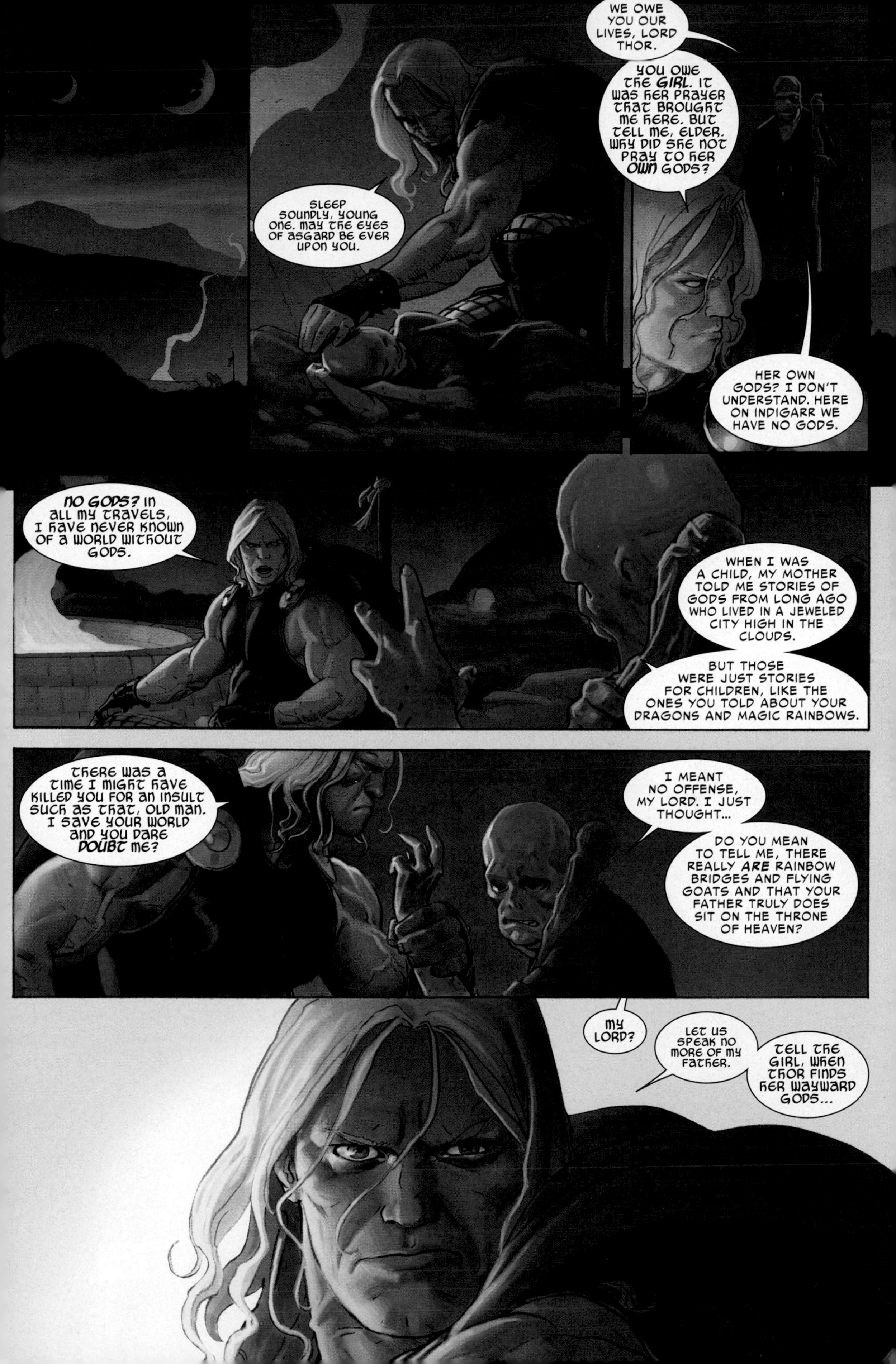

WE OWE YOU OUR LIVES, LORD THOR.
SLEEP SOUNDLY, YOUNG ONE. MAY THE EYES OF ASGARD BE EVER UPON YOU.
YOU OWE THE GIRL. IT WAS HER PRAYER THAT BROUGHT ME HERE. BUT TELL ME, ELDER. WHY DID SHE NOT PRAY TO HER OWN GODS?
HER OWN GODS? I DON'T UNDERSTAND. HERE ON INDIGARR WE HAVE NO GODS.
NO GODS? IN ALL MY TRAVELS, I HAVE NEVER KNOWN OF A WORLD WITHOUT GODS.
WHEN I WAS A CHILD, MY MOTHER TOLD ME STORIES OF GODS FROM LONG AGO WHO LIVED IN A JEWELED CITY HIGH IN THE CLOUDS.
BUT THOSE WERE JUST STORIES FOR CHILDREN, LIKE THE ONES YOU TOLD ABOUT YOUR DRAGONS AND MAGIC RAINBOWS.
THERE WAS A TIME I MIGHT HAVE KILLED YOU FOR AN INSULT SUCH AS THAT, OLD MAN. I SAVE YOUR WORLD AND YOU DARE DOUBT ME?
I MEANT NO OFFENSE, MY LORD. I JUST THOUGHT...
DO YOU MEAN TO TELL ME, THERE REALLY ARE RAINBOW BRIDGES AND FLYING GOATS AND THAT YOUR FATHER TRULY DOES SIT ON THE THRONE OF HEAVEN?
MY LORD?
LET US SPEAK NO MORE OF MY FATHER.
TELL THE GIRL, WHEN THOR FINDS HER WAYWARD GODS...

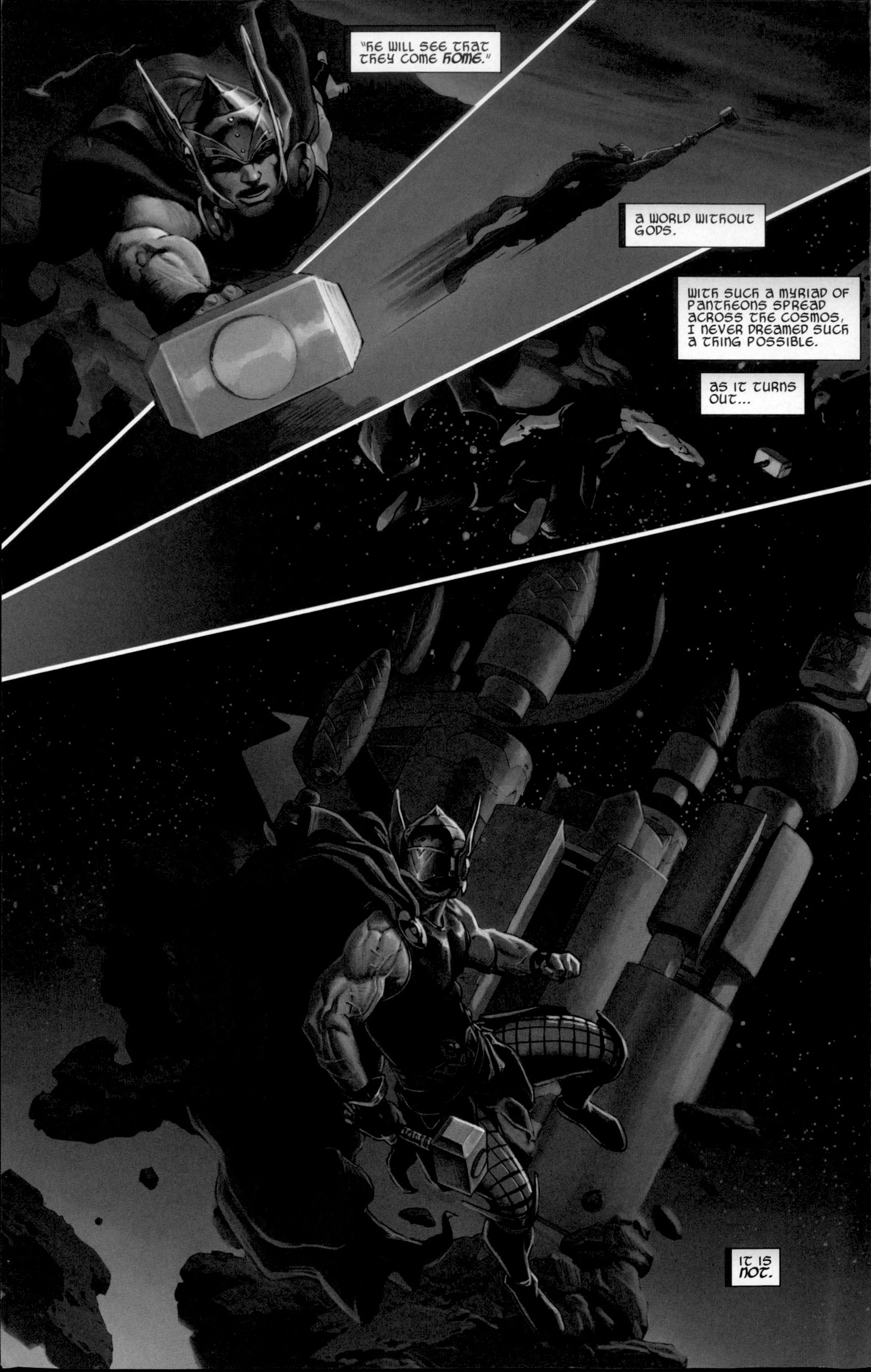
"HE WILL SEE THAT THEY COME HOME."
A WORLD WITHOUT GODS.
WITH SUCH A MYRIAD OF PANTHEONS SPREAD ACROSS THE COSMOS, I NEVER DREAMED SUCH A THING POSSIBLE.
AS IT TURNS OUT...
IT IS NOT.

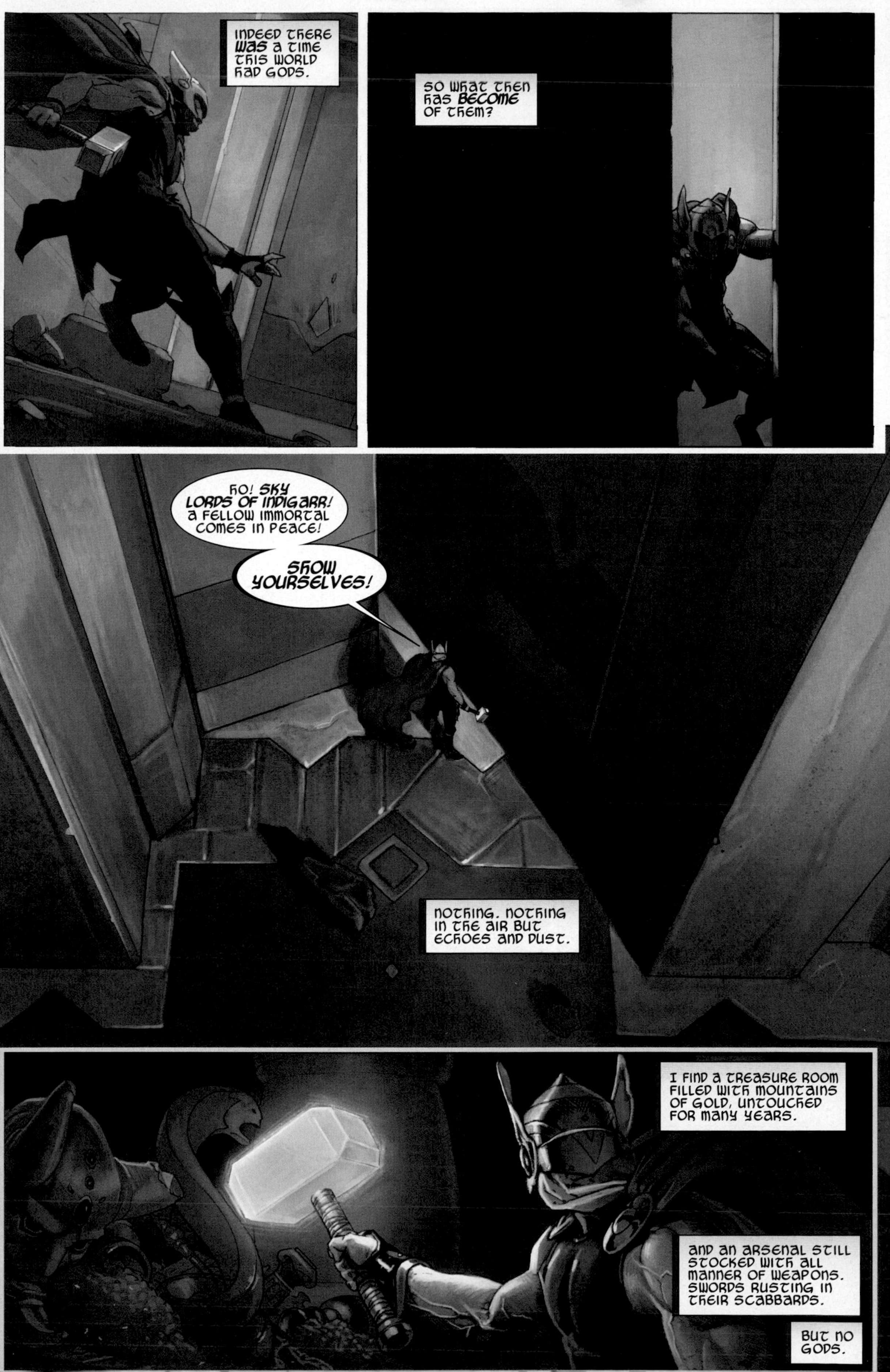
INDEED THERE WAS A TIME THIS WORLD HAD GODS.
SO WHAT THEN HAS BECOME OF THEM?
HO! SKY LORDS OF INDIGARR! A FELLOW IMMORTAL COMES IN PEACE!
SHOW YOURSELVES!
NOTHING. NOTHING IN THE AIR BUT ECHOES AND DUST.
I FIND A TREASURE ROOM FILLED WITH MOUNTAINS OF GOLD, UNTOUCHED FOR MANY YEARS.
AND AN ARSENAL STILL STOCKED WITH ALL MANNER OF WEAPONS. SWORDS RUSTING IN THEIR SCABBARDS.
BUT NO GODS.

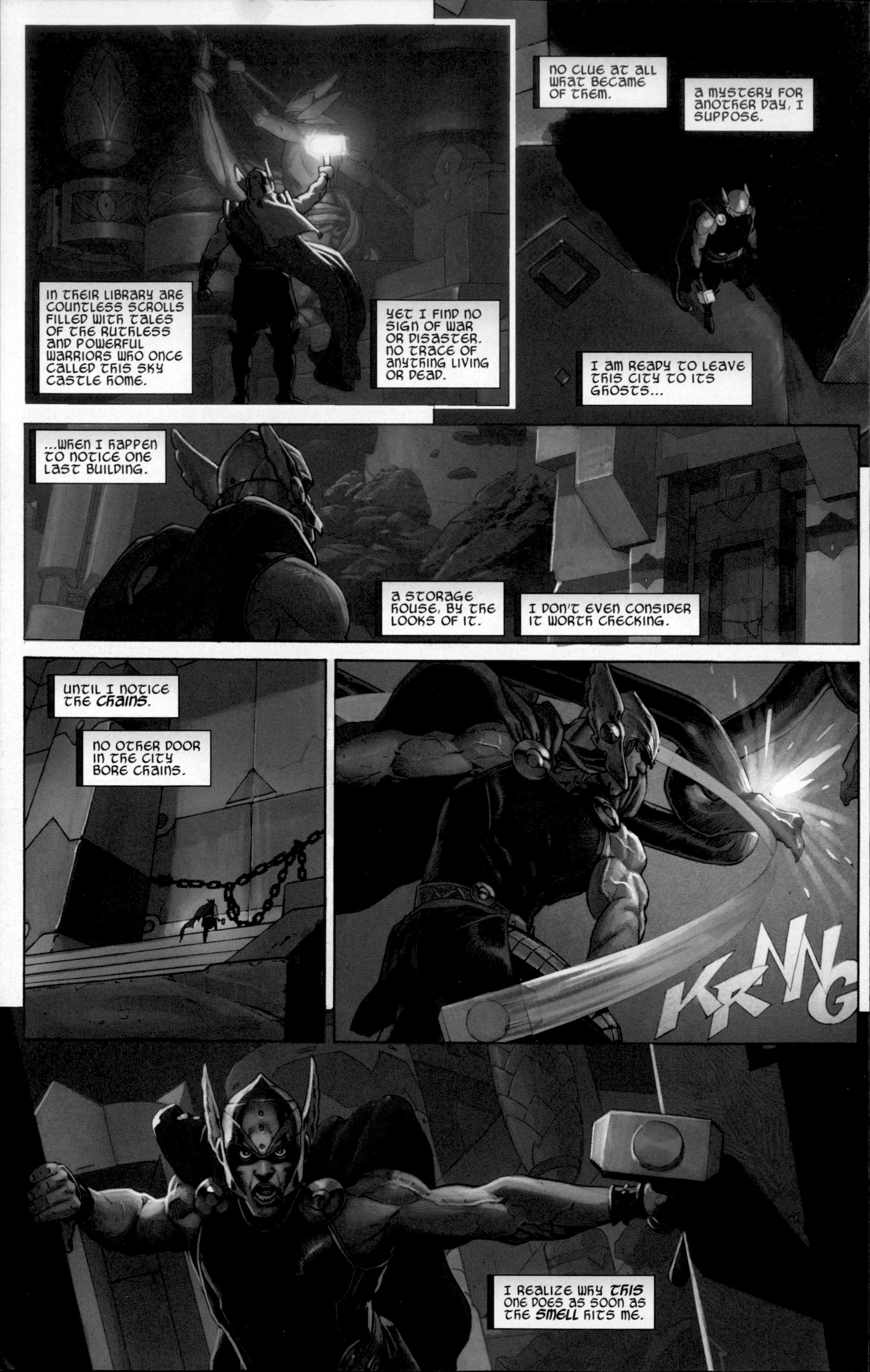
IN THEIR LIBRARY ARE COUNTLESS SCROLLS FILLED WITH TALES OF THE RUTHLESS AND POWERFUL WARRIORS WHO ONCE CALLED THIS SKY CASTLE HOME.
YET I FIND NO SIGN OF WAR OR DISASTER. NO TRACE OF ANYTHING LIVING OR DEAD.
NO CLUE AT ALL WHAT BECAME OF THEM.
A MYSTERY FOR ANOTHER DAY, I SUPPOSE.
I AM READY TO LEAVE THIS CITY TO ITS GHOSTS...
...WHEN I HAPPEN TO NOTICE ONE LAST BUILDING.
A STORAGE HOUSE, BY THE LOOKS OF IT.
I DON'T EVEN CONSIDER IT WORTH CHECKING.
UNTIL I NOTICE THE *CHAINS*.
NO OTHER DOOR IN THE CITY BORE CHAINS.
KRNNG
I REALIZE WHY *THIS* ONE DOES AS SOON AS THE *SMELL* HITS ME.

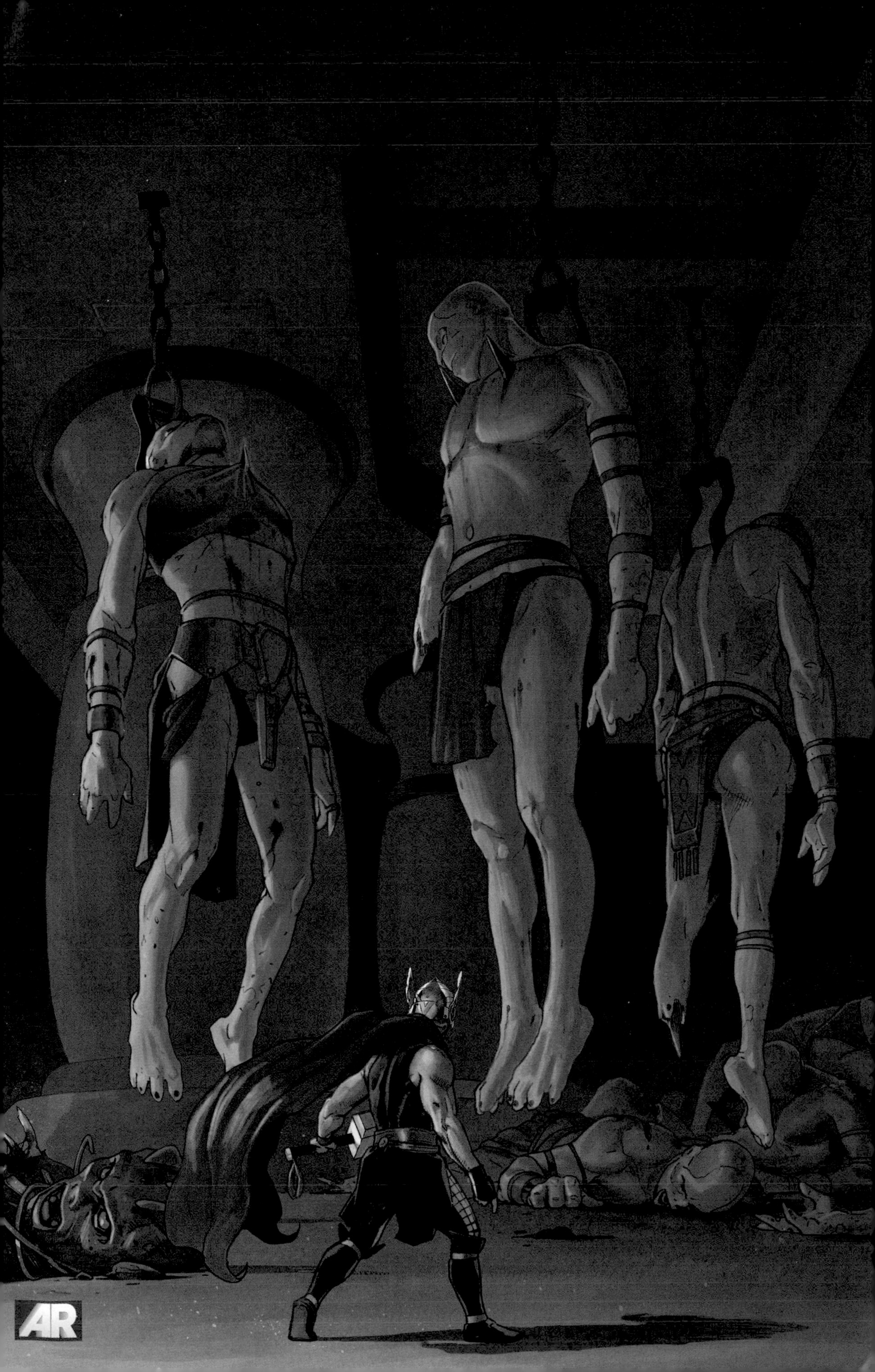

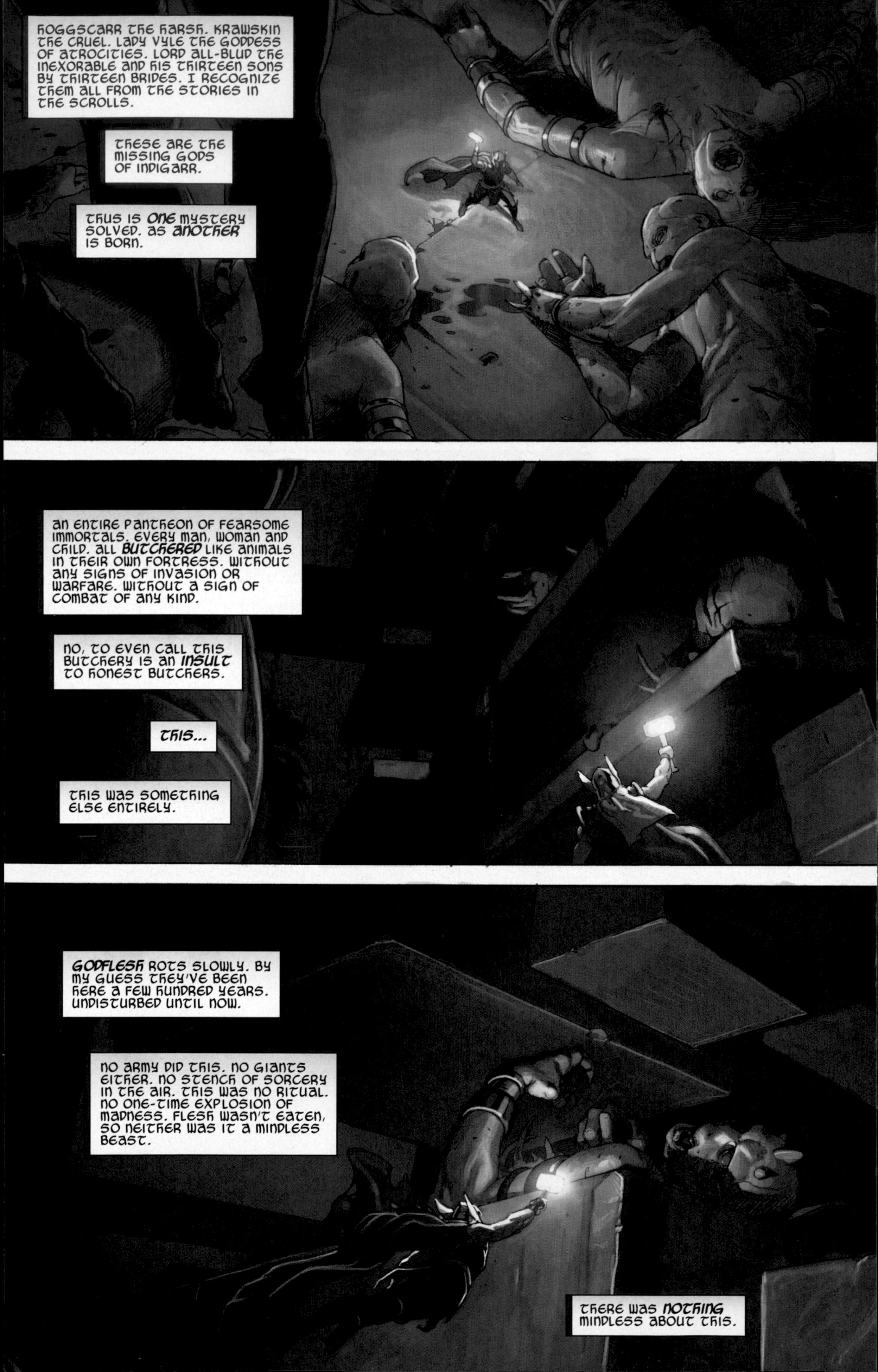
HOGGSCARR THE HARSH. KRAWSKIN THE CRUEL. LADY VYLE THE GODDESS OF ATROCITIES. LORD ALL-BLUD THE INEXORABLE AND HIS THIRTEEN SONS BY THIRTEEN BRIDES. I RECOGNIZE THEM ALL FROM THE STORIES IN THE SCROLLS.
THESE ARE THE MISSING GODS OF INDIGARR.
THUS IS ONE MYSTERY SOLVED. AS ANOTHER IS BORN.
AN ENTIRE PANTHEON OF FEARSOME IMMORTALS. EVERY MAN, WOMAN AND CHILD. ALL BUTCHERED LIKE ANIMALS IN THEIR OWN FORTRESS. WITHOUT ANY SIGNS OF INVASION OR WARFARE. WITHOUT A SIGN OF COMBAT OF ANY KIND.
NO, TO EVEN CALL THIS BUTCHERY IS AN INSULT TO HONEST BUTCHERS.
THIS...
THIS WAS SOMETHING ELSE ENTIRELY.
GODFLESH ROTS SLOWLY. BY MY GUESS THEY'VE BEEN HERE A FEW HUNDRED YEARS. UNDISTURBED UNTIL NOW.
NO ARMY DID THIS. NO GIANTS EITHER. NO STENCH OF SORCERY IN THE AIR. THIS WAS NO RITUAL. NO ONE-TIME EXPLOSION OF MADNESS. FLESH WASN'T EATEN, SO NEITHER WAS IT A MINDLESS BEAST.
THERE WAS NOTHING MINDLESS ABOUT THIS.

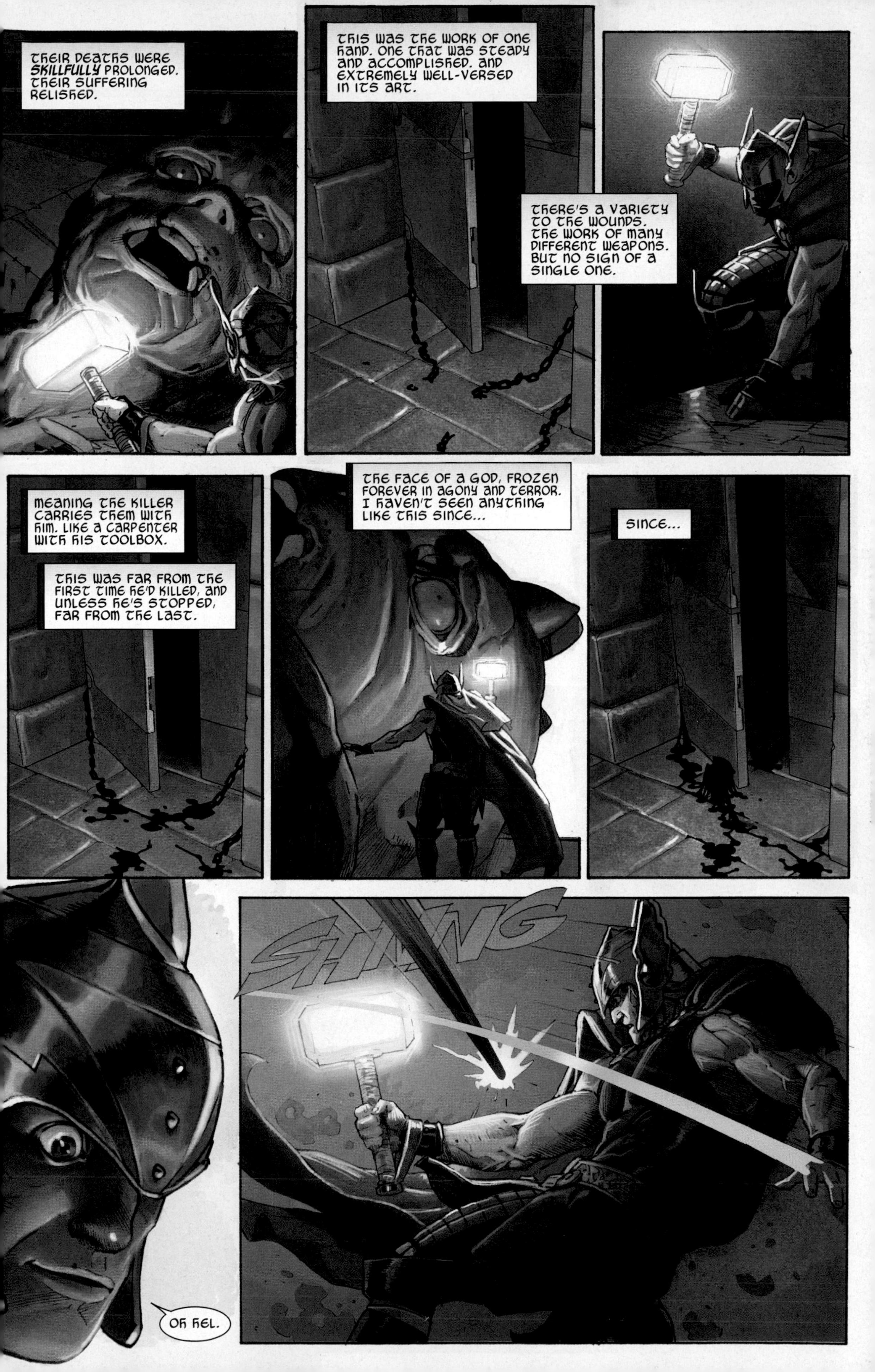

THEIR DEATHS WERE SKILLFULLY PROLONGED. THEIR SUFFERING RELISHED.
THIS WAS THE WORK OF ONE HAND. ONE THAT WAS STEADY AND ACCOMPLISHED. AND EXTREMELY WELL-VERSED IN ITS ART.
THERE'S A VARIETY TO THE WOUNDS. THE WORK OF MANY DIFFERENT WEAPONS. BUT NO SIGN OF A SINGLE ONE.
MEANING THE KILLER CARRIES THEM WITH HIM. LIKE A CARPENTER WITH HIS TOOLBOX.
THIS WAS FAR FROM THE FIRST TIME HE'D KILLED, AND UNLESS HE'S STOPPED, FAR FROM THE LAST.
THE FACE OF A GOD, FROZEN FOREVER IN AGONY AND TERROR. I HAVEN'T SEEN ANYTHING LIKE THIS SINCE...
SINCE...
OH HEL.
SHIING

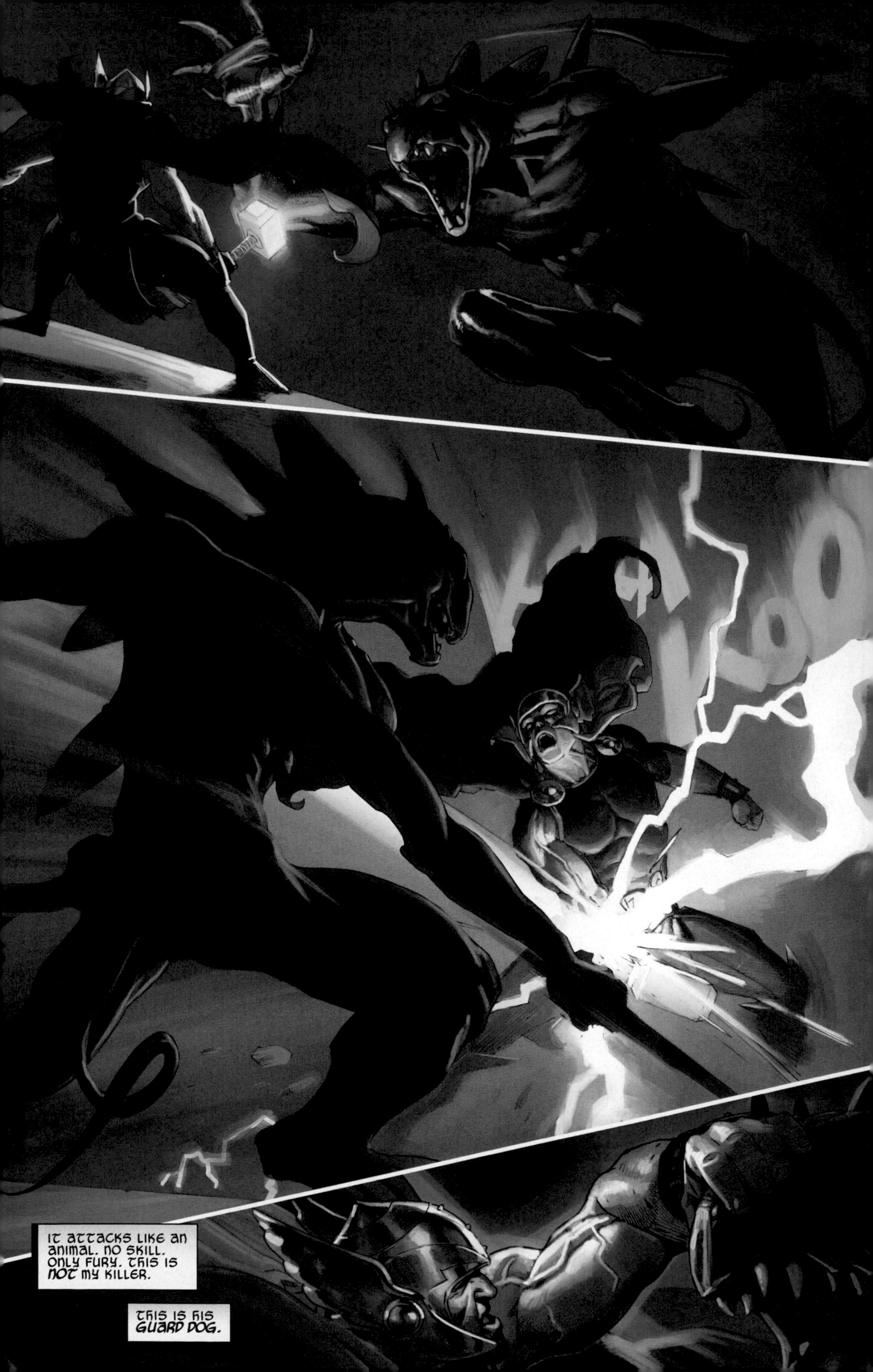
KA-VOOOM
IT ATTACKS LIKE AN ANIMAL. NO SKILL. ONLY FURY. THIS IS NOT MY KILLER.
THIS IS HIS GUARD DOG.

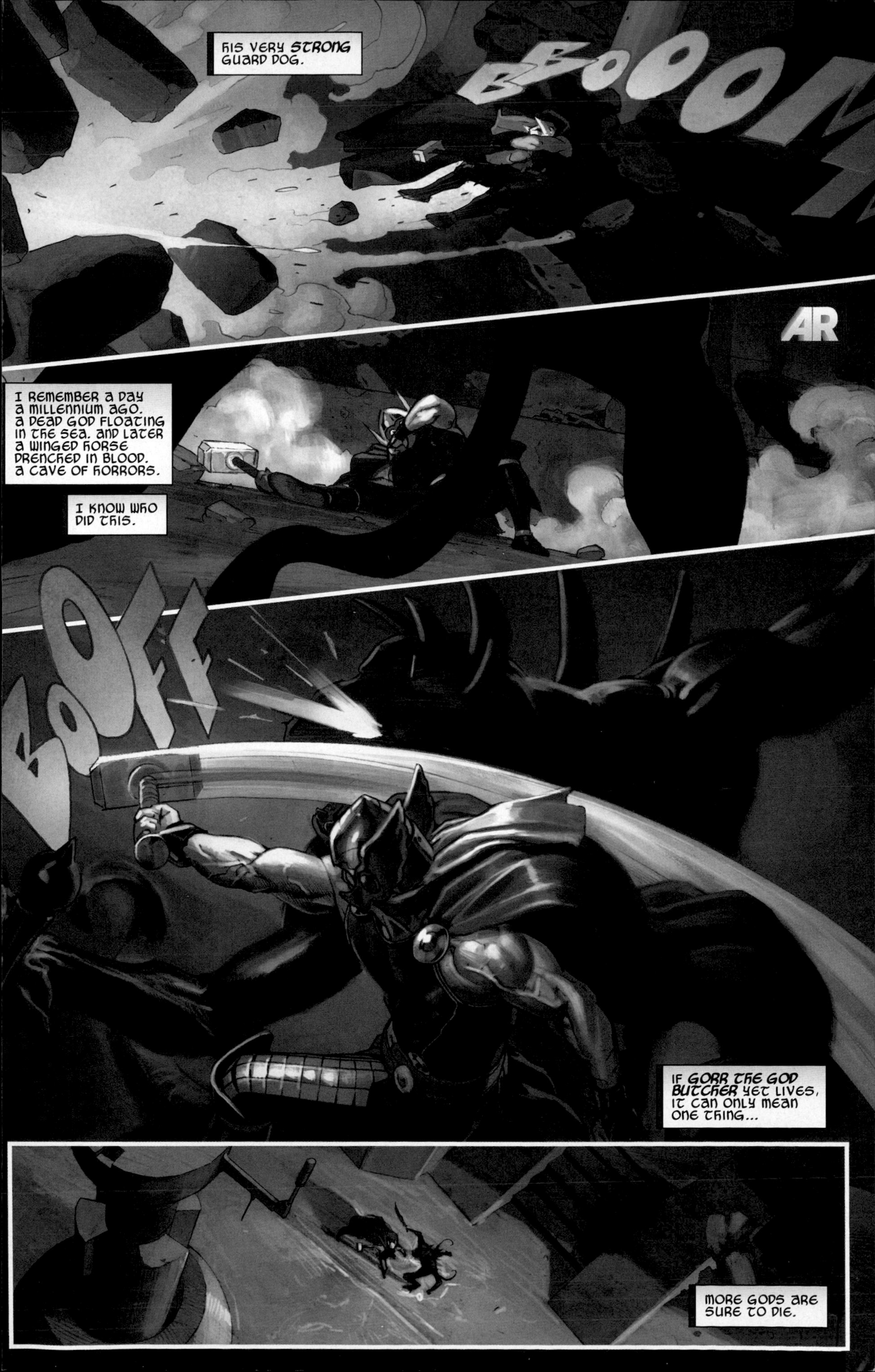
HIS VERY STRONG GUARD DOG.
BBOOOOM
AR
I REMEMBER A DAY A MILLENNIUM AGO. A DEAD GOD FLOATING IN THE SEA. AND LATER A WINGED HORSE DRENCHED IN BLOOD. A CAVE OF HORRORS.
I KNOW WHO DID THIS.
BOOFF
IF GORR THE GOD BUTCHER YET LIVES, IT CAN ONLY MEAN ONE THING...
MORE GODS ARE SURE TO DIE.

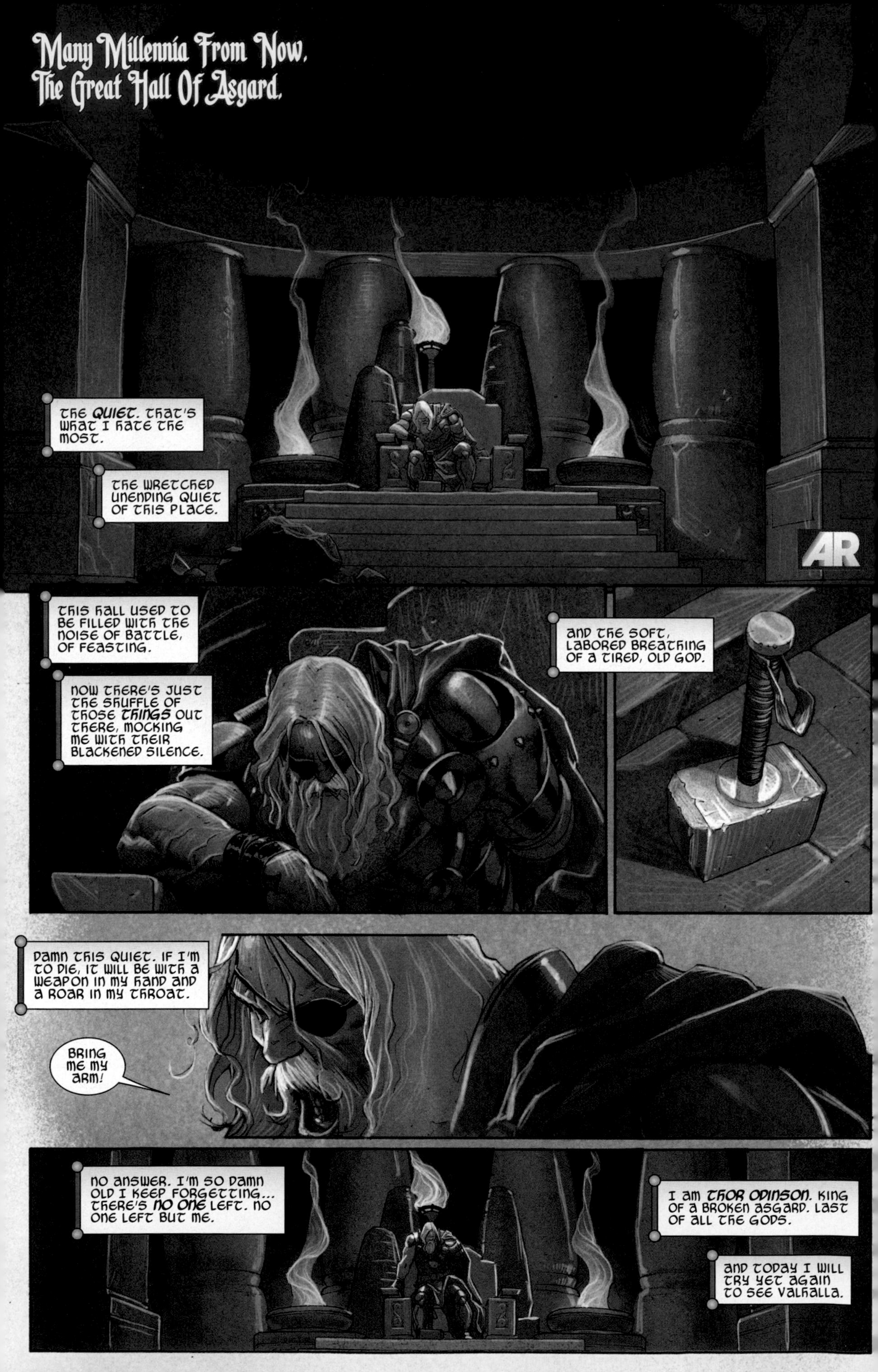
Many Millennia From Now, The Great Hall Of Asgard.
THE QUIET. THAT'S WHAT I HATE THE MOST.
THE WRETCHED UNENDING QUIET OF THIS PLACE.
AR
THIS HALL USED TO BE FILLED WITH THE NOISE OF BATTLE, OF FEASTING.
NOW THERE'S JUST THE SHUFFLE OF THOSE THINGS OUT THERE, MOCKING ME WITH THEIR BLACKENED SILENCE.
AND THE SOFT, LABORED BREATHING OF A TIRED, OLD GOD.
DAMN THIS QUIET. IF I'M TO DIE, IT WILL BE WITH A WEAPON IN MY HAND AND A ROAR IN MY THROAT.
BRING ME MY ARM!
NO ANSWER. I'M SO DAMN OLD I KEEP FORGETTING... THERE'S NO ONE LEFT. NO ONE LEFT BUT ME.
I AM THOR ODINSON. KING OF A BROKEN ASGARD. LAST OF ALL THE GODS.
AND TODAY I WILL TRY YET AGAIN TO SEE VALHALLA.

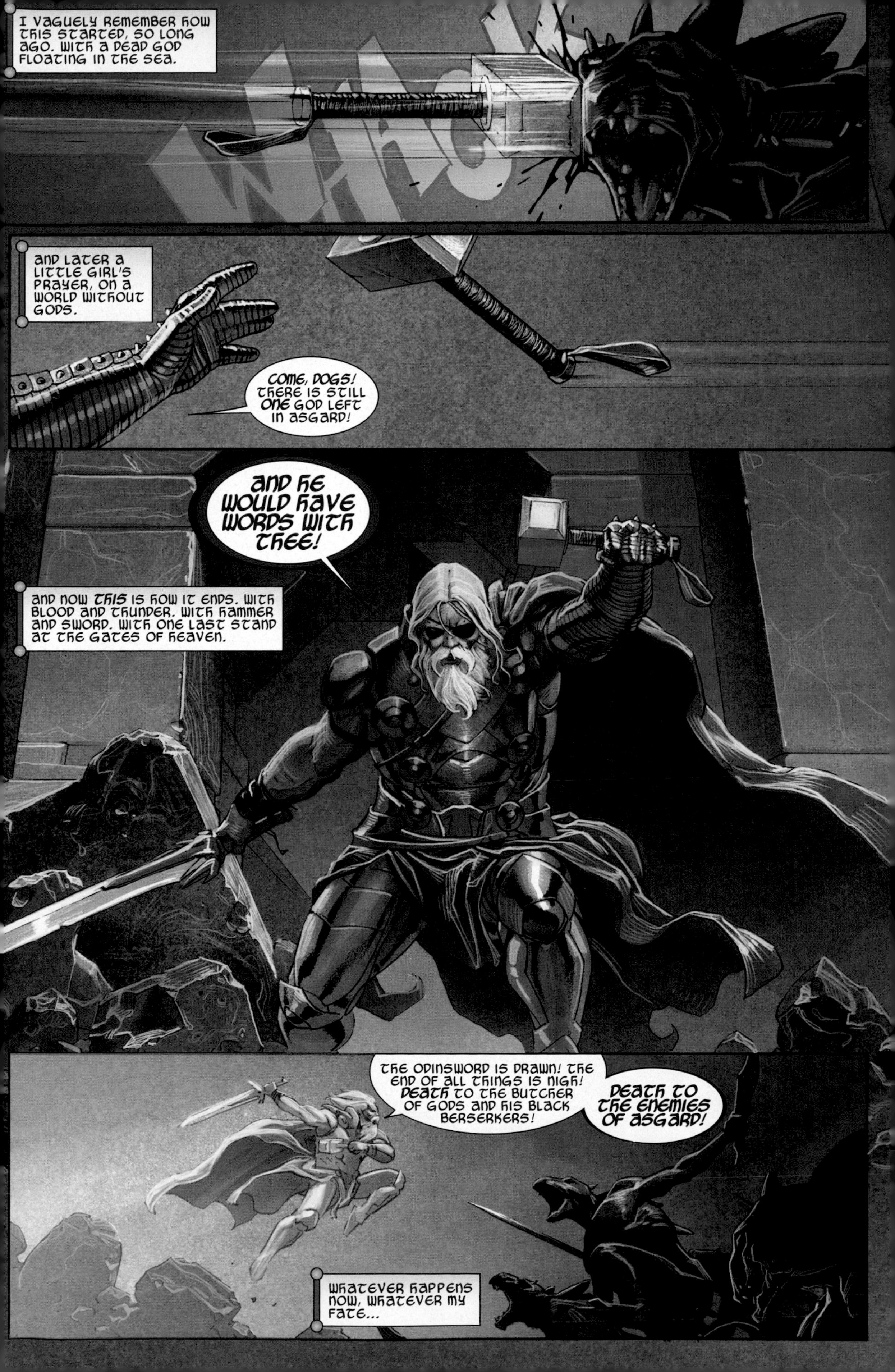
I VAGUELY REMEMBER HOW THIS STARTED, SO LONG AGO. WITH A DEAD GOD FLOATING IN THE SEA.
AND LATER A LITTLE GIRL'S PRAYER, ON A WORLD WITHOUT GODS.
COME, DOGS! THERE IS STILL ONE GOD LEFT IN ASGARD!
AND HE WOULD HAVE WORDS WITH THEE!
AND NOW THIS IS HOW IT ENDS. WITH BLOOD AND THUNDER. WITH HAMMER AND SWORD. WITH ONE LAST STAND AT THE GATES OF HEAVEN.
THE ODINSWORD IS DRAWN! THE END OF ALL THINGS IS NIGH! DEATH TO THE BUTCHER OF GODS AND HIS BLACK BERSERKERS!
DEATH TO THE ENEMIES OF ASGARD!
WHATEVER HAPPENS NOW, WHATEVER MY FATE...

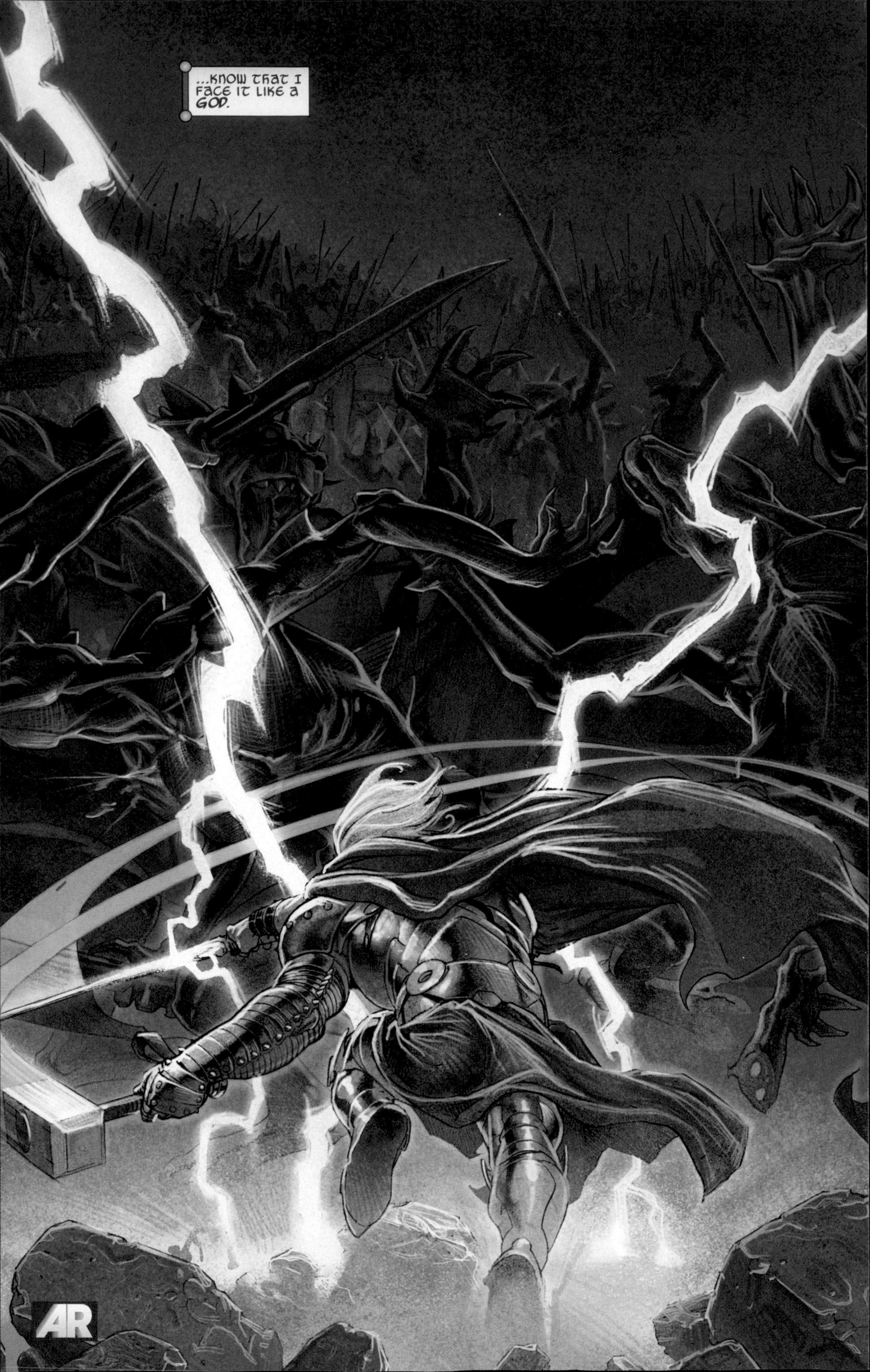
...KNOW THAT I FACE IT LIKE A GOD.

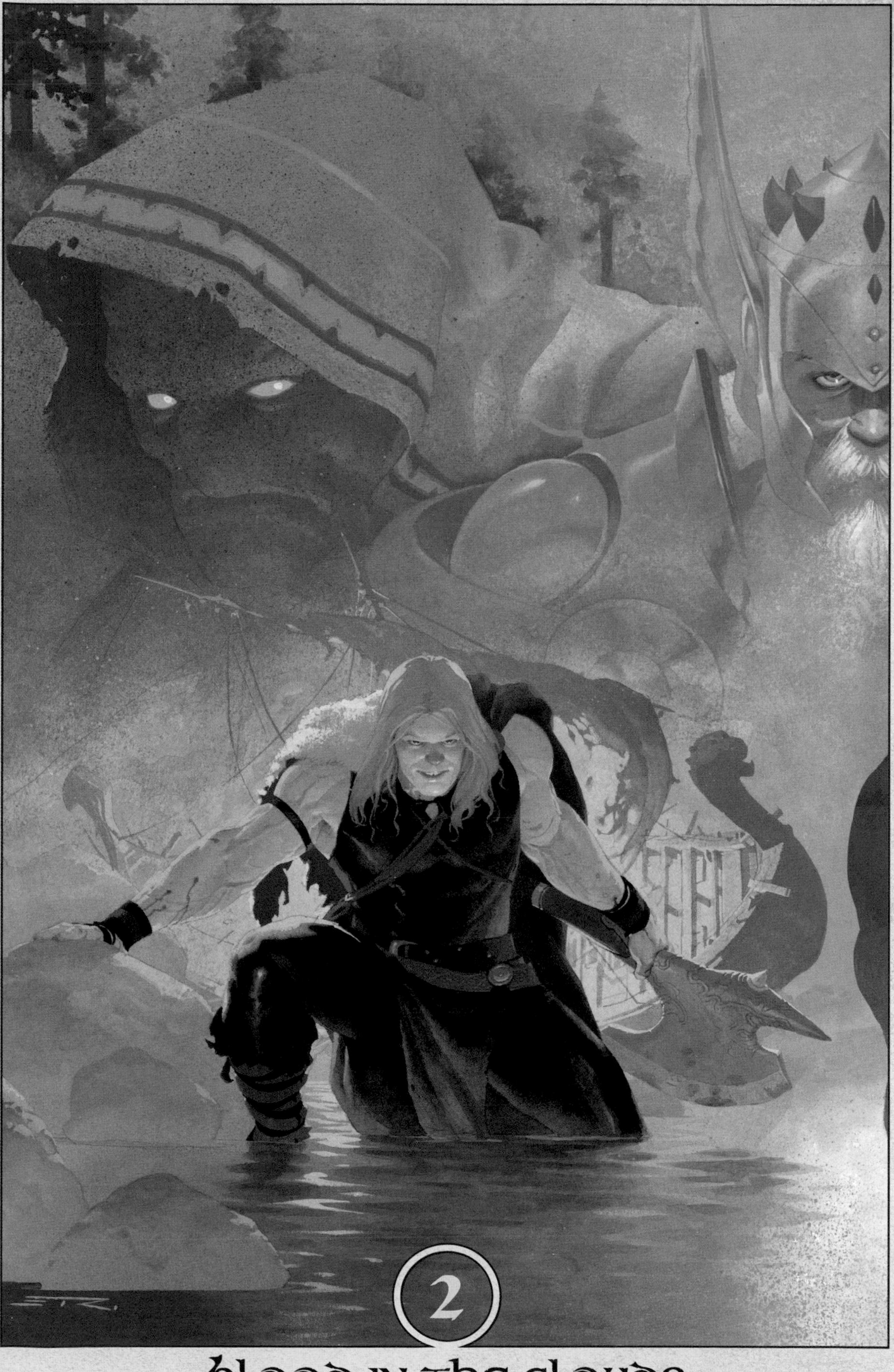
2

Blood in the Clouds

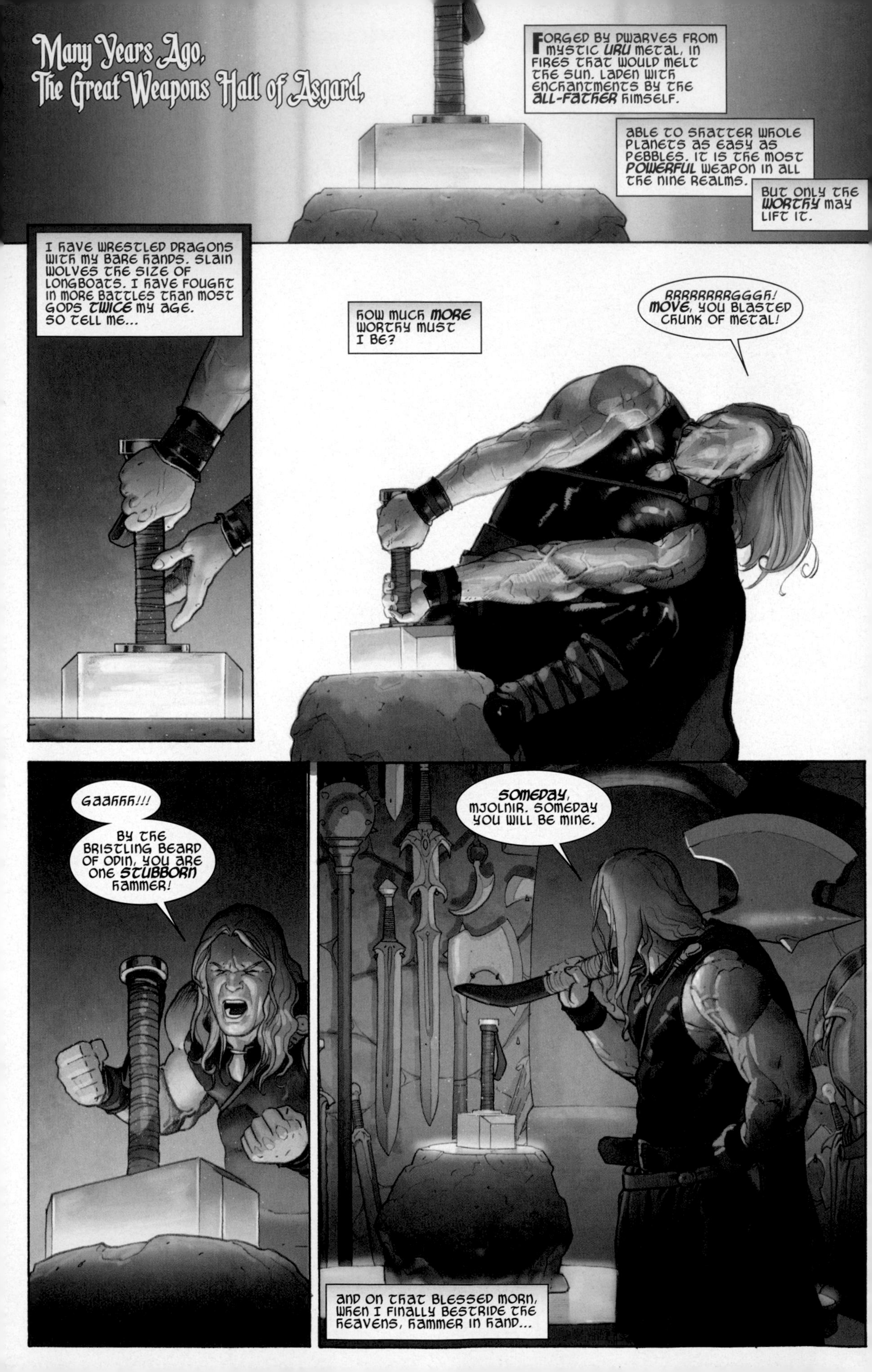
Many Years Ago, The Great Weapons Hall of Asgard,
FORGED BY DWARVES FROM MYSTIC URU METAL, IN FIRES THAT WOULD MELT THE SUN. LADEN WITH ENCHANTMENTS BY THE ALL-FATHER HIMSELF.
ABLE TO SHATTER WHOLE PLANETS AS EASY AS PEBBLES. IT IS THE MOST POWERFUL WEAPON IN ALL THE NINE REALMS.
BUT ONLY THE WORTHY MAY LIFT IT.
I HAVE WRESTLED DRAGONS WITH MY BARE HANDS. SLAIN WOLVES THE SIZE OF LONGBOATS. I HAVE FOUGHT IN MORE BATTLES THAN MOST GODS TWICE MY AGE. SO TELL ME...
HOW MUCH MORE WORTHY MUST I BE?
RRRRRRRRGGGH! MOVE, YOU BLASTED CHUNK OF METAL!
GAAHHH!!!
BY THE BRISTLING BEARD OF ODIN, YOU ARE ONE STUBBORN HAMMER!
SOMEDAY, MJOLNIR. SOMEDAY YOU WILL BE MINE.
AND ON THAT BLESSED MORN, WHEN I FINALLY BESTRIDE THE HEAVENS, HAMMER IN HAND...

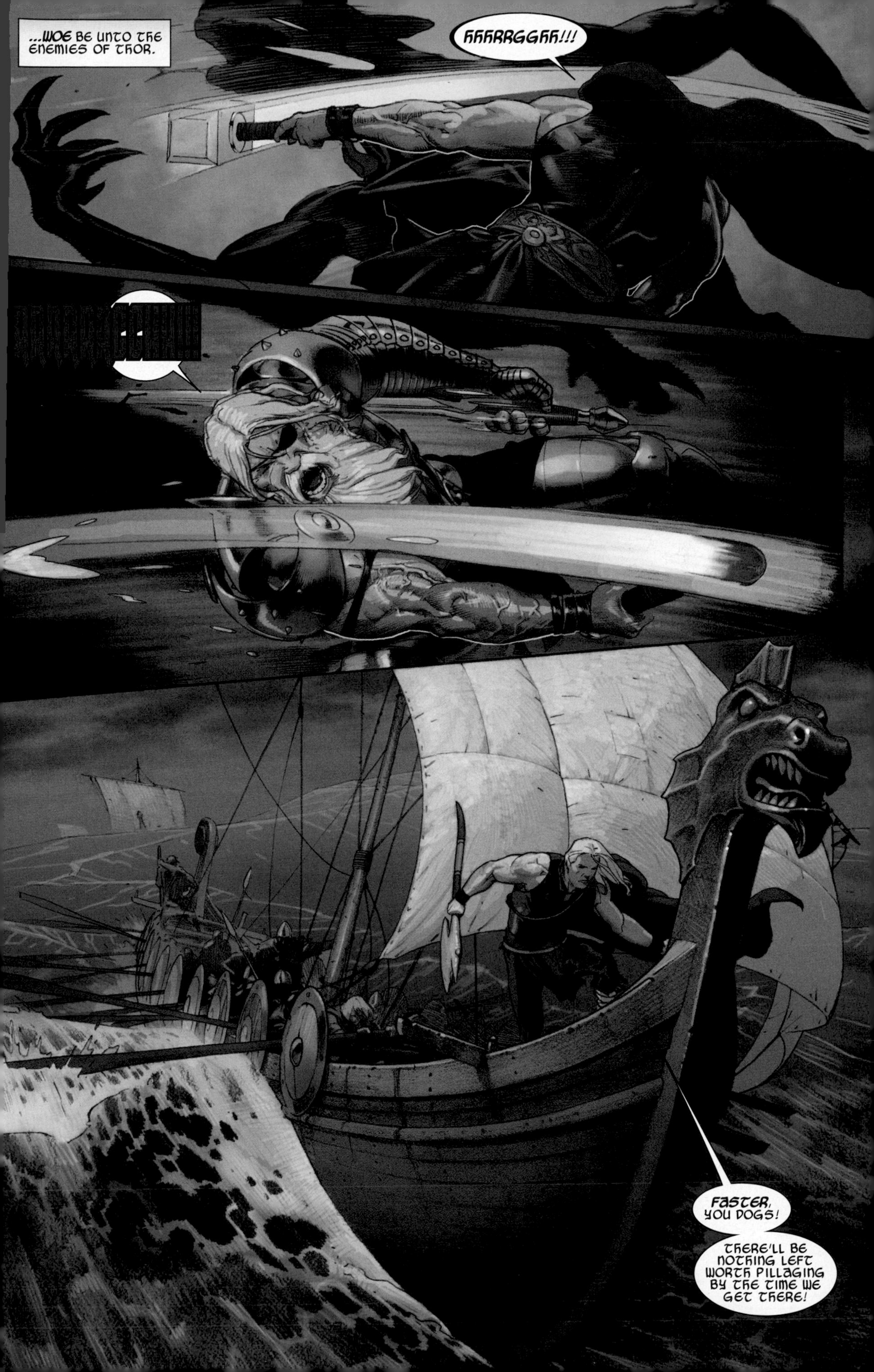
...WOE BE UNTO THE ENEMIES OF THOR.
HHHRRGGHH!!!
FASTER, YOU DOGS!
THERE'LL BE NOTHING LEFT WORTH PILLAGING BY THE TIME WE GET THERE!

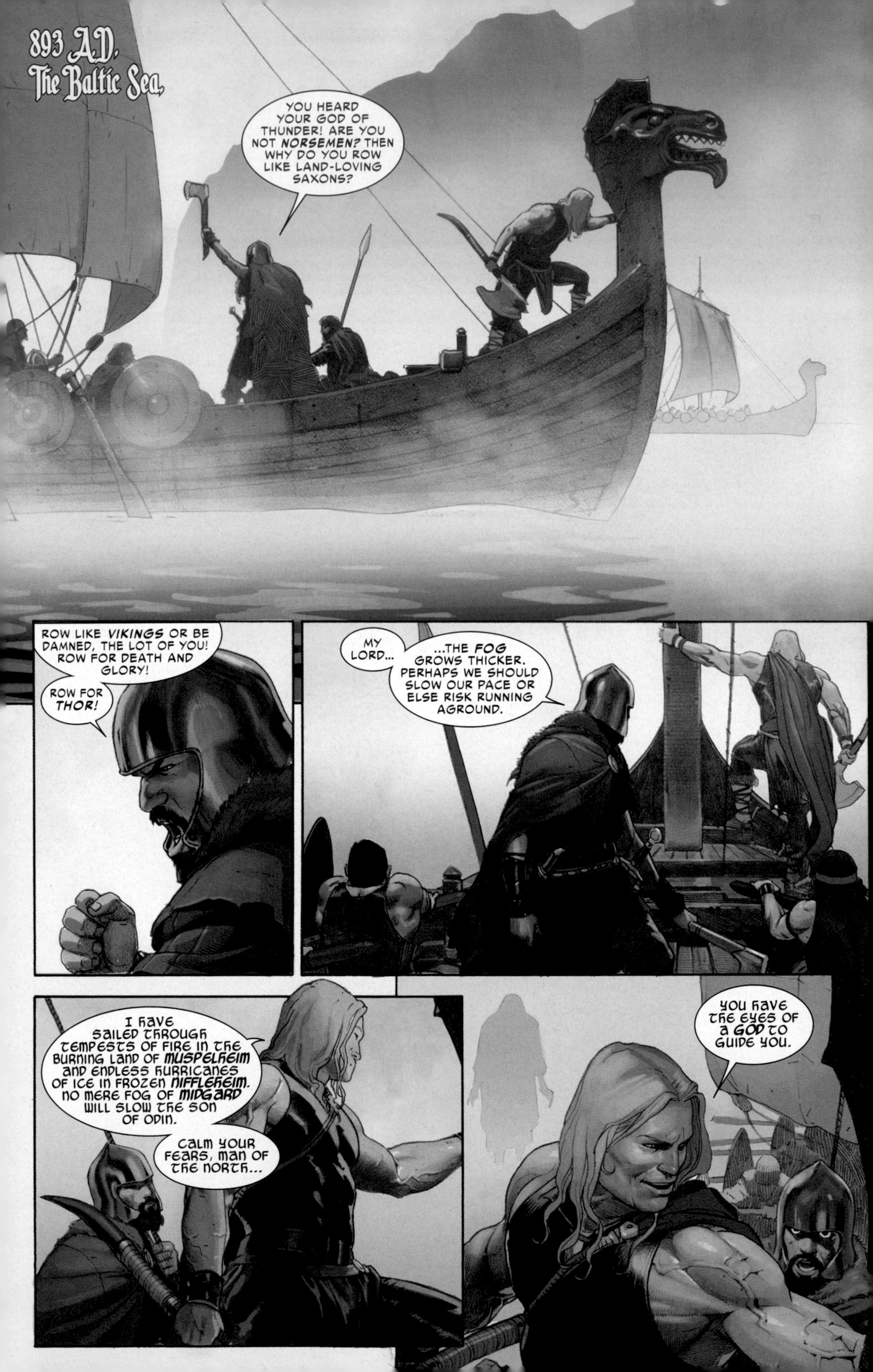
893 A.D.
The Baltic Sea.
YOU HEARD YOUR GOD OF THUNDER! ARE YOU NOT NORSEMEN? THEN WHY DO YOU ROW LIKE LAND-LOVING SAXONS?
ROW LIKE VIKINGS OR BE DAMNED, THE LOT OF YOU! ROW FOR DEATH AND GLORY!
ROW FOR THOR!
MY LORD...
...THE FOG GROWS THICKER. PERHAPS WE SHOULD SLOW OUR PACE OR ELSE RISK RUNNING AGROUND.
I HAVE SAILED THROUGH TEMPESTS OF FIRE IN THE BURNING LAND OF MUSPELHEIM AND ENDLESS HURRICANES OF ICE IN FROZEN NIFFLEHEIM. NO MERE FOG OF MIDGARD WILL SLOW THE SON OF ODIN.
CALM YOUR FEARS, MAN OF THE NORTH...
YOU HAVE THE EYES OF A GOD TO GUIDE YOU.

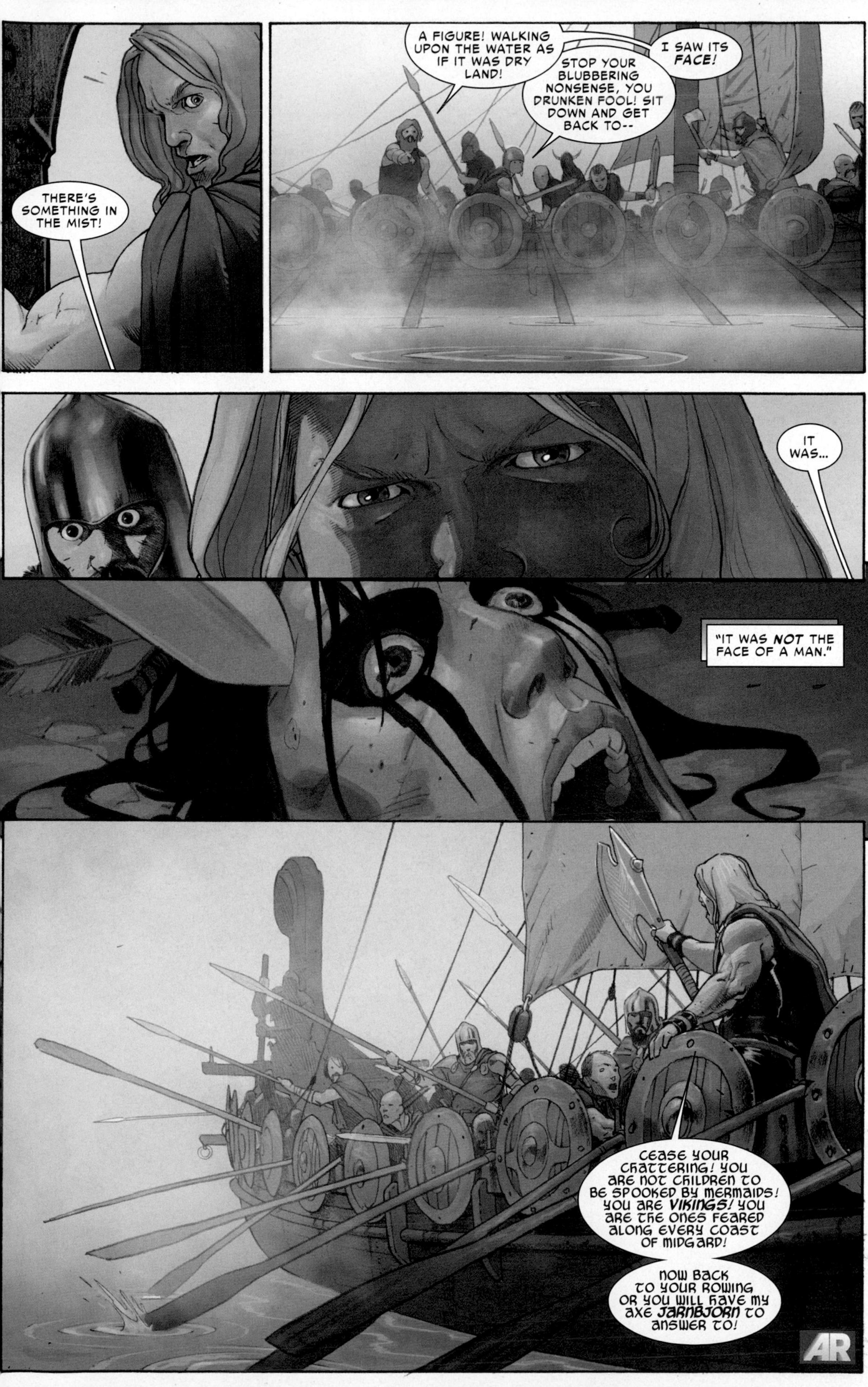
THERE'S SOMETHING IN THE MIST!
A FIGURE! WALKING UPON THE WATER AS IF IT WAS DRY LAND!
STOP YOUR BLUBBERING NONSENSE, YOU DRUNKEN FOOL! SIT DOWN AND GET BACK TO--
I SAW ITS FACE!
IT WAS...
"IT WAS NOT THE FACE OF A MAN."
CEASE YOUR CHATTERING! YOU ARE NOT CHILDREN TO BE SPOOKED BY MERMAIDS! YOU ARE VIKINGS! YOU ARE THE ONES FEARED ALONG EVERY COAST OF MIDGARD!
NOW BACK TO YOUR ROWING OR YOU WILL HAVE MY AXE JARNBJORN TO ANSWER TO!
AR

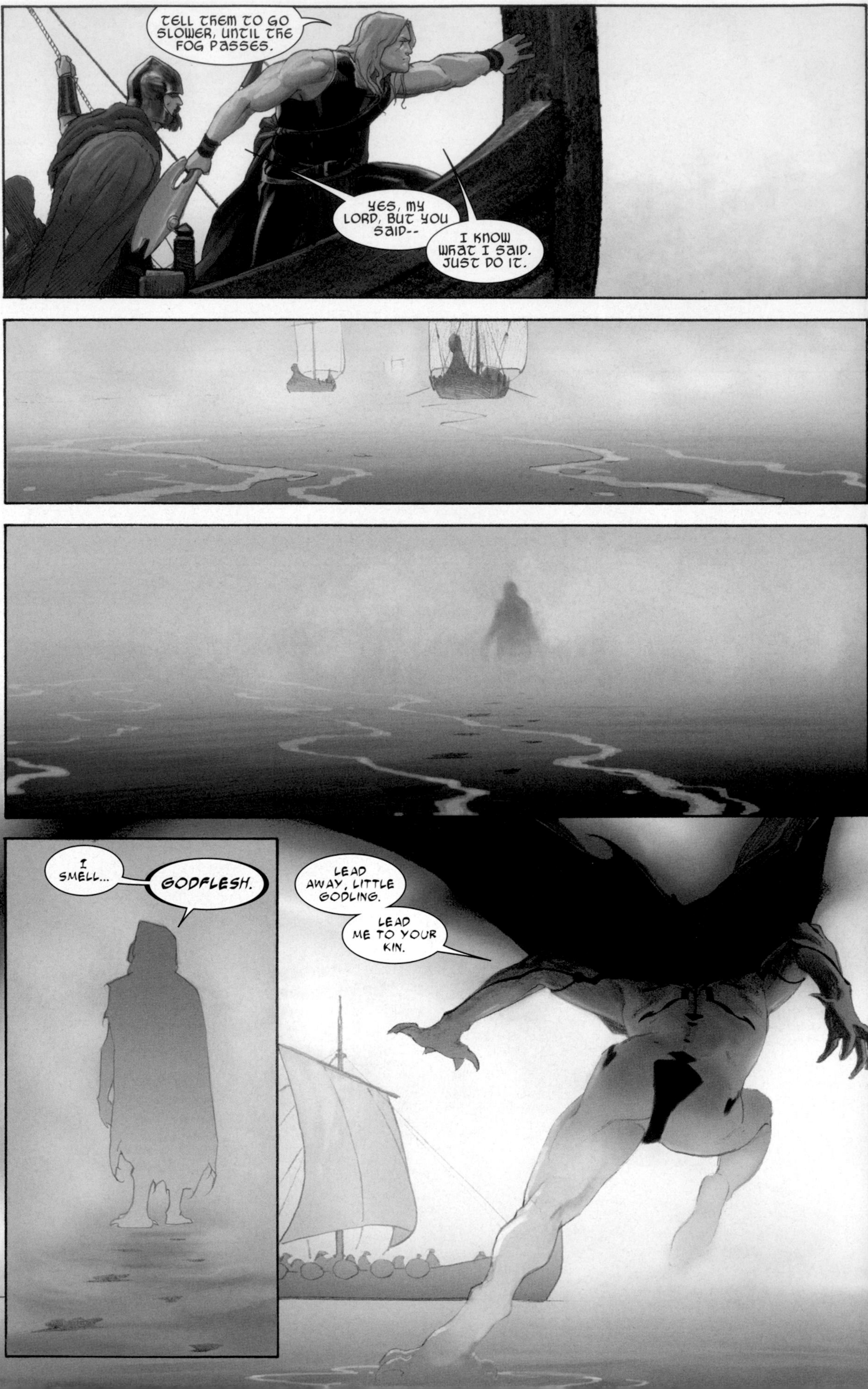
TELL THEM TO GO SLOWER, UNTIL THE FOG PASSES.
YES, MY LORD, BUT YOU SAID--
I KNOW WHAT I SAID. JUST DO IT.
I SMELL...
GODFLESH.
LEAD AWAY, LITTLE GODLING.
LEAD ME TO YOUR KIN.

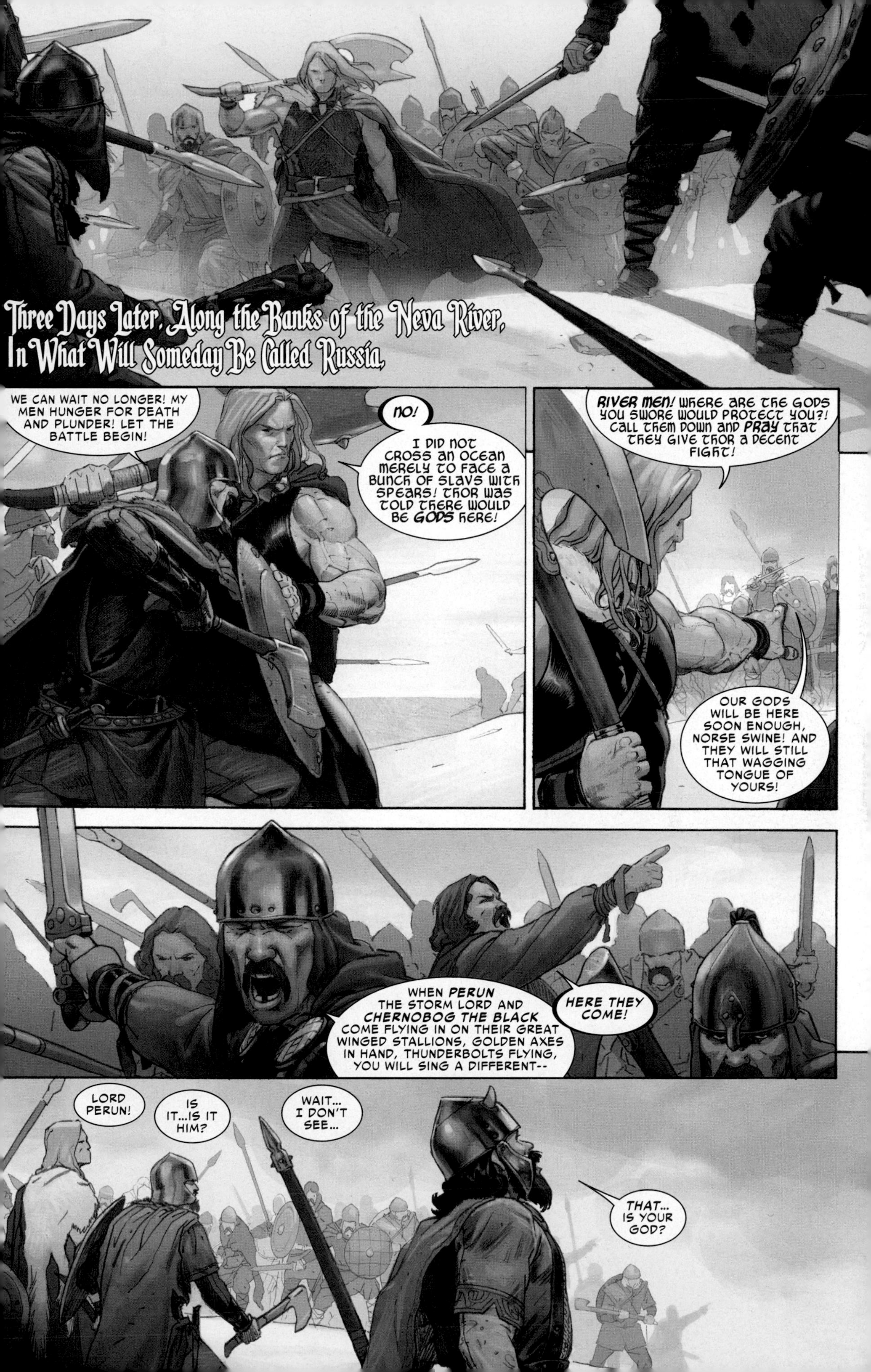

Three Days Later, Along the Banks of the Neva River, In What Will Someday Be Called Russia.
WE CAN WAIT NO LONGER! MY MEN HUNGER FOR DEATH AND PLUNDER! LET THE BATTLE BEGIN!
NO!
I DID NOT CROSS AN OCEAN MERELY TO FACE A BUNCH OF SLAVS WITH SPEARS! THOR WAS TOLD THERE WOULD BE GODS HERE!
RIVER MEN! WHERE ARE THE GODS YOU SWORE WOULD PROTECT YOU?! CALL THEM DOWN AND PRAY THAT THEY GIVE THOR A DECENT FIGHT!
OUR GODS WILL BE HERE SOON ENOUGH, NORSE SWINE! AND THEY WILL STILL THAT WAGGING TONGUE OF YOURS!
WHEN PERUN THE STORM LORD AND CHERNOBOG THE BLACK COME FLYING IN ON THEIR GREAT WINGED STALLIONS, GOLDEN AXES IN HAND, THUNDERBOLTS FLYING, YOU WILL SING A DIFFERENT--
HERE THEY COME!
LORD PERUN!
IS IT...IS IT HIM?
WAIT... I DON'T SEE...
THAT... IS YOUR GOD?

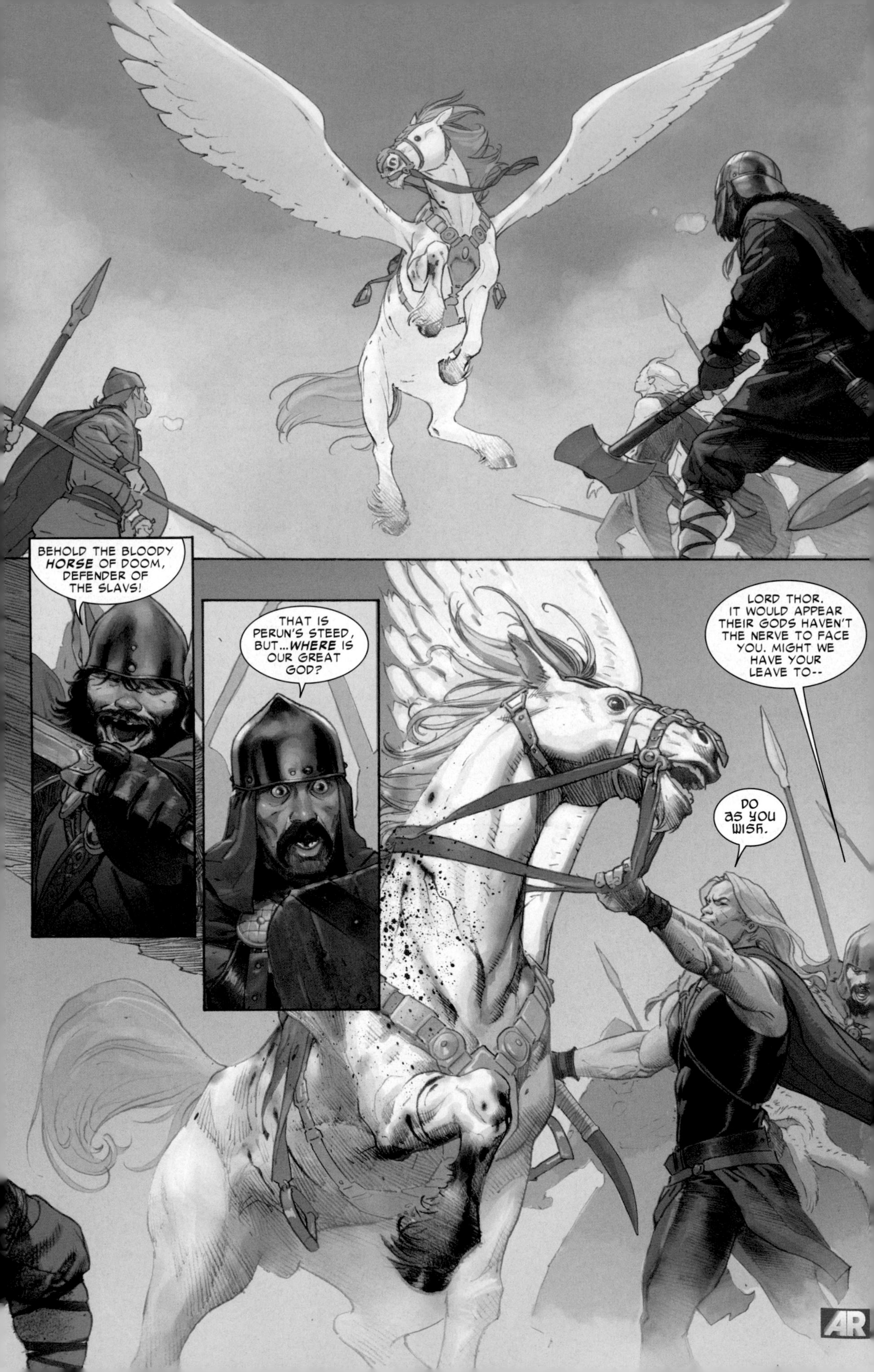

BEHOLD THE BLOODY *HORSE* OF DOOM, DEFENDER OF THE SLAVS!
THAT IS PERUN'S STEED, BUT...*WHERE* IS OUR GREAT GOD?
LORD THOR. IT WOULD APPEAR THEIR GODS HAVEN'T THE NERVE TO FACE YOU. MIGHT WE HAVE YOUR LEAVE TO--
DO AS YOU WISH.

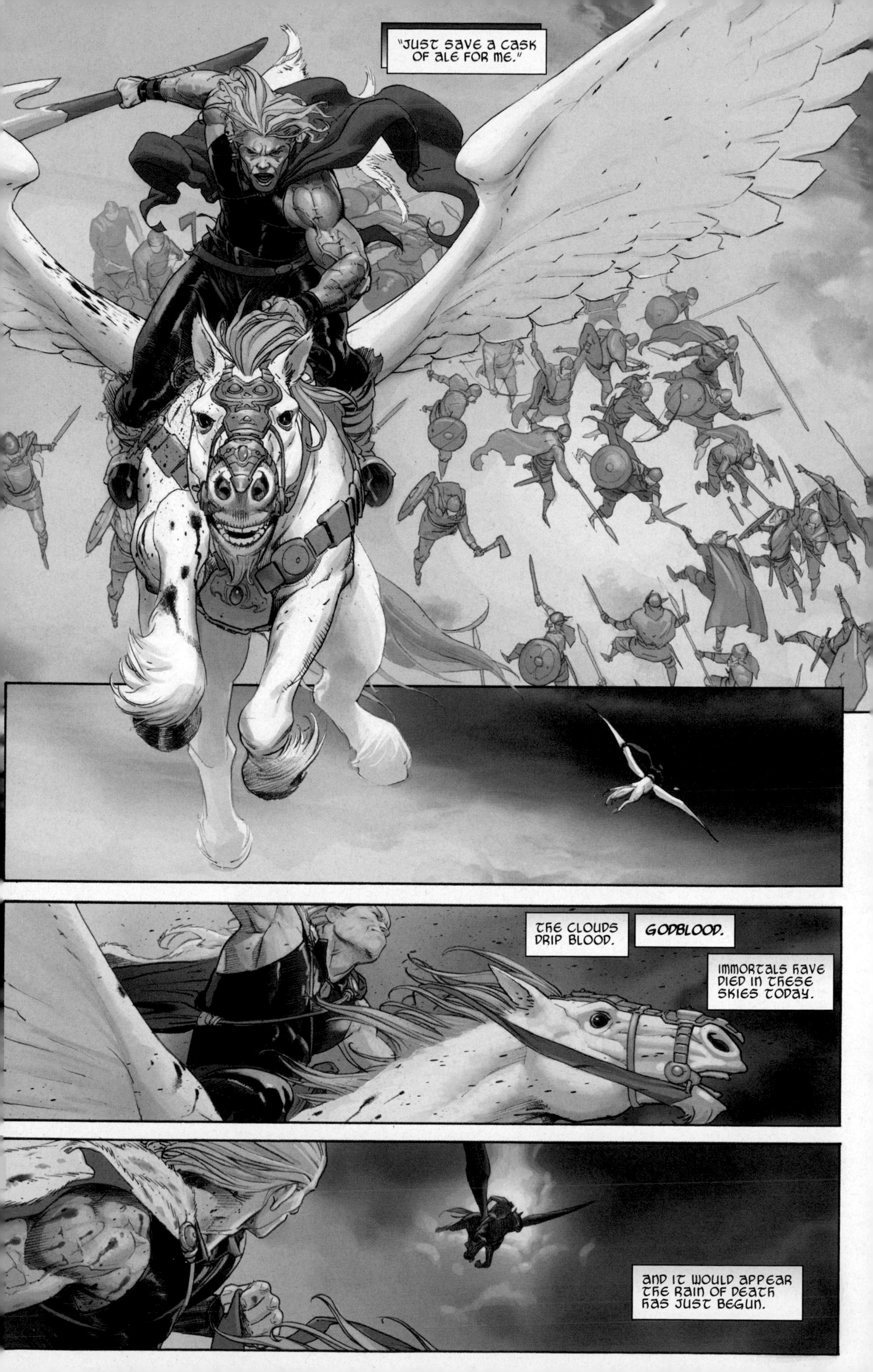
"JUST SAVE A CASK OF ALE FOR ME."
THE CLOUDS DRIP BLOOD.
GODBLOOD.
IMMORTALS HAVE DIED IN THESE SKIES TODAY.
AND IT WOULD APPEAR THE RAIN OF DEATH HAS JUST BEGUN.

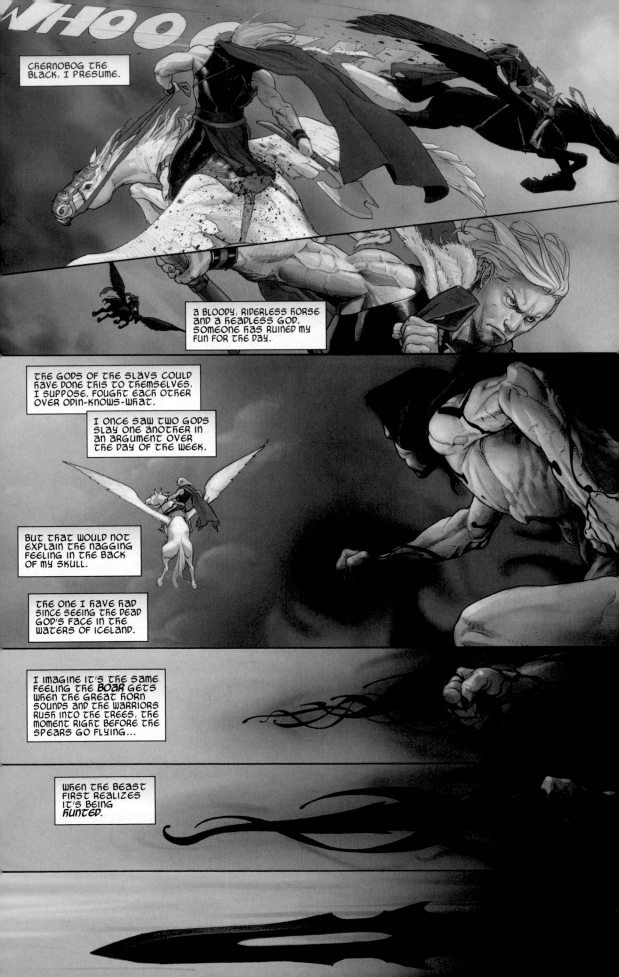

WHOO

CHERNOBOG THE BLACK, I PRESUME.

A BLOODY, RIDERLESS HORSE AND A HEADLESS GOD. SOMEONE HAS RUINED MY FUN FOR THE DAY.

THE GODS OF THE SLAVS COULD HAVE DONE THIS TO THEMSELVES, I SUPPOSE. FOUGHT EACH OTHER OVER ODIN-KNOWS-WHAT.

I ONCE SAW TWO GODS SLAY ONE ANOTHER IN AN ARGUMENT OVER THE DAY OF THE WEEK.

BUT THAT WOULD NOT EXPLAIN THE NAGGING FEELING IN THE BACK OF MY SKULL.

THE ONE I HAVE HAD SINCE SEEING THE DEAD GOD'S FACE IN THE WATERS OF ICELAND.

I IMAGINE IT'S THE SAME FEELING THE BOAR GETS WHEN THE GREAT HORN SOUNDS AND THE WARRIORS RUSH INTO THE TREES, THE MOMENT RIGHT BEFORE THE SPEARS GO FLYING...

WHEN THE BEAST FIRST REALIZES IT'S BEING HUNTED.

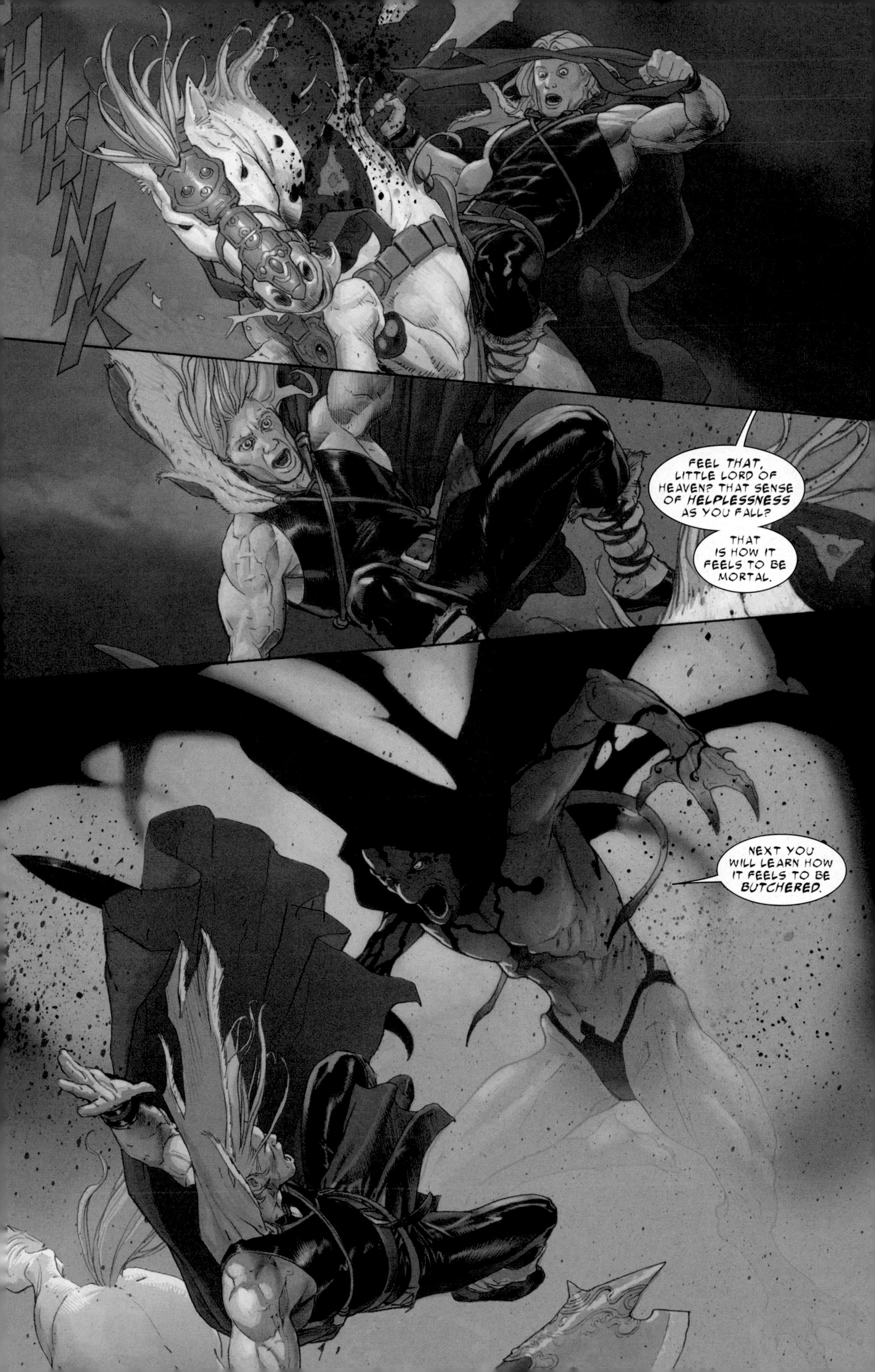
THHHHNNNK
FEEL THAT, LITTLE LORD OF HEAVEN? THAT SENSE OF HELPLESSNESS AS YOU FALL?
THAT IS HOW IT FEELS TO BE MORTAL.
NEXT YOU WILL LEARN HOW IT FEELS TO BE BUTCHERED.

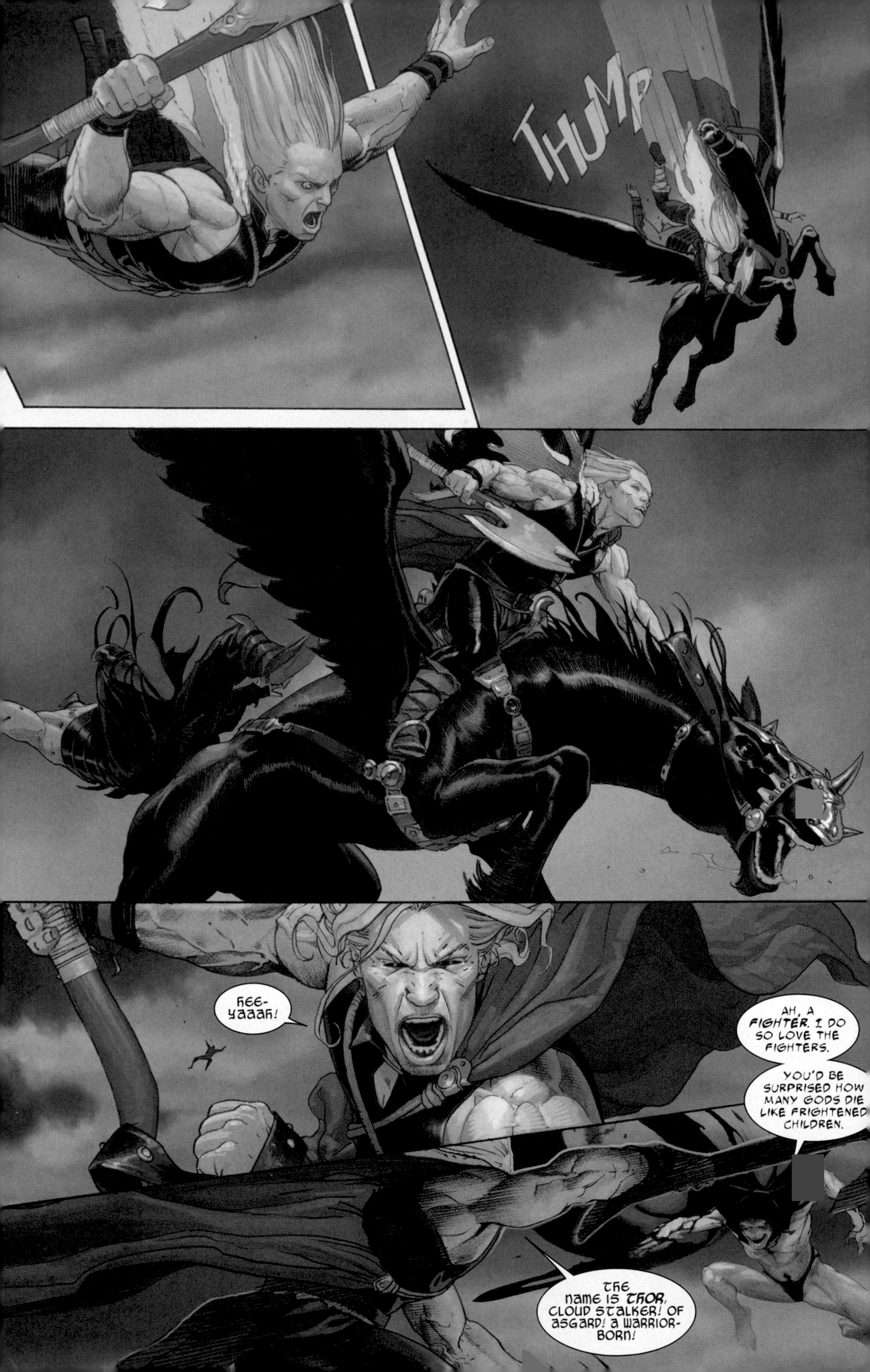
THUMP
HEE-YAAAH!
AH, A FIGHTER. I DO SO LOVE THE FIGHTERS.
YOU'D BE SURPRISED HOW MANY GODS DIE LIKE FRIGHTENED CHILDREN.
THE NAME IS THOR, CLOUD STALKER! OF ASGARD! A WARRIOR-BORN!

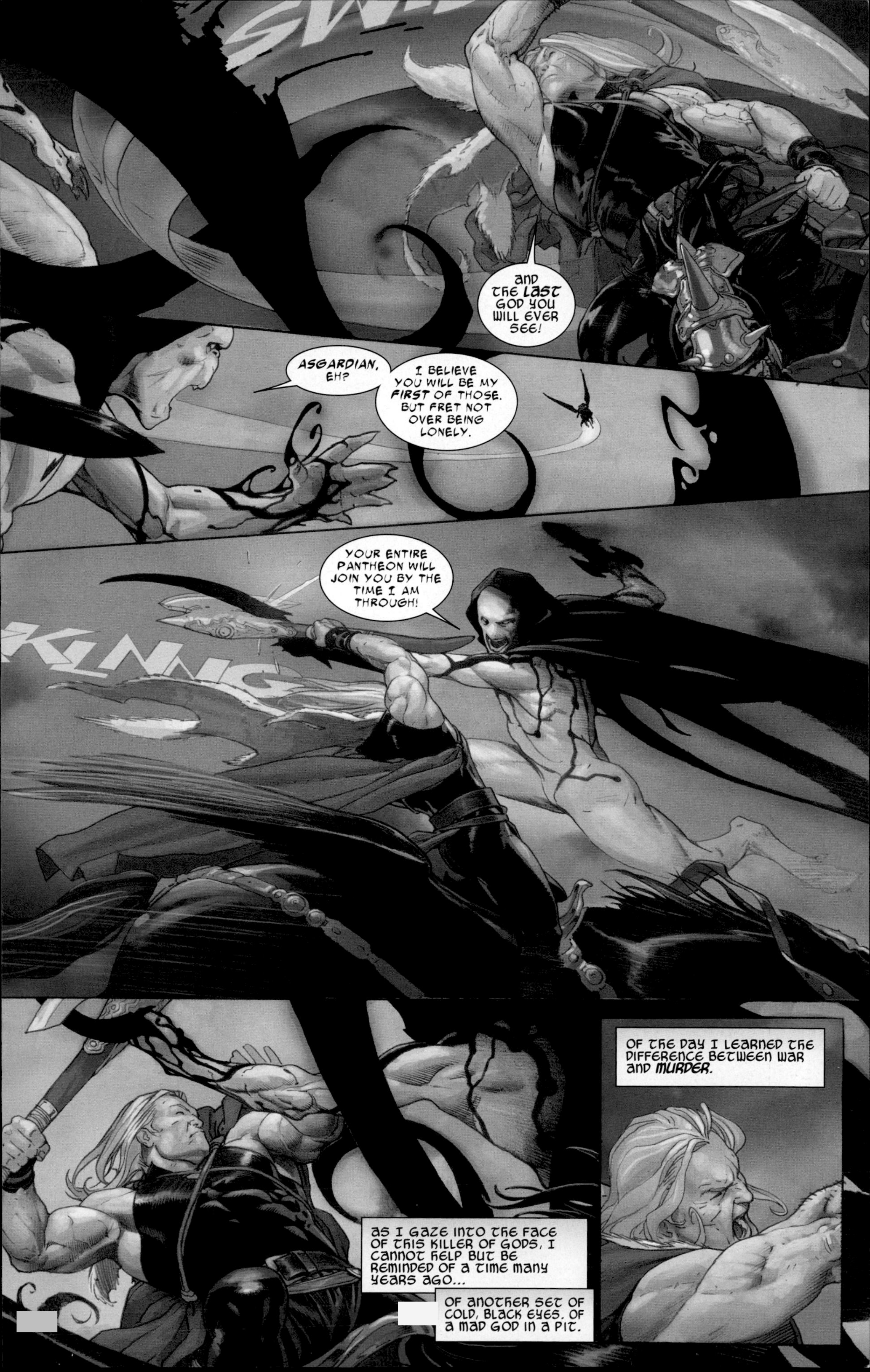
AND THE LAST GOD YOU WILL EVER SEE!
ASGARDIAN, EH?
I BELIEVE YOU WILL BE MY FIRST OF THOSE. BUT FRET NOT OVER BEING LONELY.
YOUR ENTIRE PANTHEON WILL JOIN YOU BY THE TIME I AM THROUGH!
AS I GAZE INTO THE FACE OF THIS KILLER OF GODS, I CANNOT HELP BUT BE REMINDED OF A TIME MANY YEARS AGO...
OF ANOTHER SET OF COLD, BLACK EYES. OF A MAD GOD IN A PIT.
OF THE DAY I LEARNED THE DIFFERENCE BETWEEN WAR AND MURDER.

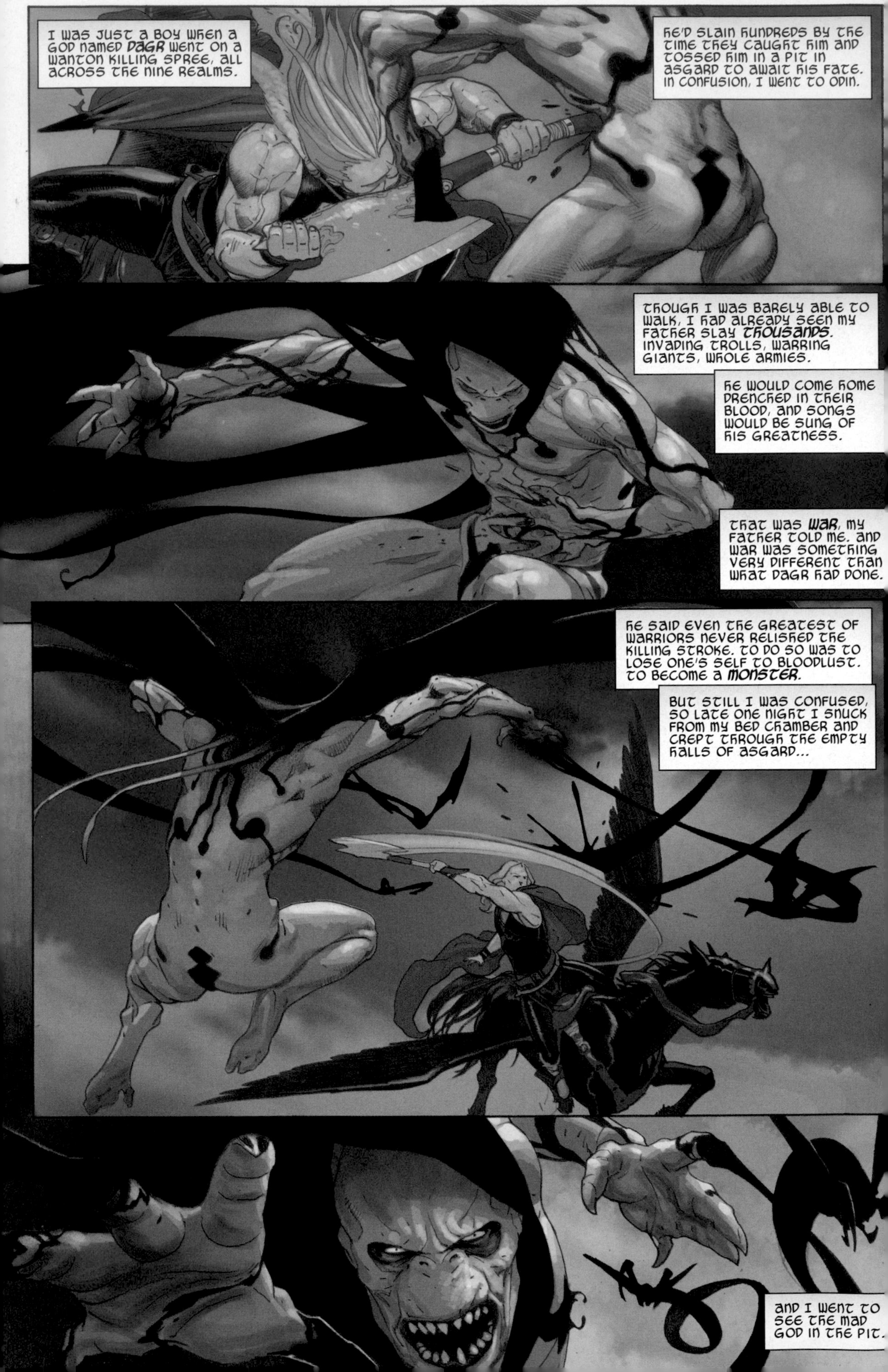
I WAS JUST A BOY WHEN A GOD NAMED DAGR WENT ON A WANTON KILLING SPREE, ALL ACROSS THE NINE REALMS.
HE'D SLAIN HUNDREDS BY THE TIME THEY CAUGHT HIM AND TOSSED HIM IN A PIT IN ASGARD TO AWAIT HIS FATE. IN CONFUSION, I WENT TO ODIN.
THOUGH I WAS BARELY ABLE TO WALK, I HAD ALREADY SEEN MY FATHER SLAY THOUSANDS. INVADING TROLLS, WARRING GIANTS, WHOLE ARMIES.
HE WOULD COME HOME DRENCHED IN THEIR BLOOD, AND SONGS WOULD BE SUNG OF HIS GREATNESS.
THAT WAS WAR, MY FATHER TOLD ME. AND WAR WAS SOMETHING VERY DIFFERENT THAN WHAT DAGR HAD DONE.
HE SAID EVEN THE GREATEST OF WARRIORS NEVER RELISHED THE KILLING STROKE. TO DO SO WAS TO LOSE ONE'S SELF TO BLOODLUST. TO BECOME A MONSTER.
BUT STILL I WAS CONFUSED, SO LATE ONE NIGHT I SNUCK FROM MY BED CHAMBER AND CREPT THROUGH THE EMPTY HALLS OF ASGARD...
AND I WENT TO SEE THE MAD GOD IN THE PIT.

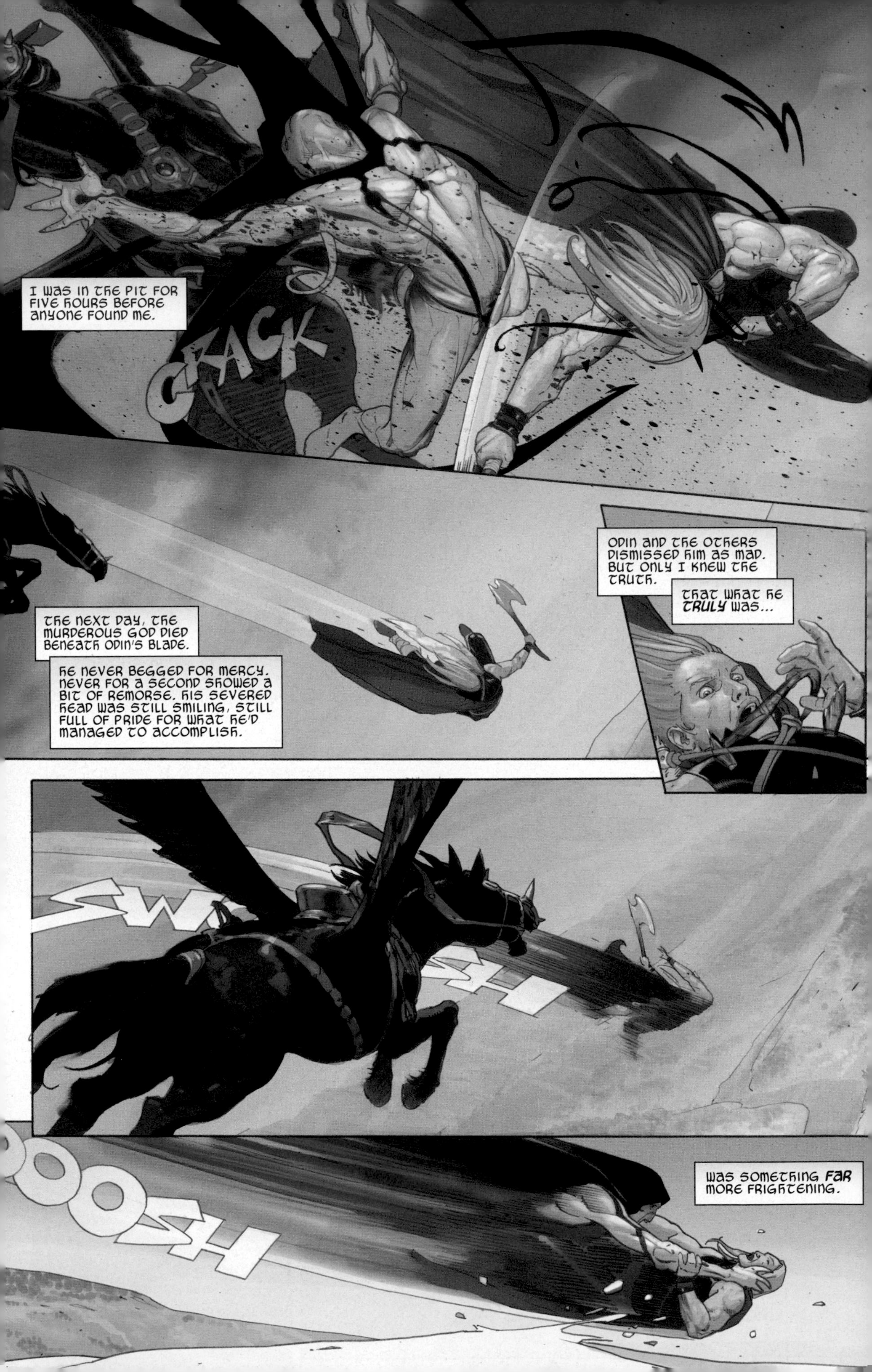
I WAS IN THE PIT FOR FIVE HOURS BEFORE ANYONE FOUND ME.
CRACK
THE NEXT DAY, THE MURDEROUS GOD DIED BENEATH ODIN'S BLADE.
HE NEVER BEGGED FOR MERCY. NEVER FOR A SECOND SHOWED A BIT OF REMORSE. HIS SEVERED HEAD WAS STILL SMILING, STILL FULL OF PRIDE FOR WHAT HE'D MANAGED TO ACCOMPLISH.
ODIN AND THE OTHERS DISMISSED HIM AS MAD. BUT ONLY I KNEW THE TRUTH.
THAT WHAT HE TRULY WAS...
WAS SOMETHING FAR MORE FRIGHTENING.

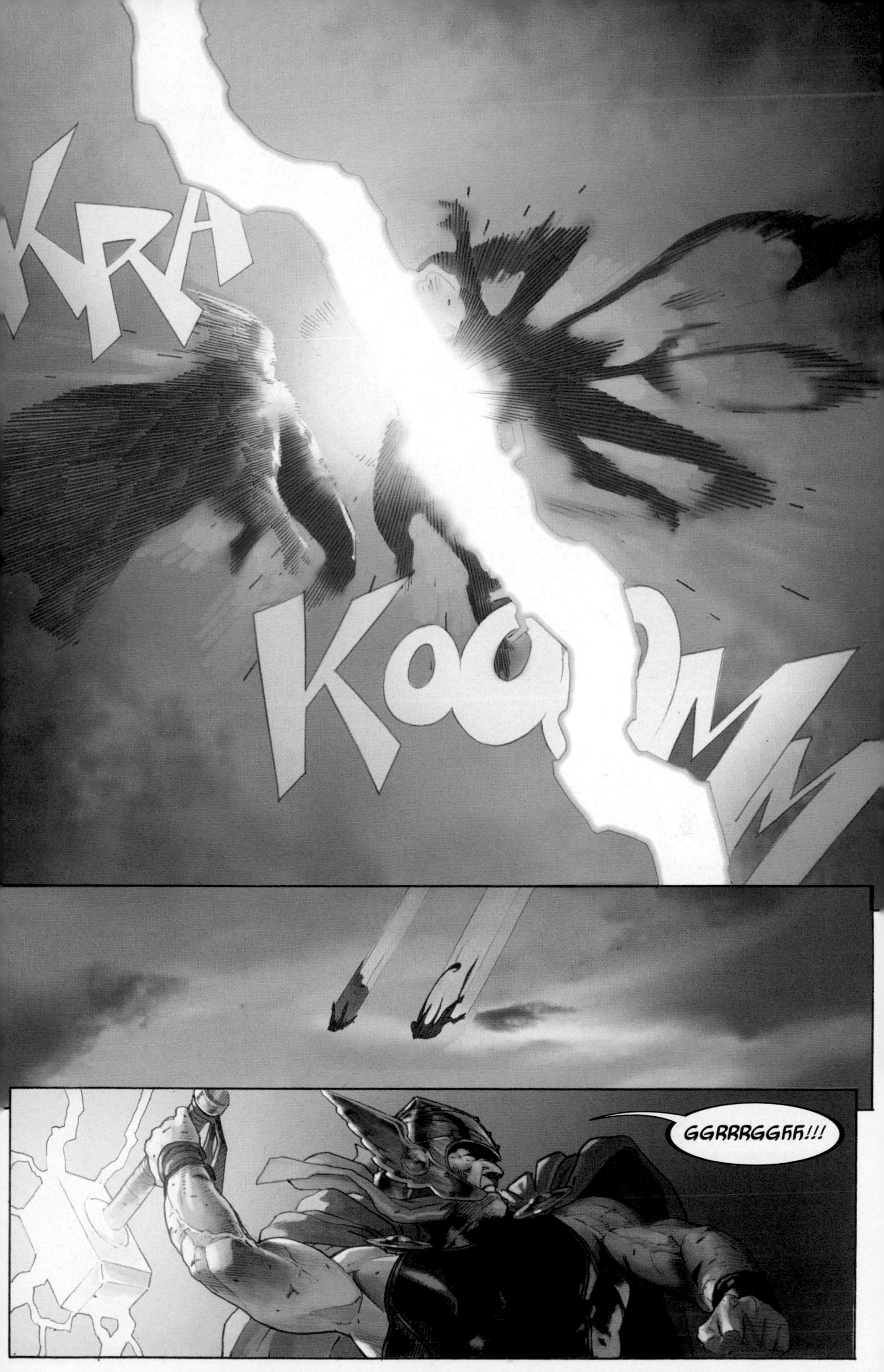
KRA
KOOOOM
GGRRRGGHH!!!

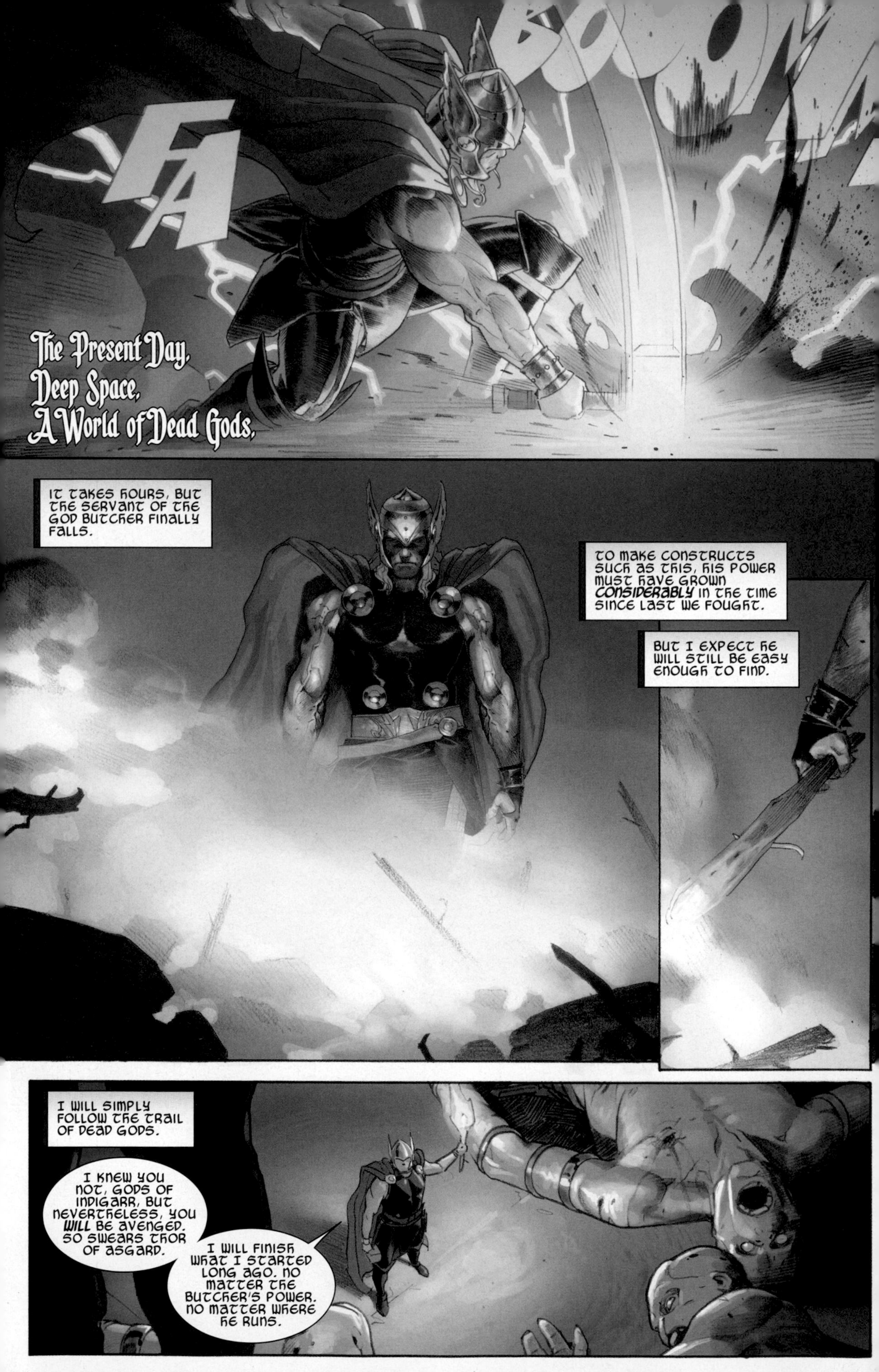
FA
BOOM
The Present Day,
Deep Space,
A World of Dead Gods,
IT TAKES HOURS, BUT THE SERVANT OF THE GOD BUTCHER FINALLY FALLS.
TO MAKE CONSTRUCTS SUCH AS THIS, HIS POWER MUST HAVE GROWN CONSIDERABLY IN THE TIME SINCE LAST WE FOUGHT.
BUT I EXPECT HE WILL STILL BE EASY ENOUGH TO FIND.
I WILL SIMPLY FOLLOW THE TRAIL OF DEAD GODS.
I KNEW YOU NOT, GODS OF INDIGARR, BUT NEVERTHELESS, YOU WILL BE AVENGED. SO SWEARS THOR OF ASGARD.
I WILL FINISH WHAT I STARTED LONG AGO. NO MATTER THE BUTCHER'S POWER. NO MATTER WHERE HE RUNS.

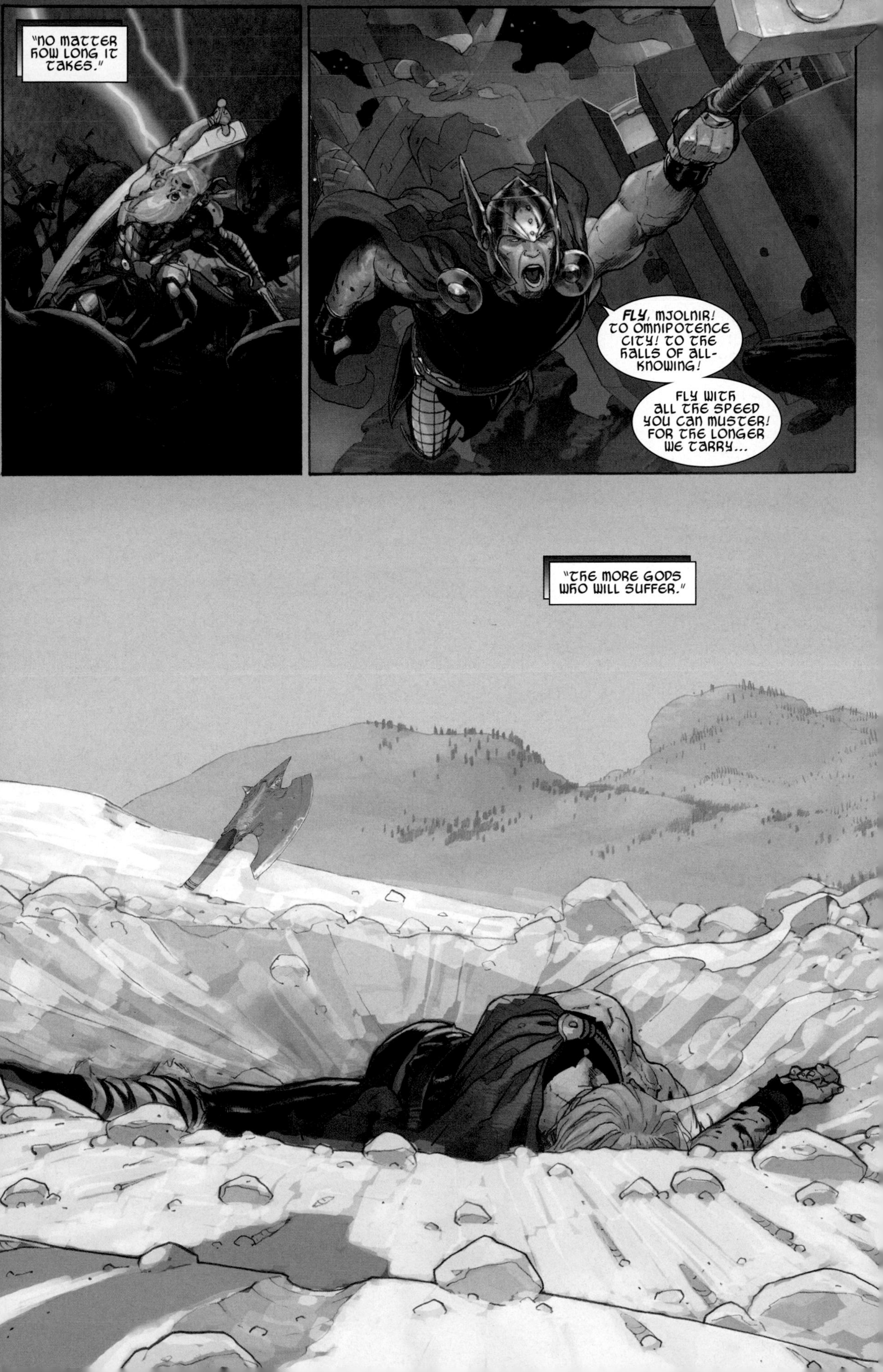
"NO MATTER HOW LONG IT TAKES."
FLY, MJOLNIR! TO OMNIPOTENCE CITY! TO THE HALLS OF ALL-KNOWING!
FLY WITH ALL THE SPEED YOU CAN MUSTER! FOR THE LONGER WE TARRY...
"THE MORE GODS WHO WILL SUFFER."

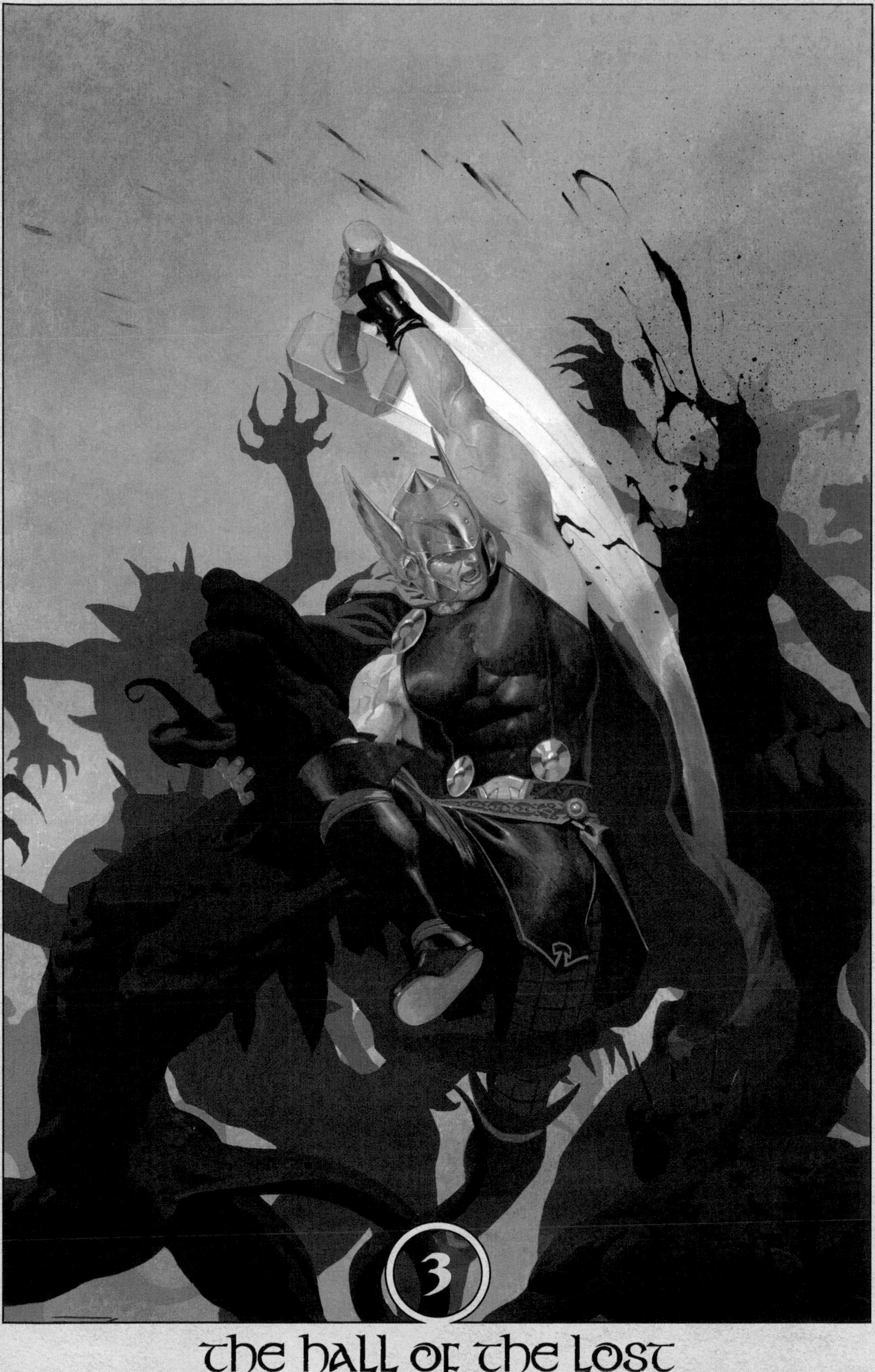
3

THE HALL OF THE LOST

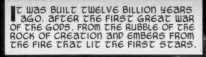

IT WAS BUILT TWELVE BILLION YEARS AGO, AFTER THE FIRST GREAT WAR OF THE GODS. FROM THE RUBBLE OF THE ROCK OF CREATION AND EMBERS FROM THE FIRE THAT LIT THE FIRST STARS.

IT WAS BUILT BY THE LORDS OF THE DAWN, BY THE FIRST OF THE ELDER GODS, AS A PLACE OF DIVINE FELLOWSHIP. A PLACE WHERE IMMORTALS FROM ALL CORNERS OF REALITY WOULD FOREVER BE WELCOME.

HERE ETERNAL TREATIES ARE SIGNED. SACRED COVENANTS SWORN THAT SAVE THE LIVES OF MILLIONS. HERE GODS ARE MARRIED AND TRIED. HERE WORLDS ARE BORN AND BARTERED.

HERE IS THE HOME OF THE PARLIAMENT OF PANTHEONS AND THE HIGH HOLY COURT. THE GENESIS BAZAARS AND THE HALLS OF ALL-KNOWING. THE MOON-SIZED JEWELS OF THE UNIVERSAL CROWN.

HERE IN THE CENTER OF INFINITY IS THE HEAVEN OF HEAVENS, A SITE NO MORTAL EYES WILL EVER SEE.

HERE IS *OMNIPOTENCE CITY*, NEXUS OF ALL THE GODS.

HERE HAVE I COME SEEKING ANSWERS.

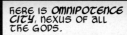

THOR OF ASGARD. I MUST SAY, I NEVER EXPECTED TO SEE YOU HERE AGAIN.

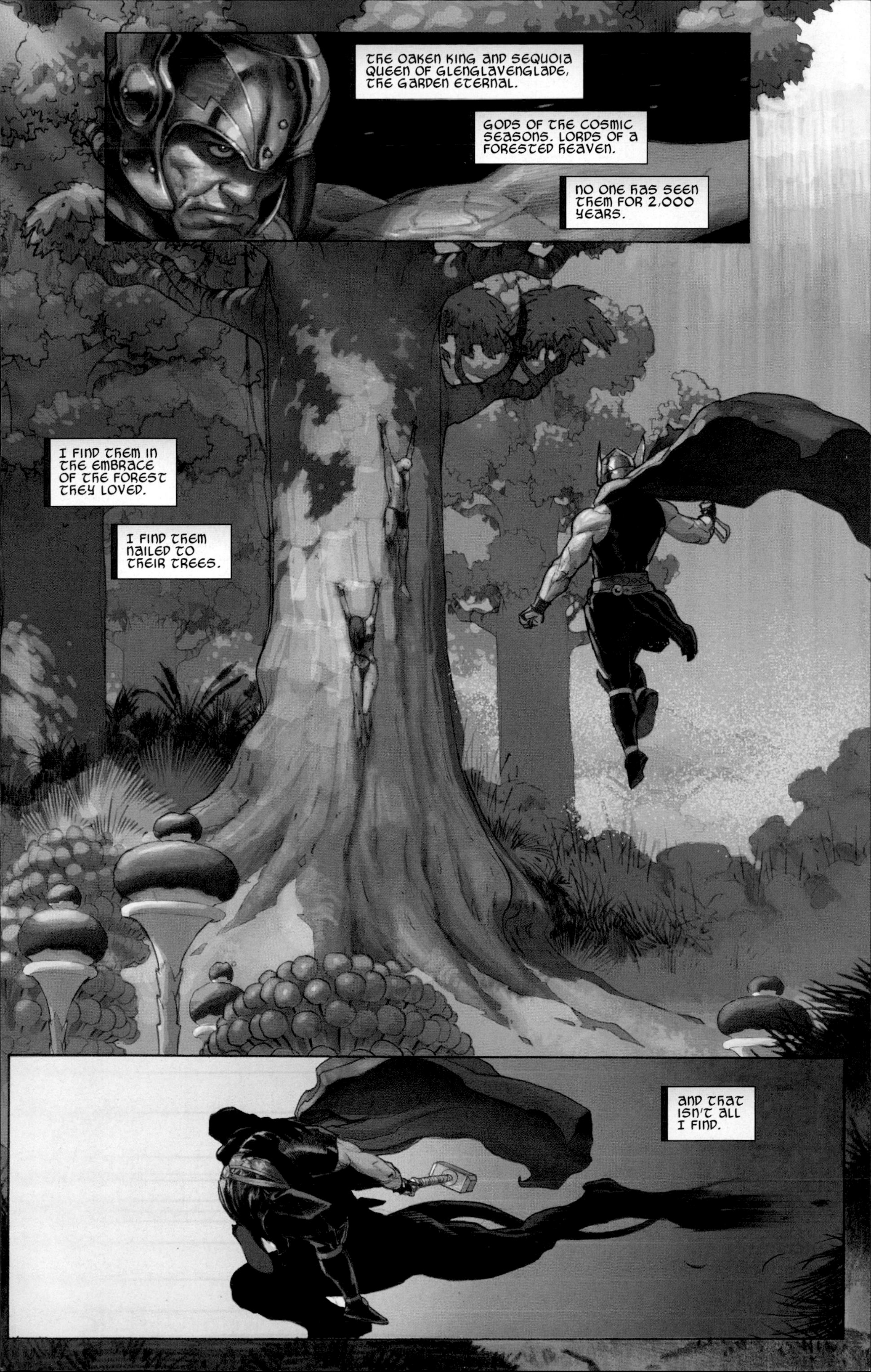
THE OAKEN KING AND SEQUOIA QUEEN OF GLENGLAVENGLADE, THE GARDEN ETERNAL.
GODS OF THE COSMIC SEASONS. LORDS OF A FORESTED HEAVEN.
NO ONE HAS SEEN THEM FOR 2,000 YEARS.
I FIND THEM IN THE EMBRACE OF THE FOREST THEY LOVED.
I FIND THEM NAILED TO THEIR TREES.
AND THAT ISN'T ALL I FIND.

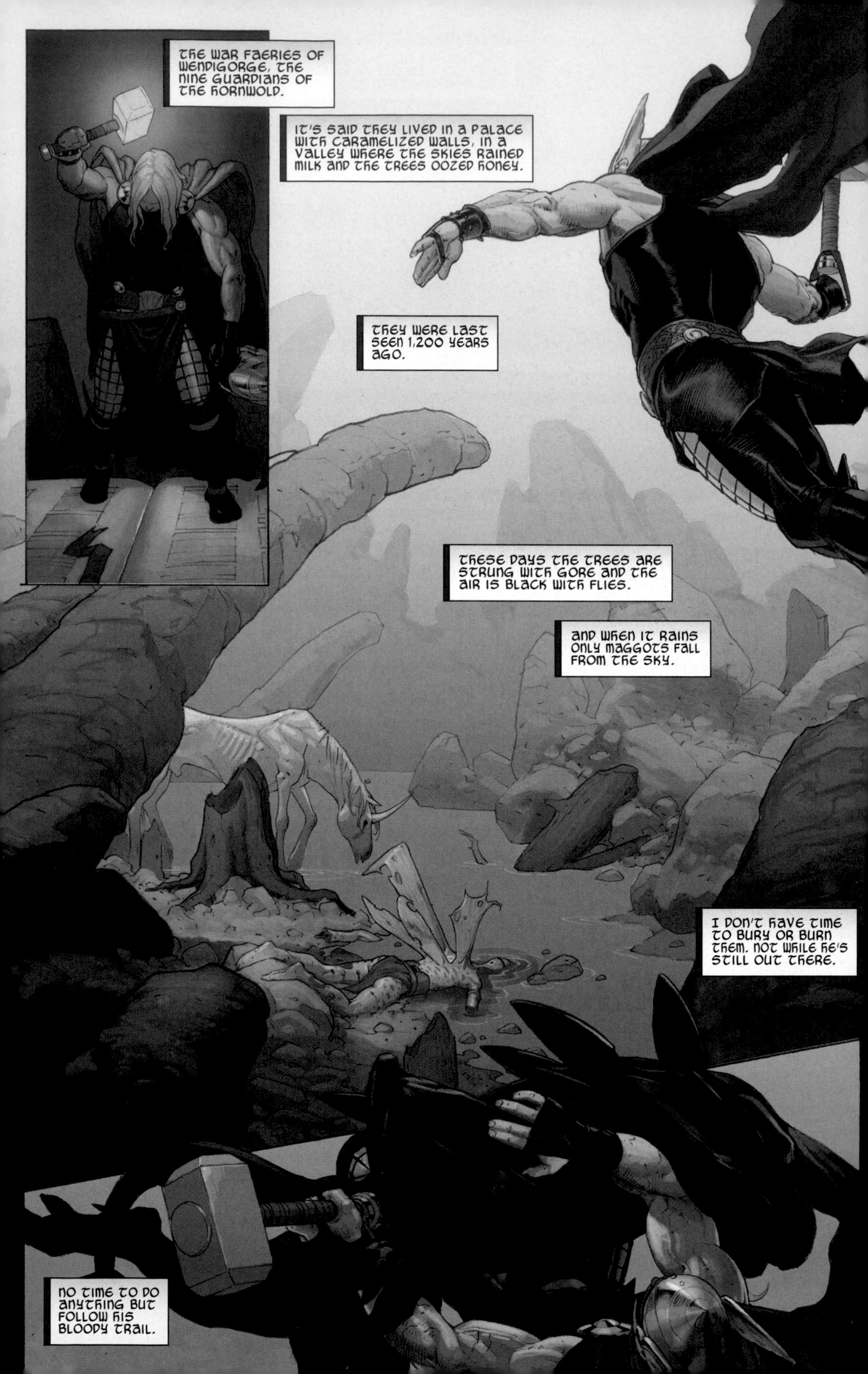
THE WAR FAERIES OF WENDIGORGE, THE NINE GUARDIANS OF THE HORNWOLD.
IT'S SAID THEY LIVED IN A PALACE WITH CARAMELIZED WALLS, IN A VALLEY WHERE THE SKIES RAINED MILK AND THE TREES OOZED HONEY.
THEY WERE LAST SEEN 1,200 YEARS AGO.
THESE DAYS THE TREES ARE STRUNG WITH GORE AND THE AIR IS BLACK WITH FLIES.
AND WHEN IT RAINS ONLY MAGGOTS FALL FROM THE SKY.
I DON'T HAVE TIME TO BURY OR BURN THEM. NOT WHILE HE'S STILL OUT THERE.
NO TIME TO DO ANYTHING BUT FOLLOW HIS BLOODY TRAIL.

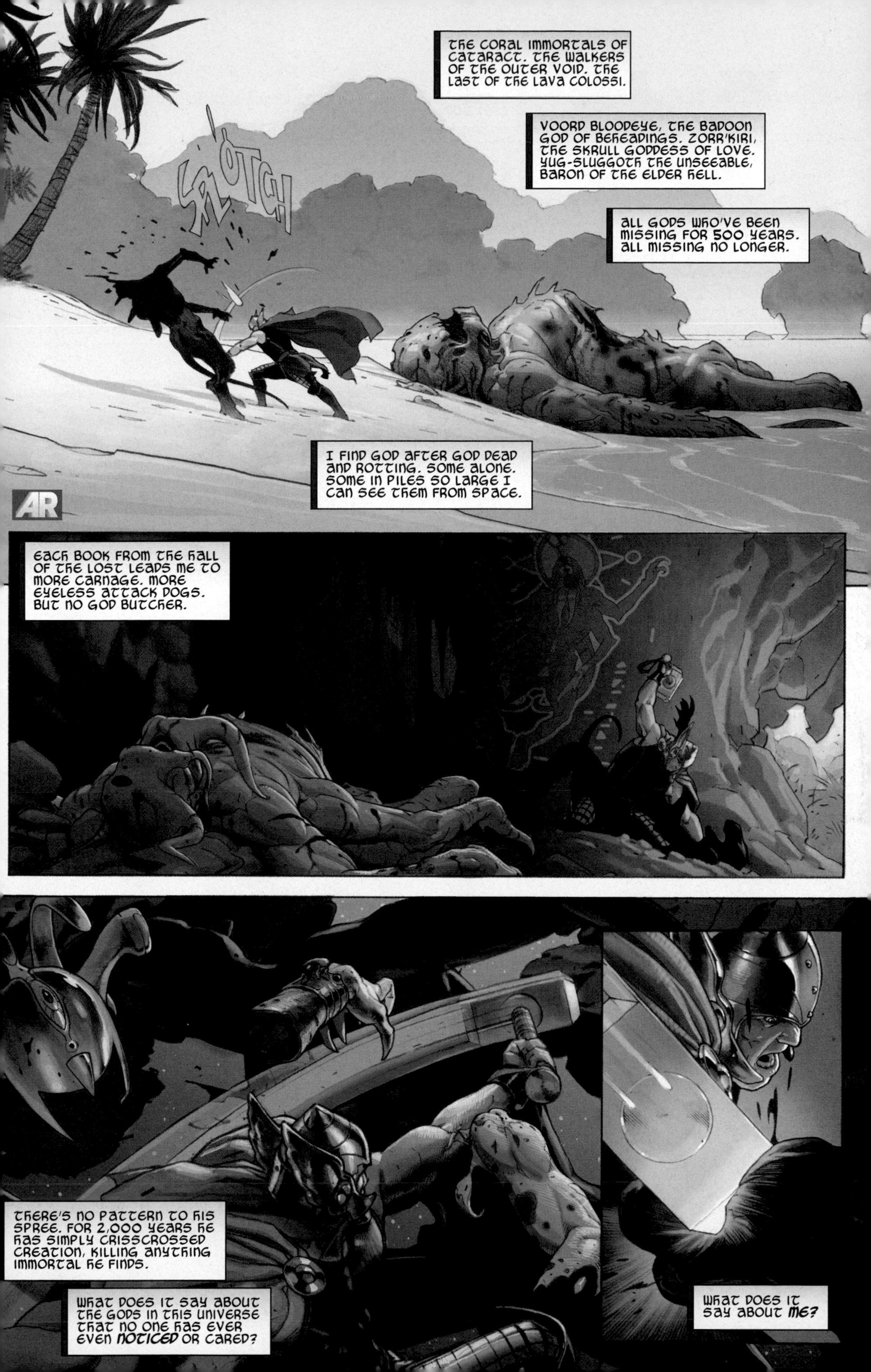

THE CORAL IMMORTALS OF CATARACT. THE WALKERS OF THE OUTER VOID. THE LAST OF THE LAVA COLOSSI.
VOORD BLOODEYE, THE BADOON GOD OF BEHEADINGS. ZORR'KIRI, THE SKRULL GODDESS OF LOVE. YUG-SLUGGOTH THE UNSEEABLE, BARON OF THE ELDER HELL.
SKLOTCH
ALL GODS WHO'VE BEEN MISSING FOR 500 YEARS. ALL MISSING NO LONGER.
I FIND GOD AFTER GOD DEAD AND ROTTING. SOME ALONE. SOME IN PILES SO LARGE I CAN SEE THEM FROM SPACE.
EACH BOOK FROM THE HALL OF THE LOST LEADS ME TO MORE CARNAGE. MORE EYELESS ATTACK DOGS. BUT NO GOD BUTCHER.
THERE'S NO PATTERN TO HIS SPREE. FOR 2,000 YEARS HE HAS SIMPLY CRISSCROSSED CREATION, KILLING ANYTHING IMMORTAL HE FINDS.
WHAT DOES IT SAY ABOUT THE GODS IN THIS UNIVERSE THAT NO ONE HAS EVER EVEN *NOTICED* OR CARED?
WHAT DOES IT SAY ABOUT *ME?*

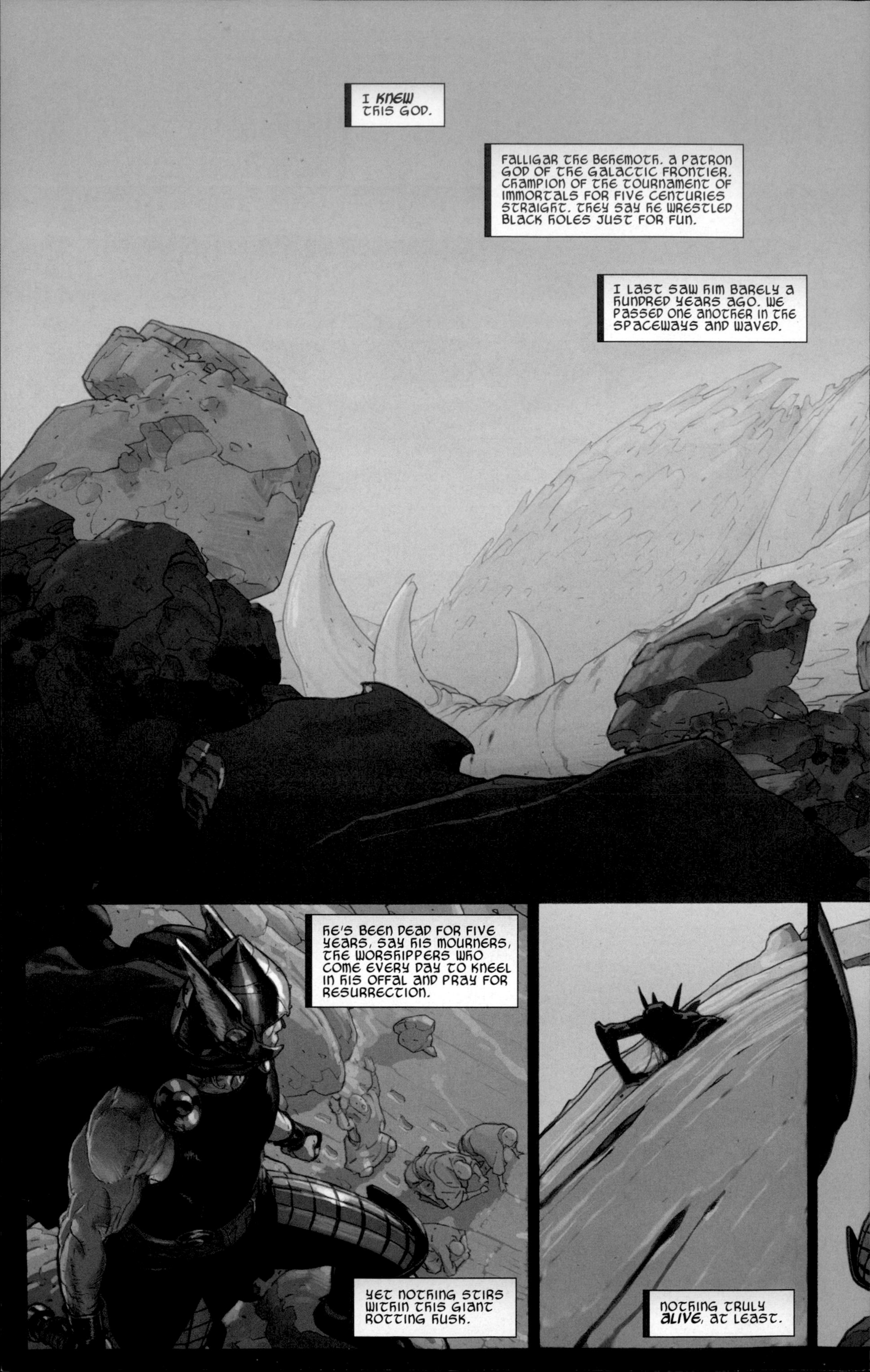
I KNEW THIS GOD.
FALLIGAR THE BEHEMOTH. A PATRON GOD OF THE GALACTIC FRONTIER. CHAMPION OF THE TOURNAMENT OF IMMORTALS FOR FIVE CENTURIES STRAIGHT. THEY SAY HE WRESTLED BLACK HOLES JUST FOR FUN.
I LAST SAW HIM BARELY A HUNDRED YEARS AGO. WE PASSED ONE ANOTHER IN THE SPACEWAYS AND WAVED.
HE'S BEEN DEAD FOR FIVE YEARS, SAY HIS MOURNERS, THE WORSHIPPERS WHO COME EVERY DAY TO KNEEL IN HIS OFFAL AND PRAY FOR RESURRECTION.
YET NOTHING STIRS WITHIN THIS GIANT ROTTING HUSK.
NOTHING TRULY ALIVE, AT LEAST.

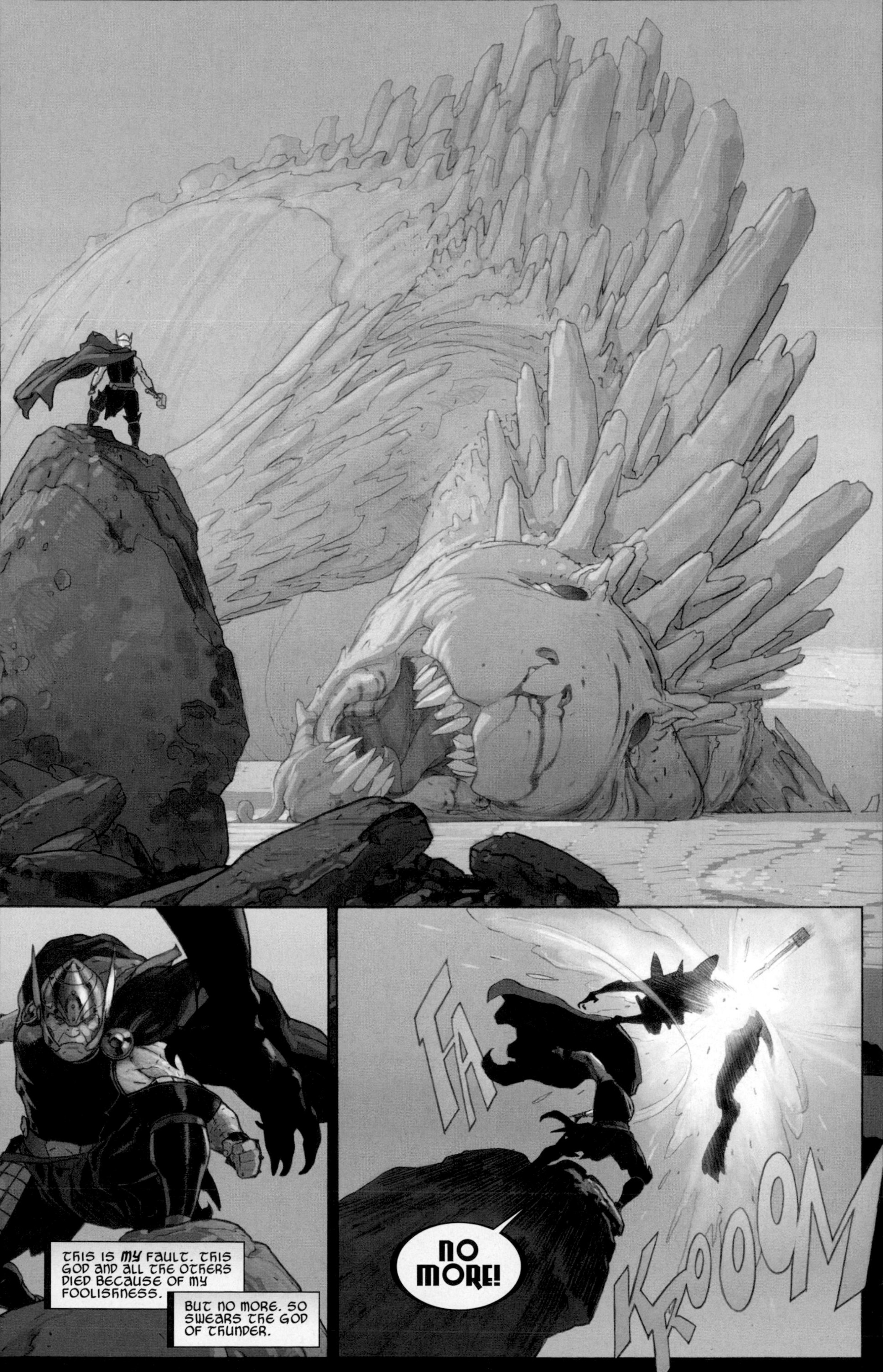
THIS IS MY FAULT. THIS GOD AND ALL THE OTHERS DIED BECAUSE OF MY FOOLISHNESS.
BUT NO MORE. SO SWEARS THE GOD OF THUNDER.
FA
NO MORE!
KROOOM

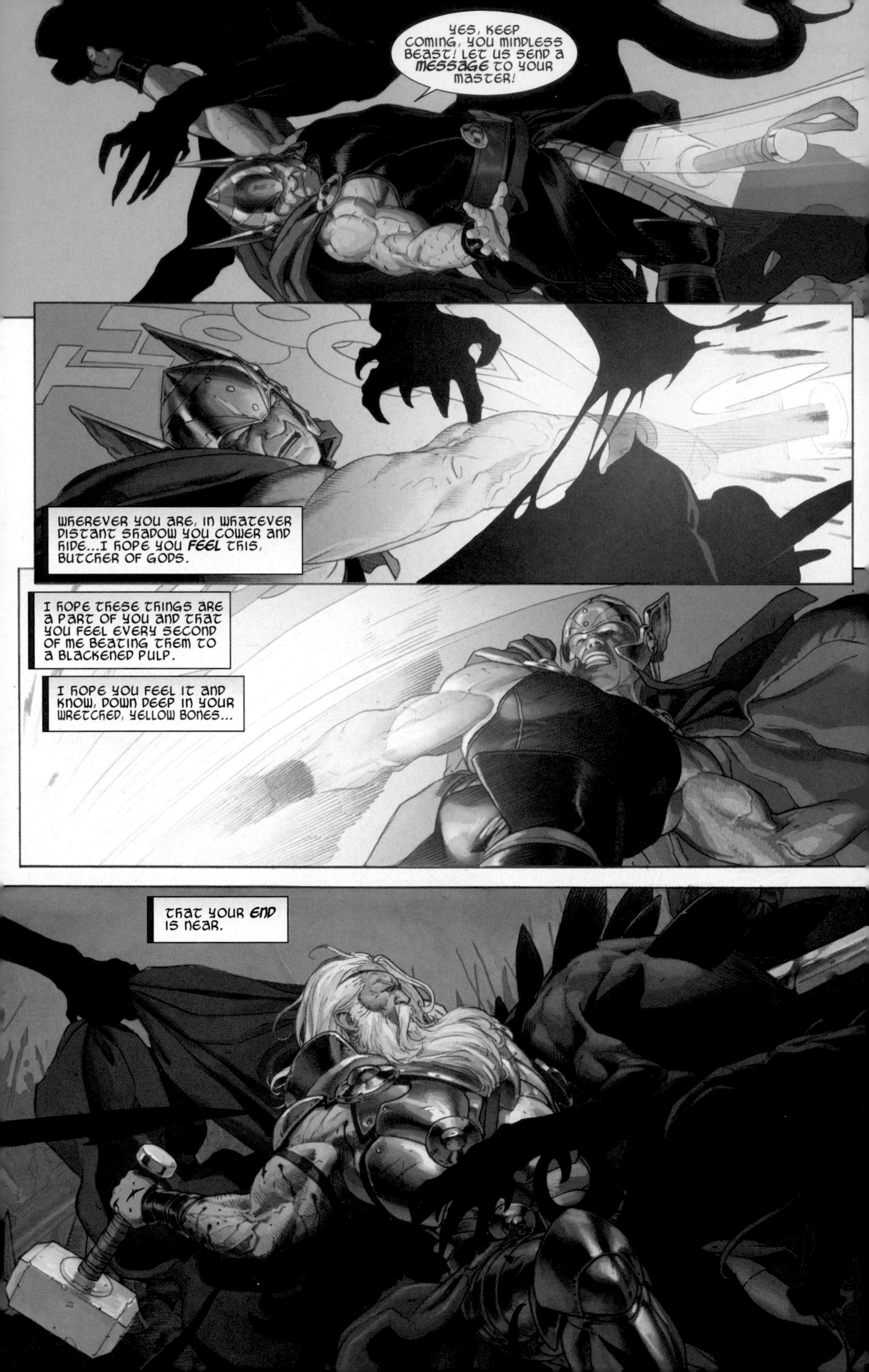

YES, KEEP COMING, YOU MINDLESS BEAST! LET US SEND A MESSAGE TO YOUR MASTER!
WHEREVER YOU ARE, IN WHATEVER DISTANT SHADOW YOU COWER AND HIDE...I HOPE YOU FEEL THIS, BUTCHER OF GODS.
I HOPE THESE THINGS ARE A PART OF YOU AND THAT YOU FEEL EVERY SECOND OF ME BEATING THEM TO A BLACKENED PULP.
I HOPE YOU FEEL IT AND KNOW, DOWN DEEP IN YOUR WRETCHED, YELLOW BONES...
THAT YOUR END IS NEAR.

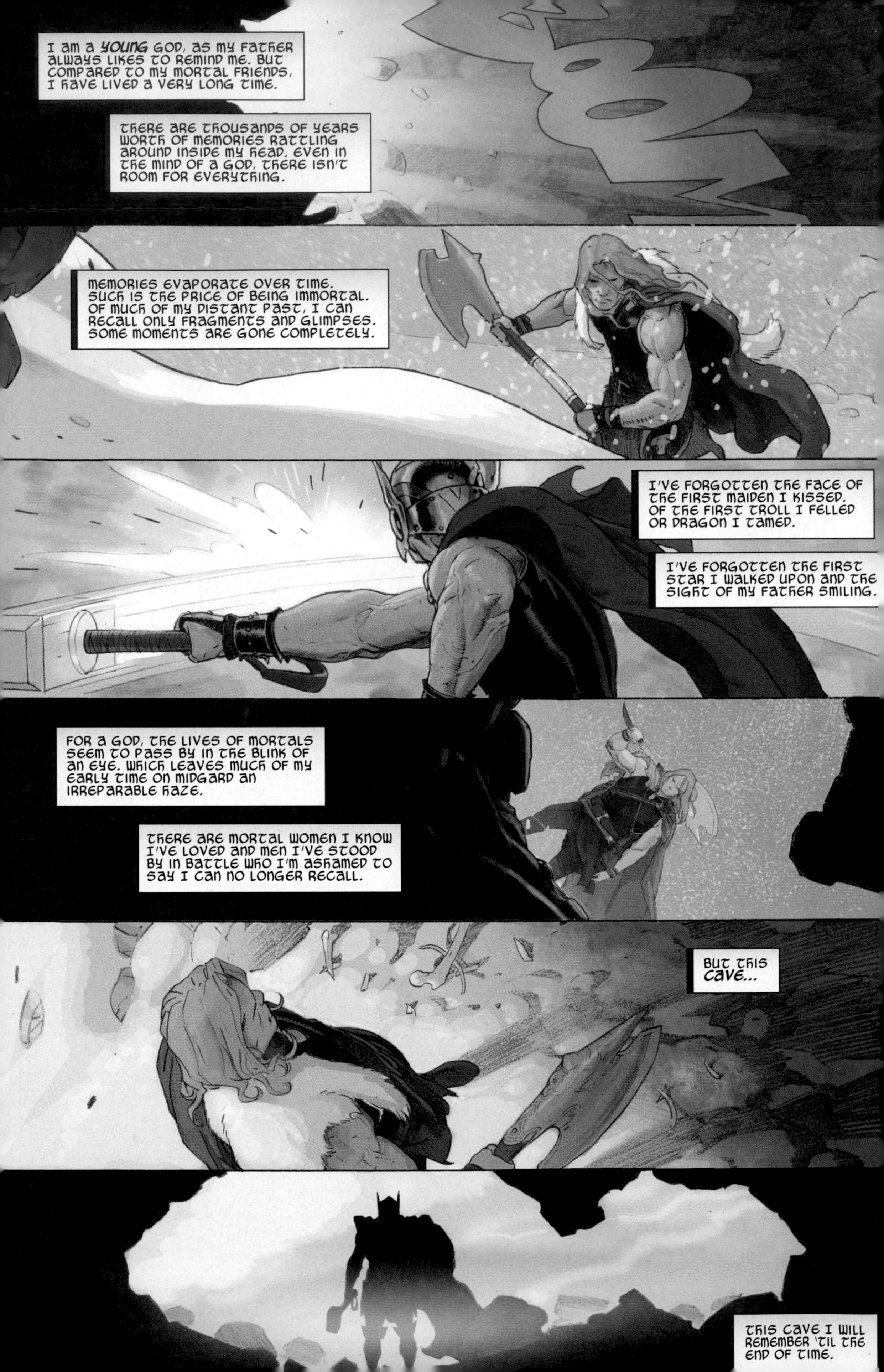
I AM A *YOUNG* GOD, AS MY FATHER ALWAYS LIKES TO REMIND ME. BUT COMPARED TO MY MORTAL FRIENDS, I HAVE LIVED A VERY LONG TIME.
THERE ARE THOUSANDS OF YEARS WORTH OF MEMORIES RATTLING AROUND INSIDE MY HEAD. EVEN IN THE MIND OF A GOD, THERE ISN'T ROOM FOR EVERYTHING.
MEMORIES EVAPORATE OVER TIME. SUCH IS THE PRICE OF BEING IMMORTAL. OF MUCH OF MY DISTANT PAST, I CAN RECALL ONLY FRAGMENTS AND GLIMPSES. SOME MOMENTS ARE GONE COMPLETELY.
I'VE FORGOTTEN THE FACE OF THE FIRST MAIDEN I KISSED. OF THE FIRST TROLL I FELLED OR DRAGON I TAMED.
I'VE FORGOTTEN THE FIRST STAR I WALKED UPON AND THE SIGHT OF MY FATHER SMILING.
FOR A GOD, THE LIVES OF MORTALS SEEM TO PASS BY IN THE BLINK OF AN EYE. WHICH LEAVES MUCH OF MY EARLY TIME ON MIDGARD AN IRREPARABLE HAZE.
THERE ARE MORTAL WOMEN I KNOW I'VE LOVED AND MEN I'VE STOOD BY IN BATTLE WHO I'M ASHAMED TO SAY I CAN NO LONGER RECALL.
BUT THIS *CAVE*...
THIS CAVE I WILL REMEMBER 'TIL THE END OF TIME.

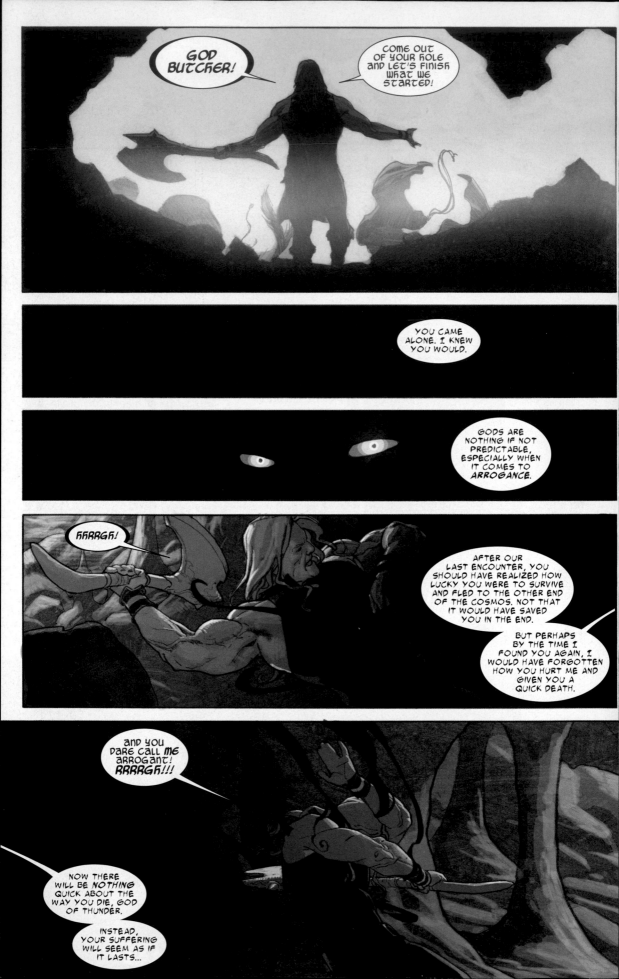

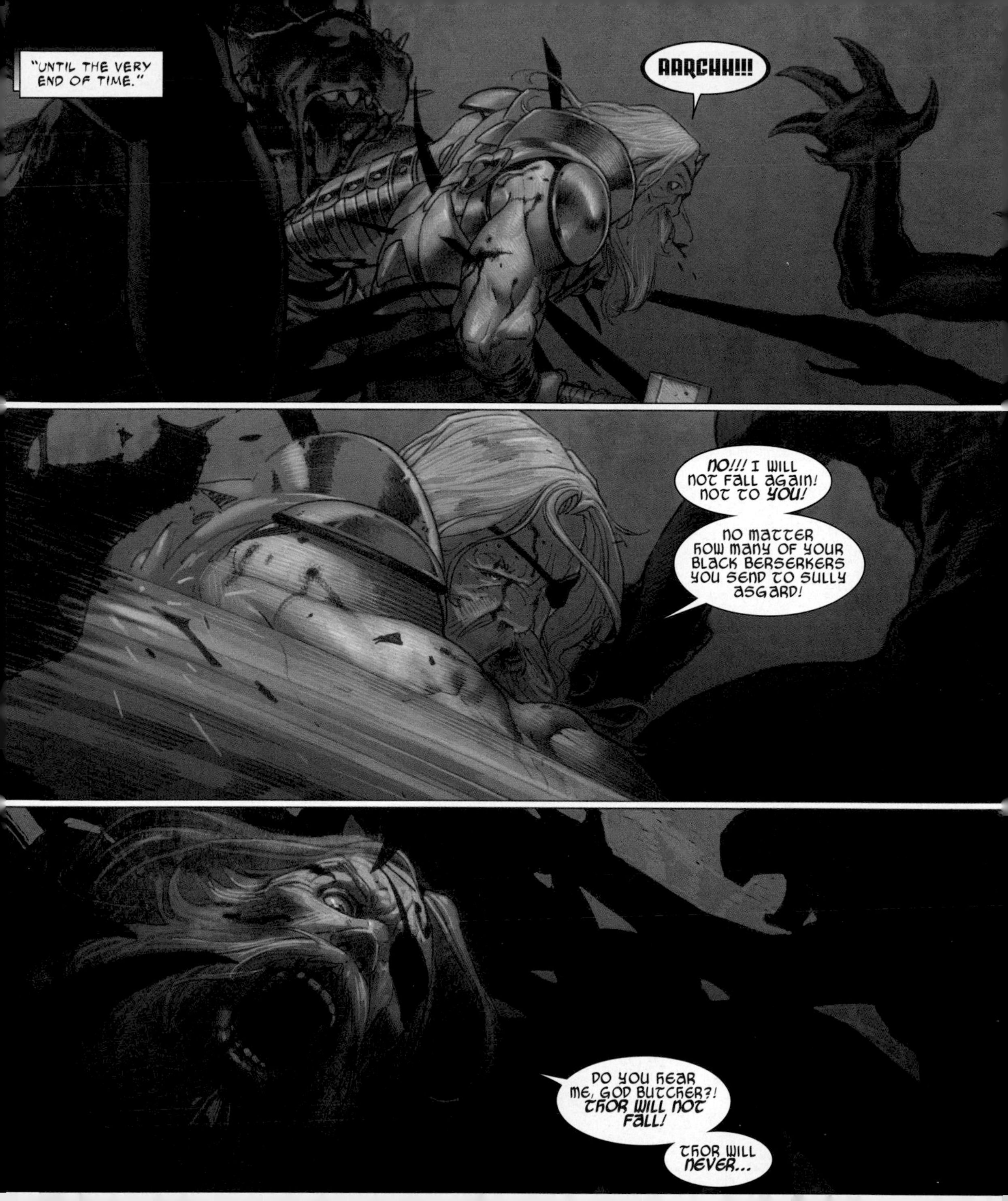
"UNTIL THE VERY END OF TIME."
AARCHH!!!
NO!!! I WILL NOT FALL AGAIN! NOT TO YOU!
NO MATTER HOW MANY OF YOUR BLACK BERSERKERS YOU SEND TO SULLY ASGARD!
DO YOU HEAR ME, GOD BUTCHER?! THOR WILL NOT FALL!
THOR WILL NEVER...

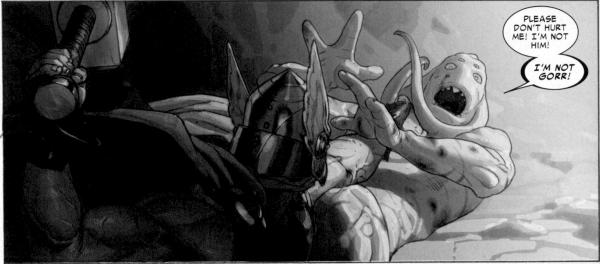

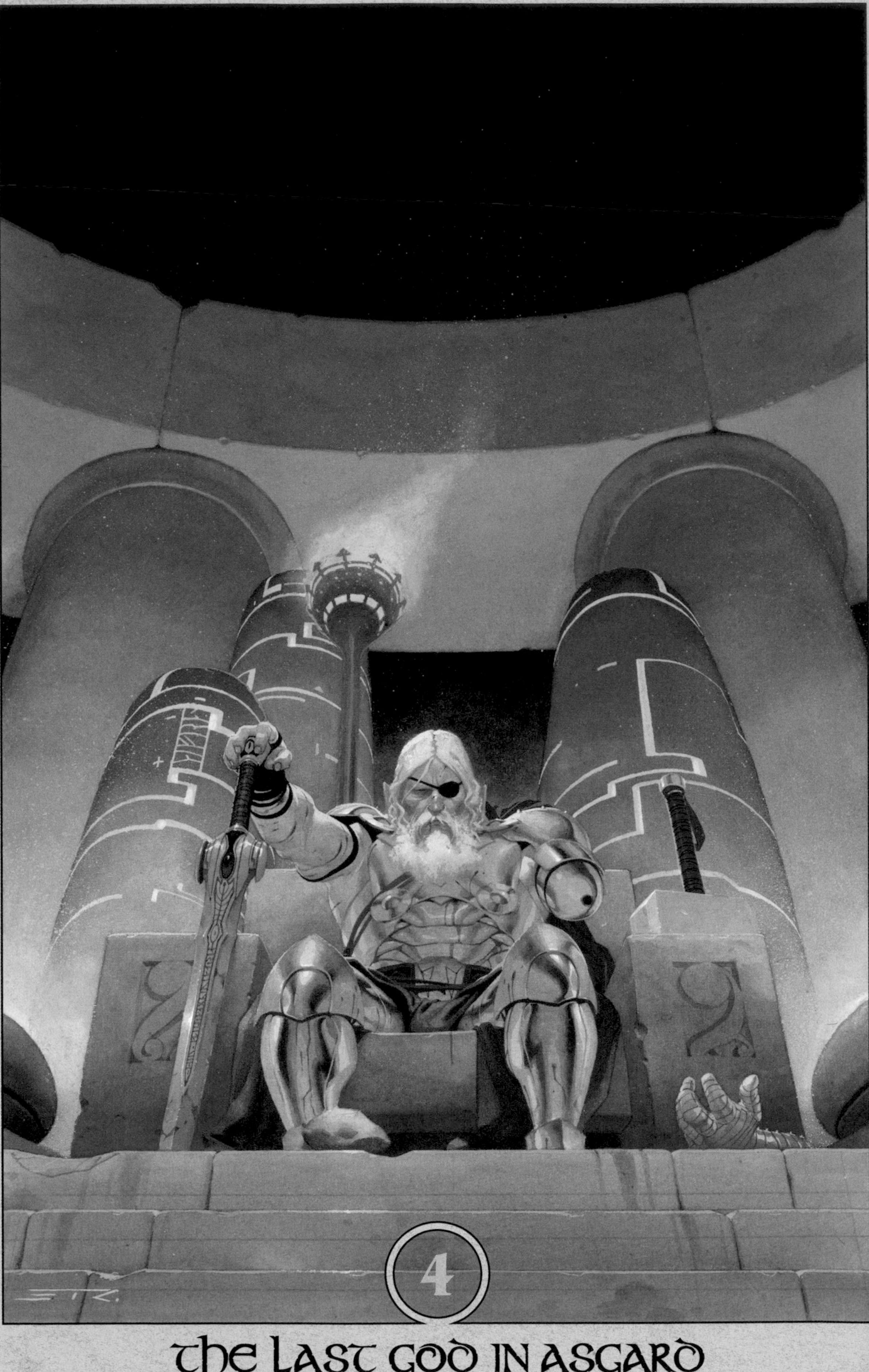
4

THE LAST GOD IN ASGARD

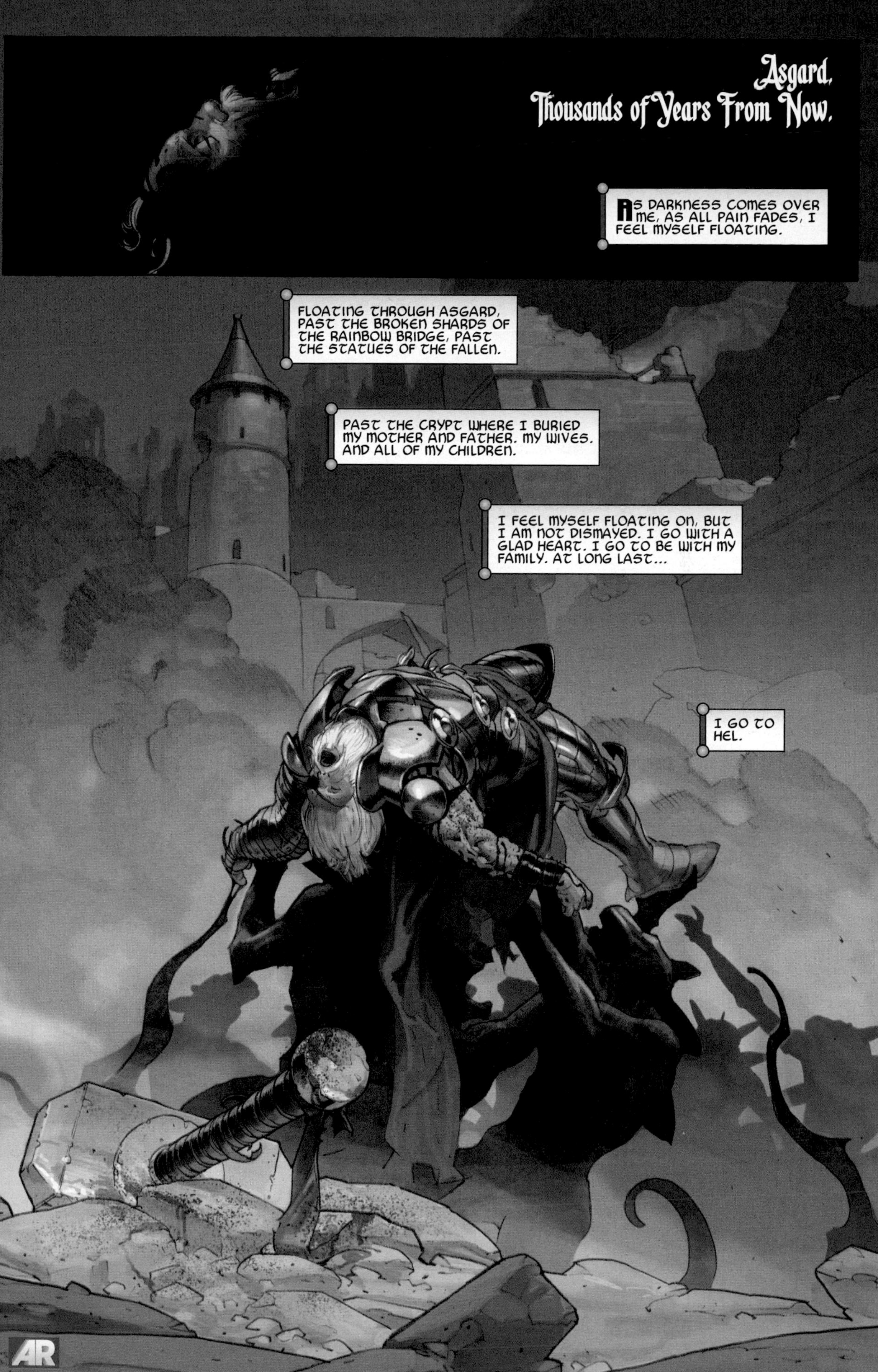
Asgard,
Thousands of Years From Now.
AS DARKNESS COMES OVER ME, AS ALL PAIN FADES, I FEEL MYSELF FLOATING.
FLOATING THROUGH ASGARD, PAST THE BROKEN SHARDS OF THE RAINBOW BRIDGE, PAST THE STATUES OF THE FALLEN.
PAST THE CRYPT WHERE I BURIED MY MOTHER AND FATHER. MY WIVES. AND ALL OF MY CHILDREN.
I FEEL MYSELF FLOATING ON, BUT I AM NOT DISMAYED. I GO WITH A GLAD HEART. I GO TO BE WITH MY FAMILY. AT LONG LAST...
I GO TO HEL.

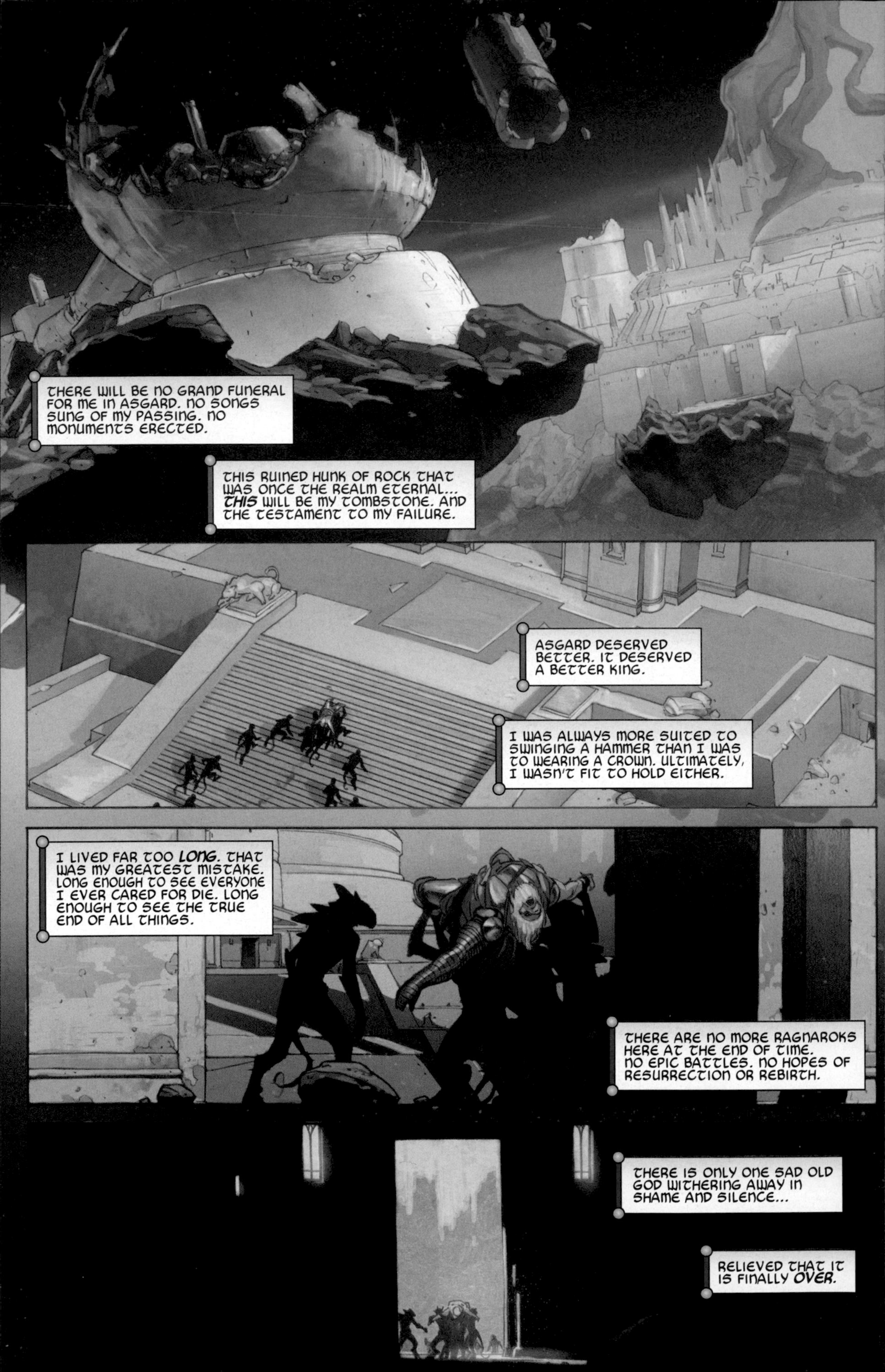
THERE WILL BE NO GRAND FUNERAL FOR ME IN ASGARD. NO SONGS SUNG OF MY PASSING. NO MONUMENTS ERECTED.
THIS RUINED HUNK OF ROCK THAT WAS ONCE THE REALM ETERNAL... *THIS* WILL BE MY TOMBSTONE. AND THE TESTAMENT TO MY FAILURE.
ASGARD DESERVED BETTER. IT DESERVED A BETTER KING.
I WAS ALWAYS MORE SUITED TO SWINGING A HAMMER THAN I WAS TO WEARING A CROWN. ULTIMATELY, I WASN'T FIT TO HOLD EITHER.
I LIVED FAR TOO *LONG*. THAT WAS MY GREATEST MISTAKE. LONG ENOUGH TO SEE EVERYONE I EVER CARED FOR DIE. LONG ENOUGH TO SEE THE TRUE END OF ALL THINGS.
THERE ARE NO MORE RAGNAROKS HERE AT THE END OF TIME. NO EPIC BATTLES. NO HOPES OF RESURRECTION OR REBIRTH.
THERE IS ONLY ONE SAD OLD GOD WITHERING AWAY IN SHAME AND SILENCE...
RELIEVED THAT IT IS FINALLY *OVER*.

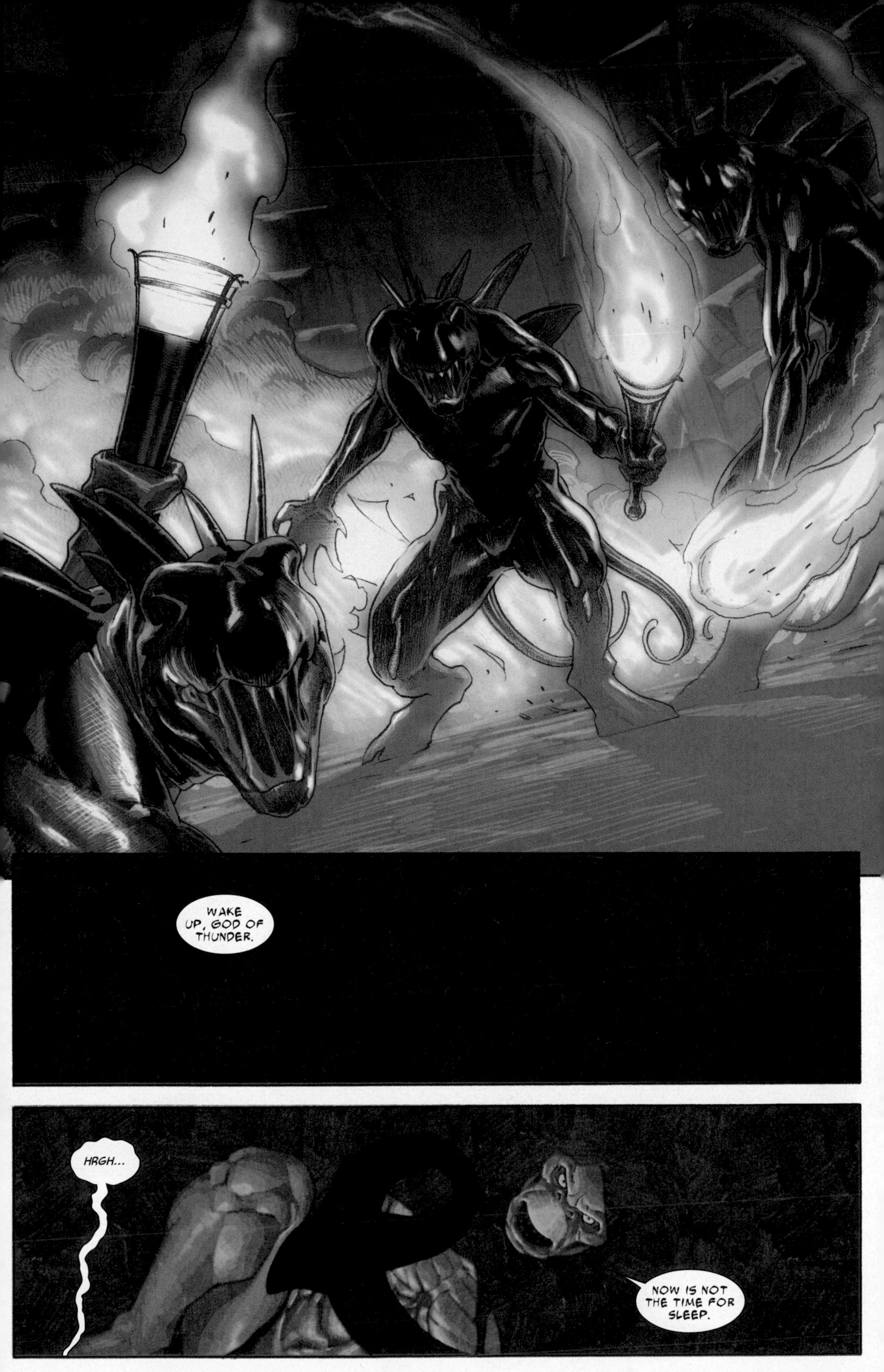
WAKE UP, GOD OF THUNDER.
HRGH...
NOW IS NOT THE TIME FOR SLEEP.

893 A.D.
The Cave of The God Butcher.

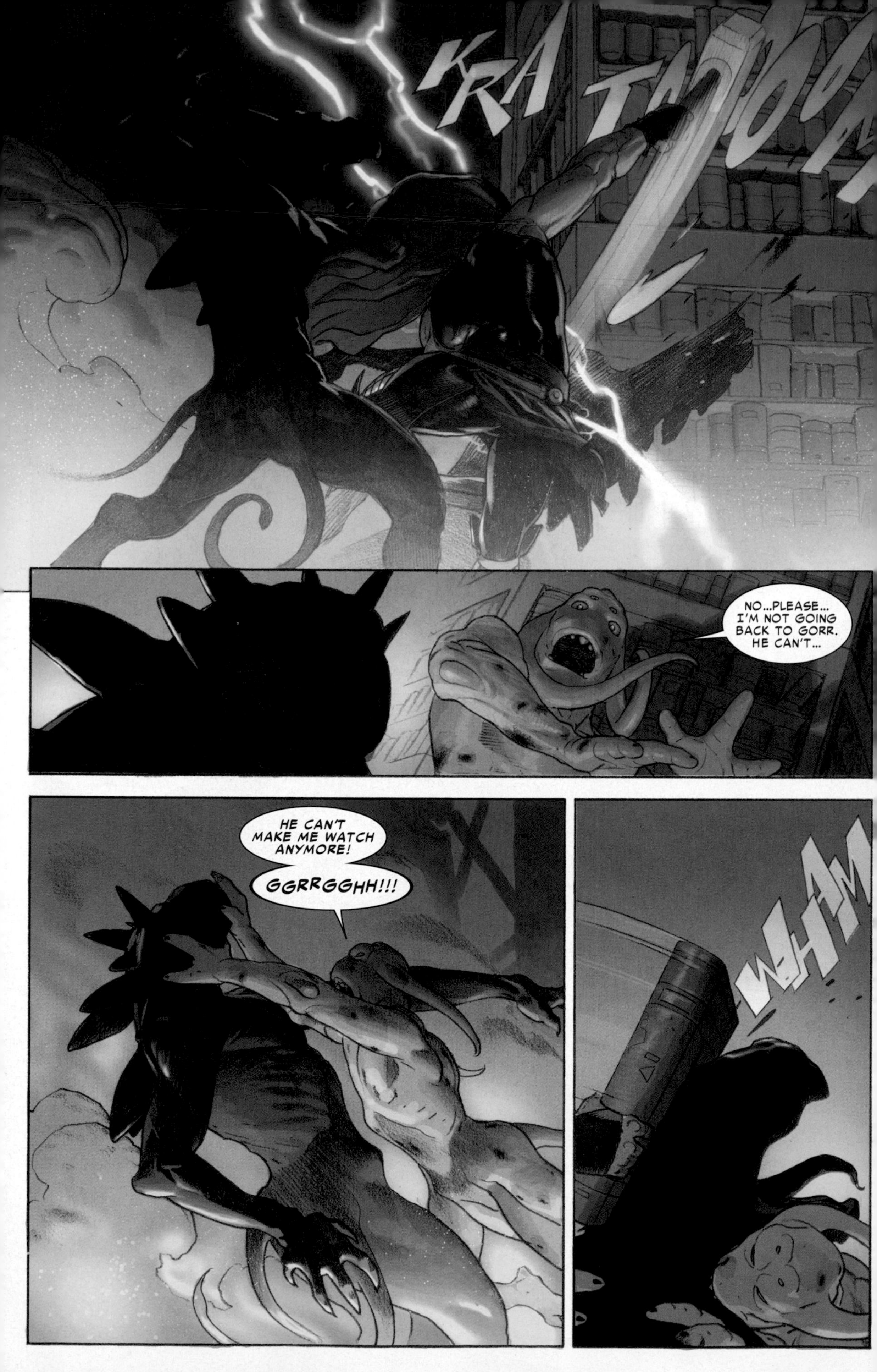
KRA TADOOM
NO...PLEASE... I'M NOT GOING BACK TO GORR. HE CAN'T...
HE CAN'T MAKE ME WATCH ANYMORE!
GGRRGGHH!!!
WHAM

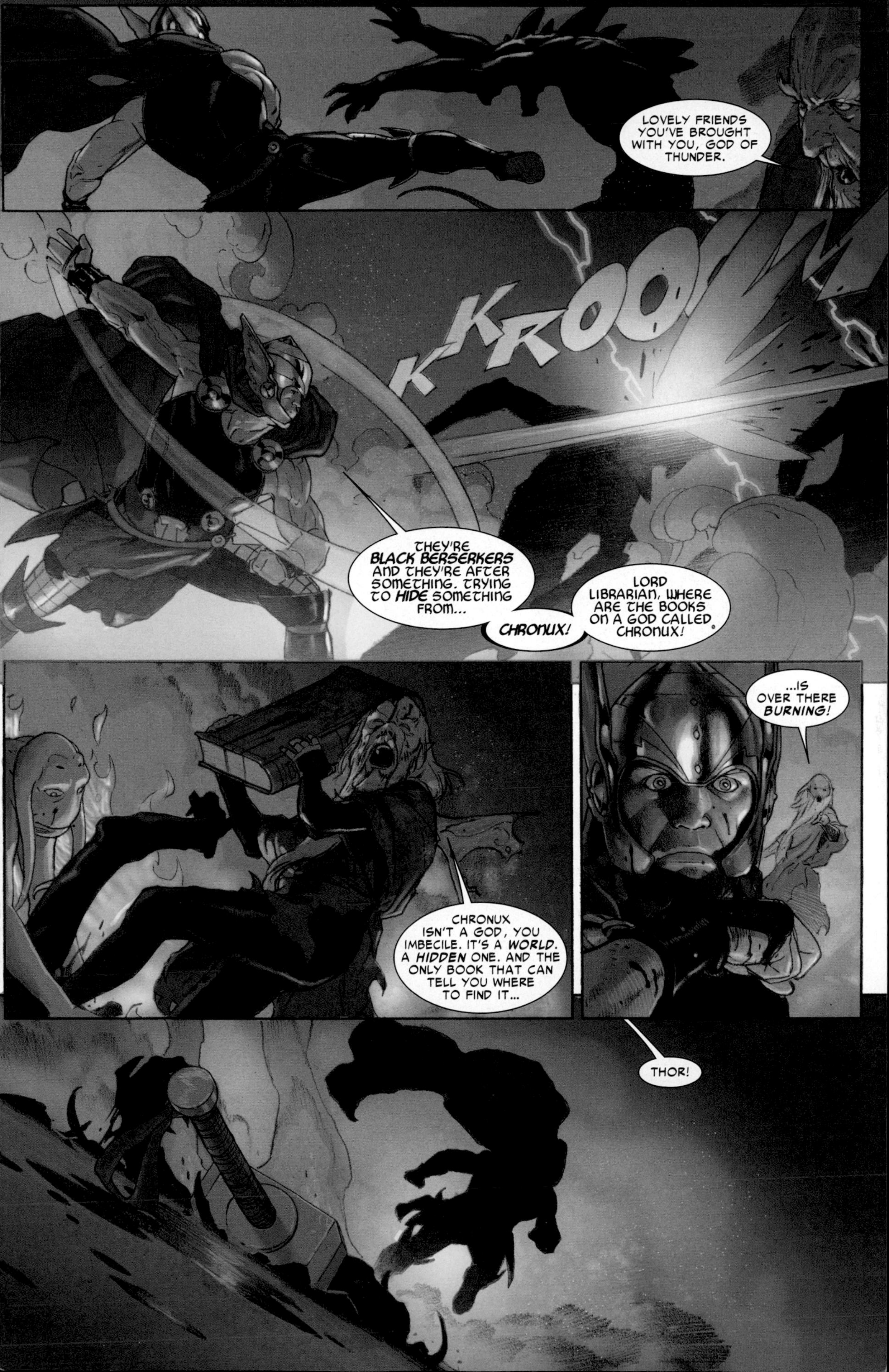
LOVELY FRIENDS YOU'VE BROUGHT WITH YOU, GOD OF THUNDER.
KKKROOOM
THEY'RE **BLACK BERSERKERS** AND THEY'RE AFTER SOMETHING. TRYING TO ***HIDE*** SOMETHING FROM...
CHRONUX!
LORD LIBRARIAN, WHERE ARE THE BOOKS ON A GOD CALLED CHRONUX!
CHRONUX ISN'T A GOD, YOU IMBECILE. IT'S A ***WORLD***. A ***HIDDEN*** ONE. AND THE ONLY BOOK THAT CAN TELL YOU WHERE TO FIND IT...
...IS OVER THERE ***BURNING!***
THOR!

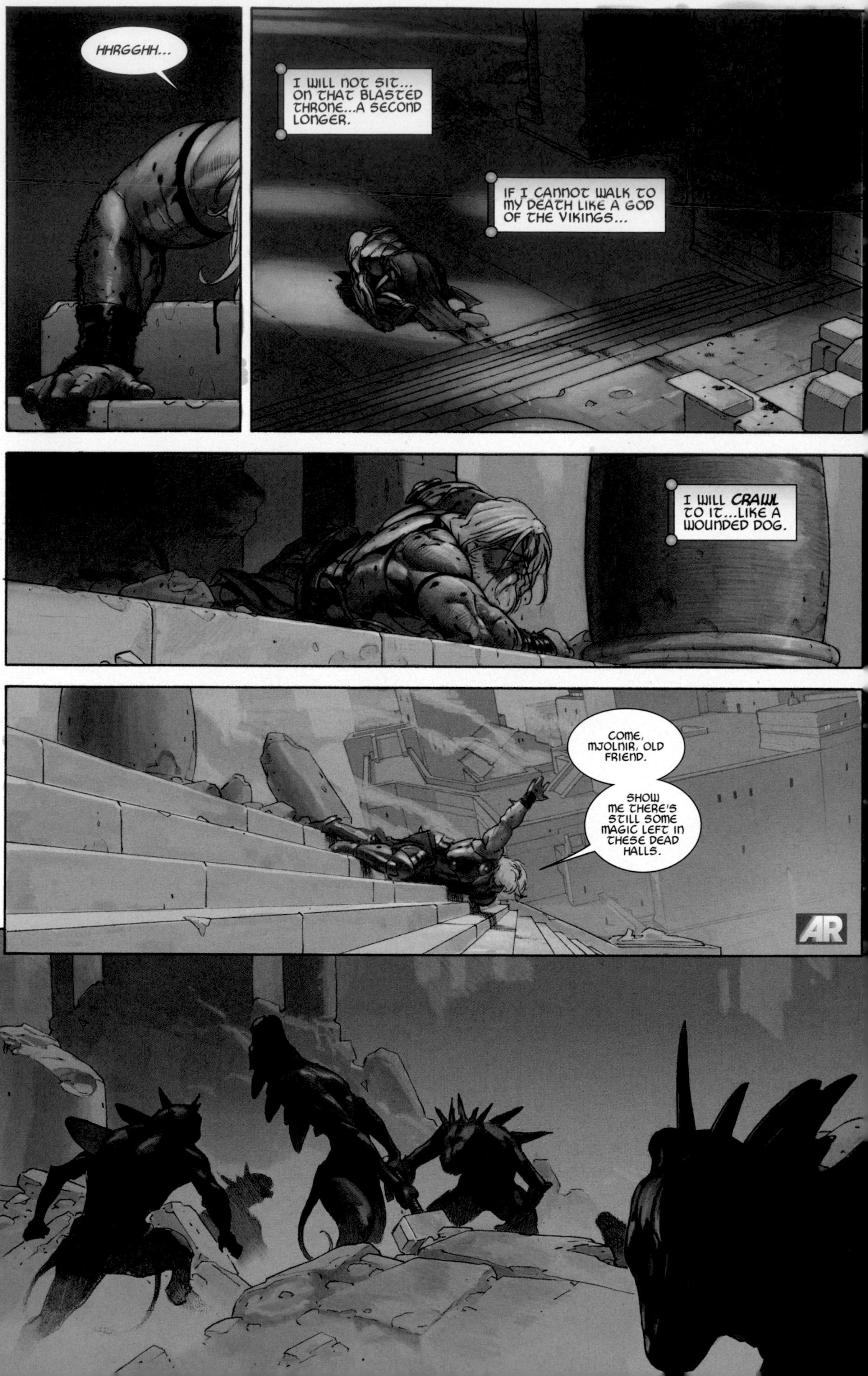

HHRGGHH...
I WILL NOT SIT... ON THAT BLASTED THRONE...A SECOND LONGER.
IF I CANNOT WALK TO MY DEATH LIKE A GOD OF THE VIKINGS...
I WILL CRAWL TO IT...LIKE A WOUNDED DOG.
COME, MJOLNIR, OLD FRIEND.
SHOW ME THERE'S STILL SOME MAGIC LEFT IN THESE DEAD HALLS.
AR

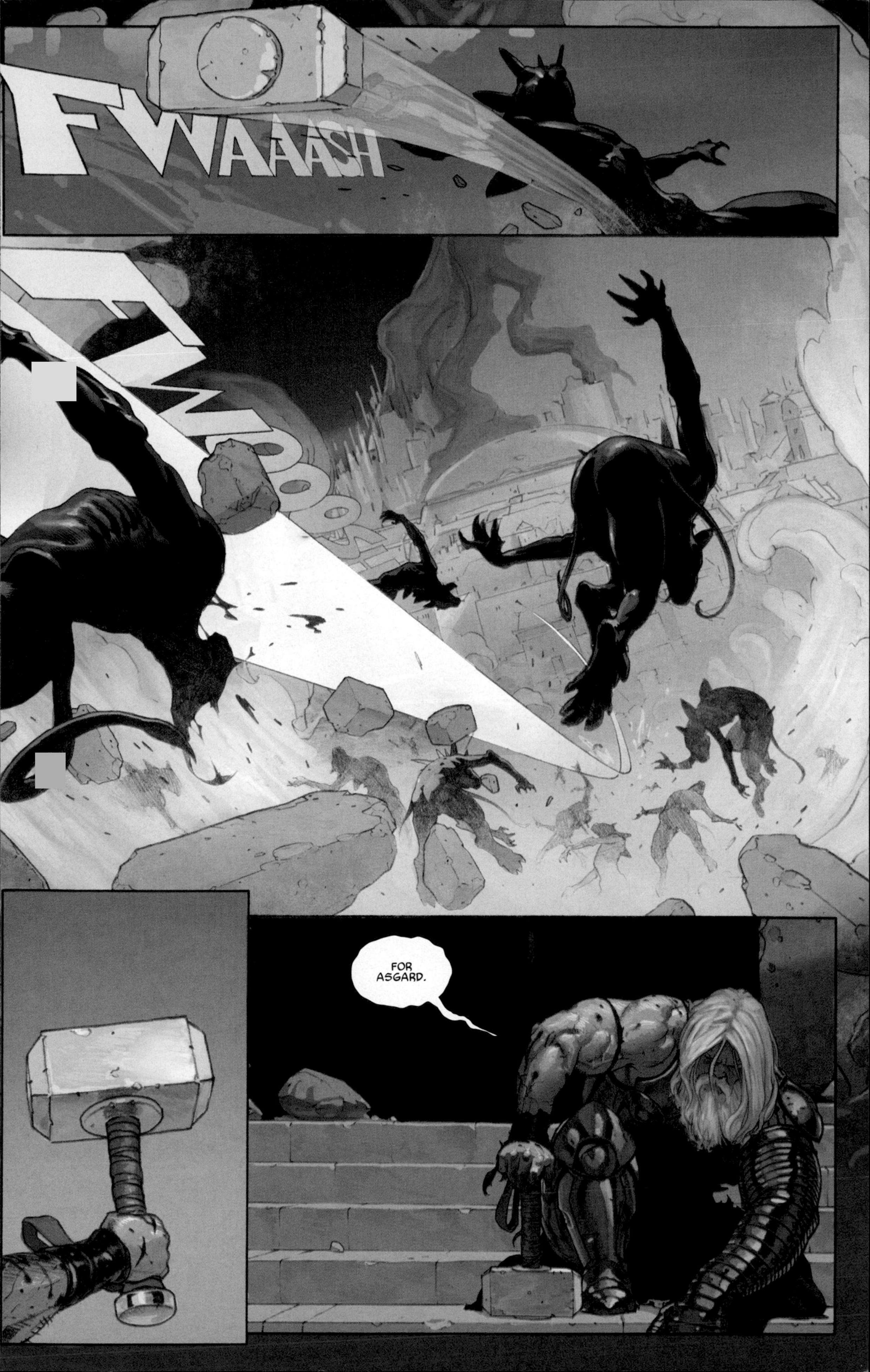
FWAAASH
FOR ASGARD.

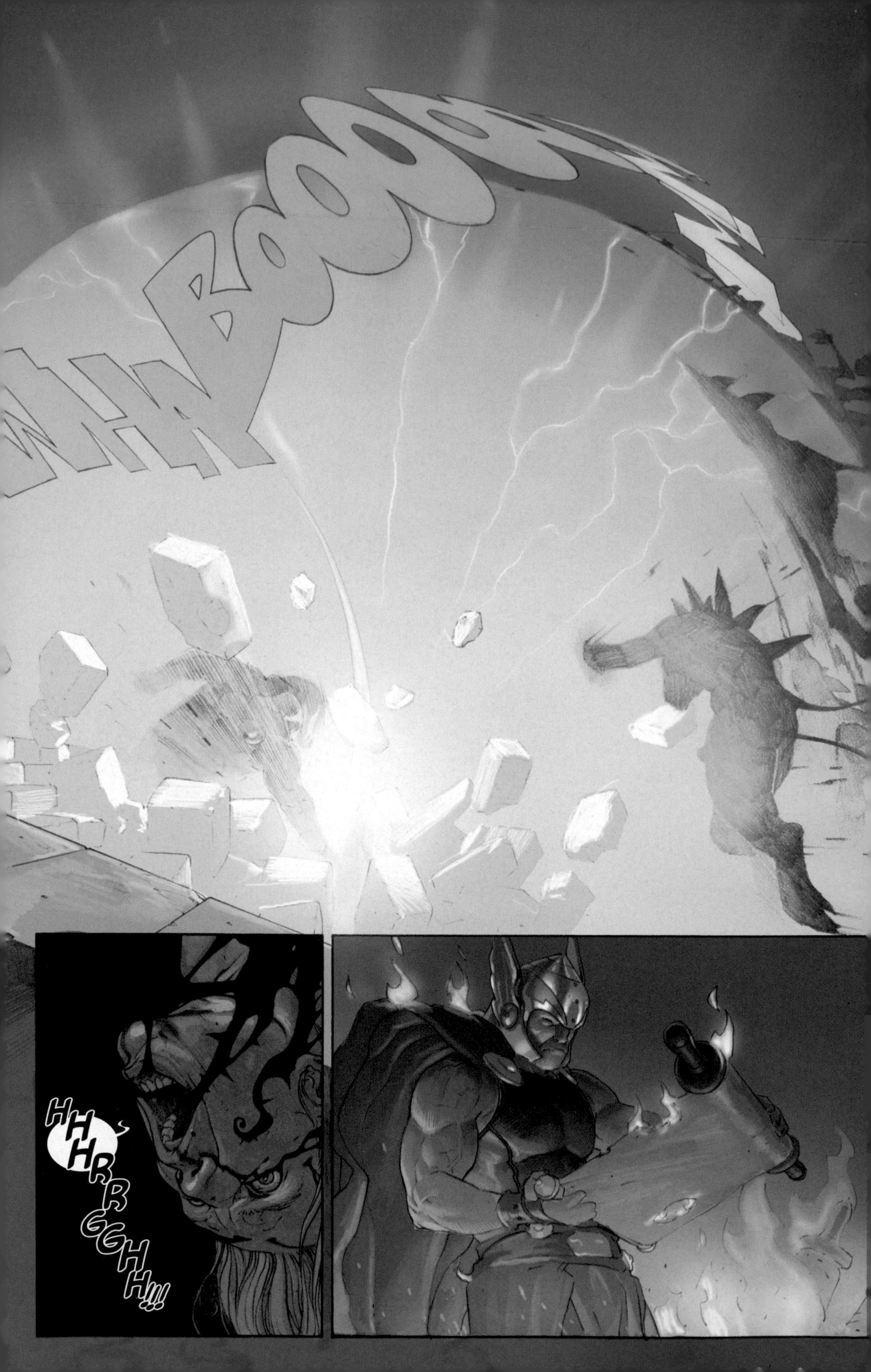
HHHRRGGHH!!!

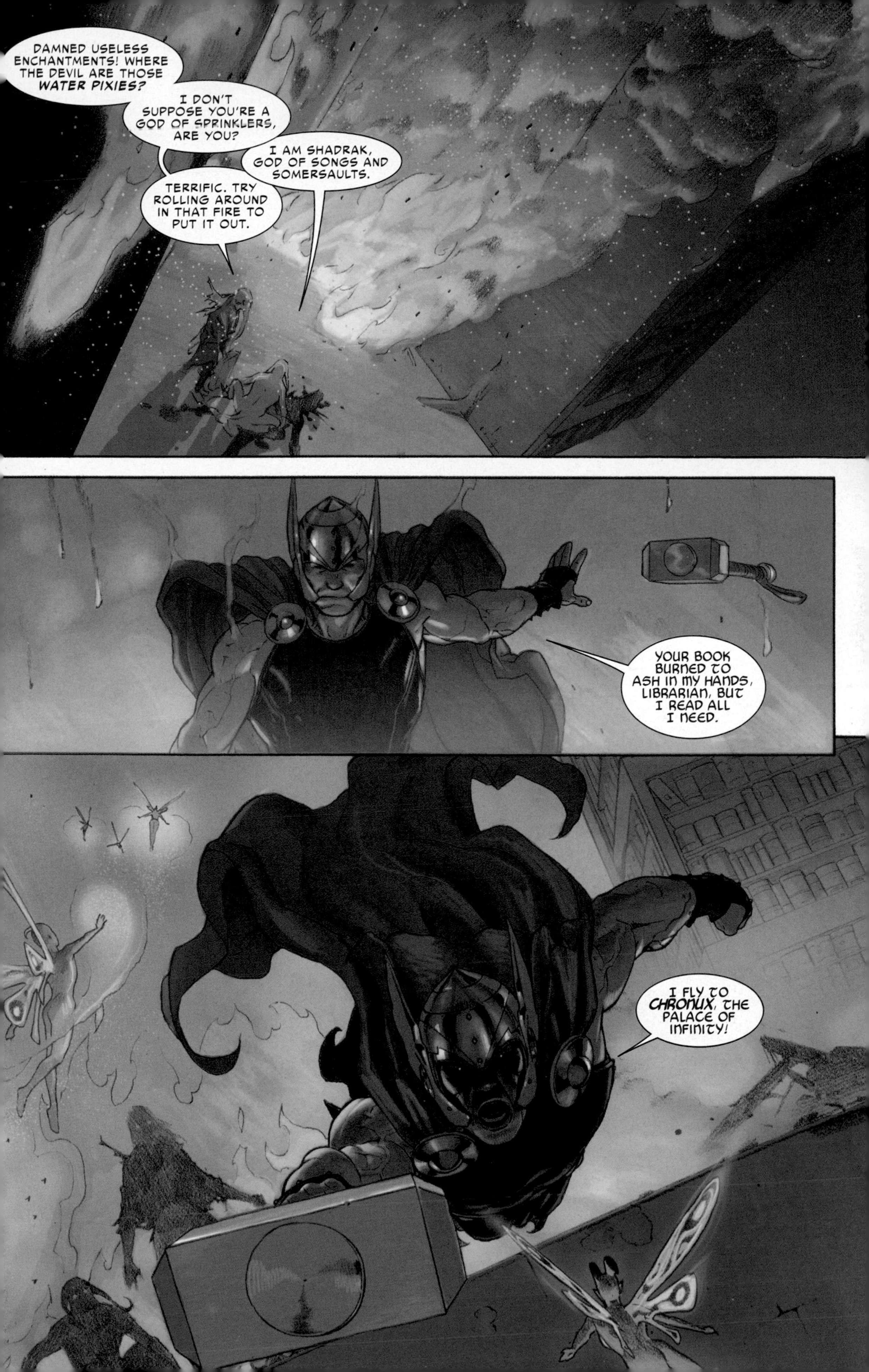
DAMNED USELESS ENCHANTMENTS! WHERE THE DEVIL ARE THOSE WATER PIXIES?
I DON'T SUPPOSE YOU'RE A GOD OF SPRINKLERS, ARE YOU?
I AM SHADRAK, GOD OF SONGS AND SOMERSAULTS.
TERRIFIC. TRY ROLLING AROUND IN THAT FIRE TO PUT IT OUT.
YOUR BOOK BURNED TO ASH IN MY HANDS, LIBRARIAN, BUT I READ ALL I NEED.
I FLY TO CHRONUX, THE PALACE OF INFINITY!

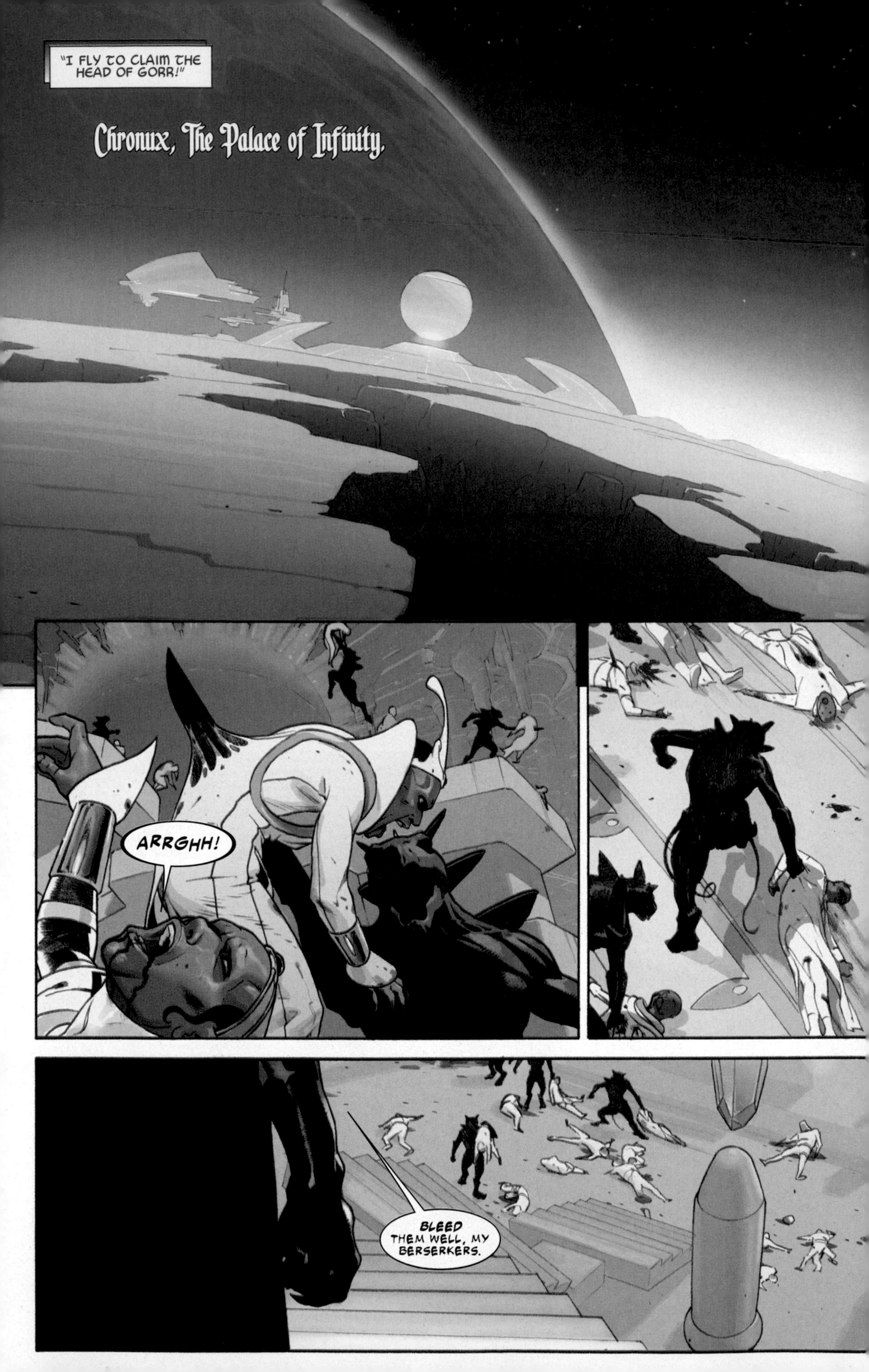
"I FLY TO CLAIM THE HEAD OF GORR!"
Chronux, The Palace of Infinity.
ARRGHH!
BLEED THEM WELL, MY BERSERKERS.

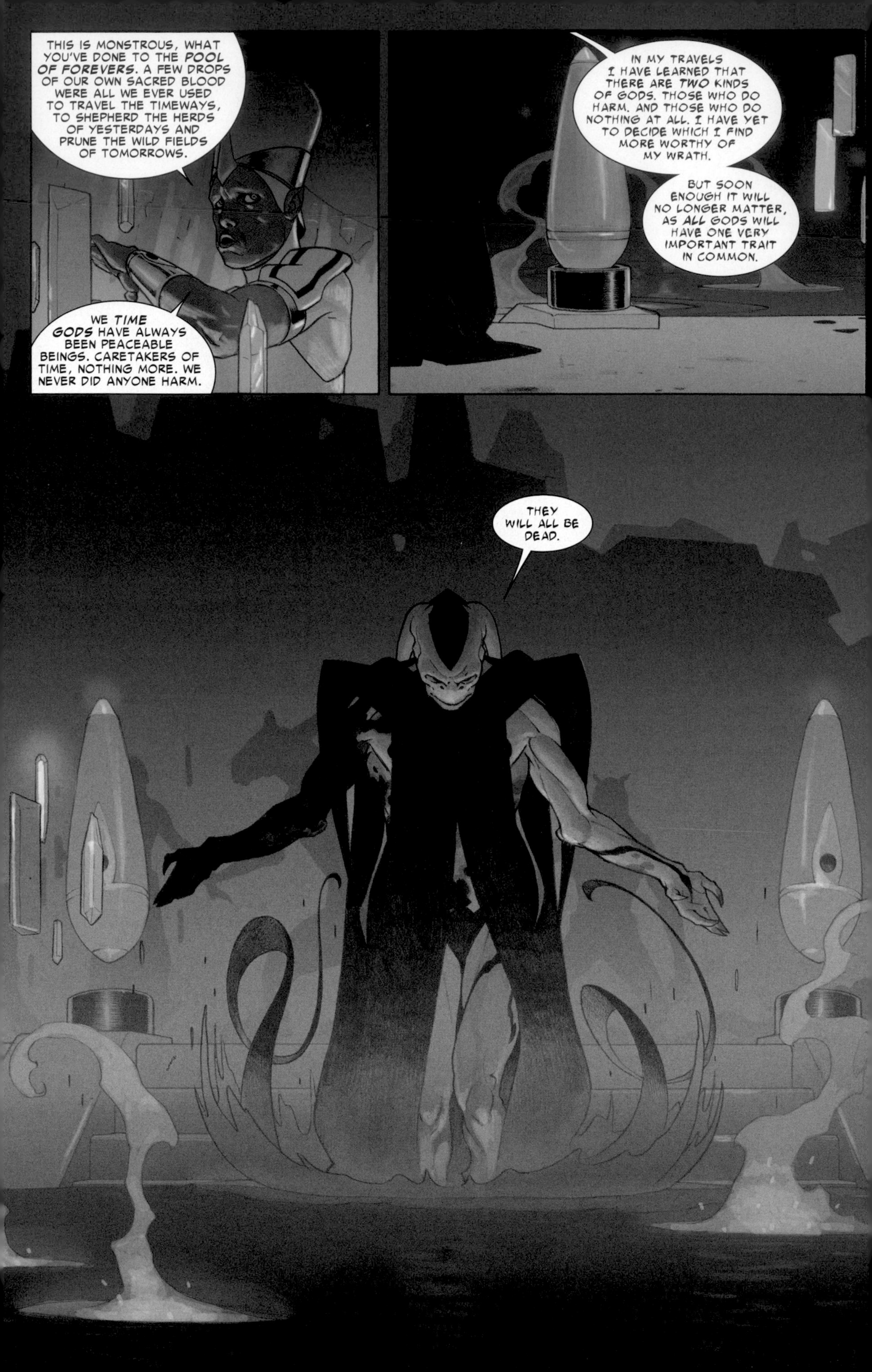
THIS IS MONSTROUS, WHAT YOU'VE DONE TO THE *POOL OF FOREVERS*. A FEW DROPS OF OUR OWN SACRED BLOOD WERE ALL WE EVER USED TO TRAVEL THE TIMEWAYS, TO SHEPHERD THE HERDS OF YESTERDAYS AND PRUNE THE WILD FIELDS OF TOMORROWS.
WE *TIME GODS* HAVE ALWAYS BEEN PEACEABLE BEINGS. CARETAKERS OF TIME, NOTHING MORE. WE NEVER DID ANYONE HARM.
IN MY TRAVELS I HAVE LEARNED THAT THERE ARE *TWO* KINDS OF GODS. THOSE WHO DO HARM. AND THOSE WHO DO NOTHING AT ALL. I HAVE YET TO DECIDE WHICH I FIND MORE WORTHY OF MY WRATH.
BUT SOON ENOUGH IT WILL NO LONGER MATTER, AS *ALL* GODS WILL HAVE ONE VERY IMPORTANT TRAIT IN COMMON.
THEY WILL ALL BE DEAD.

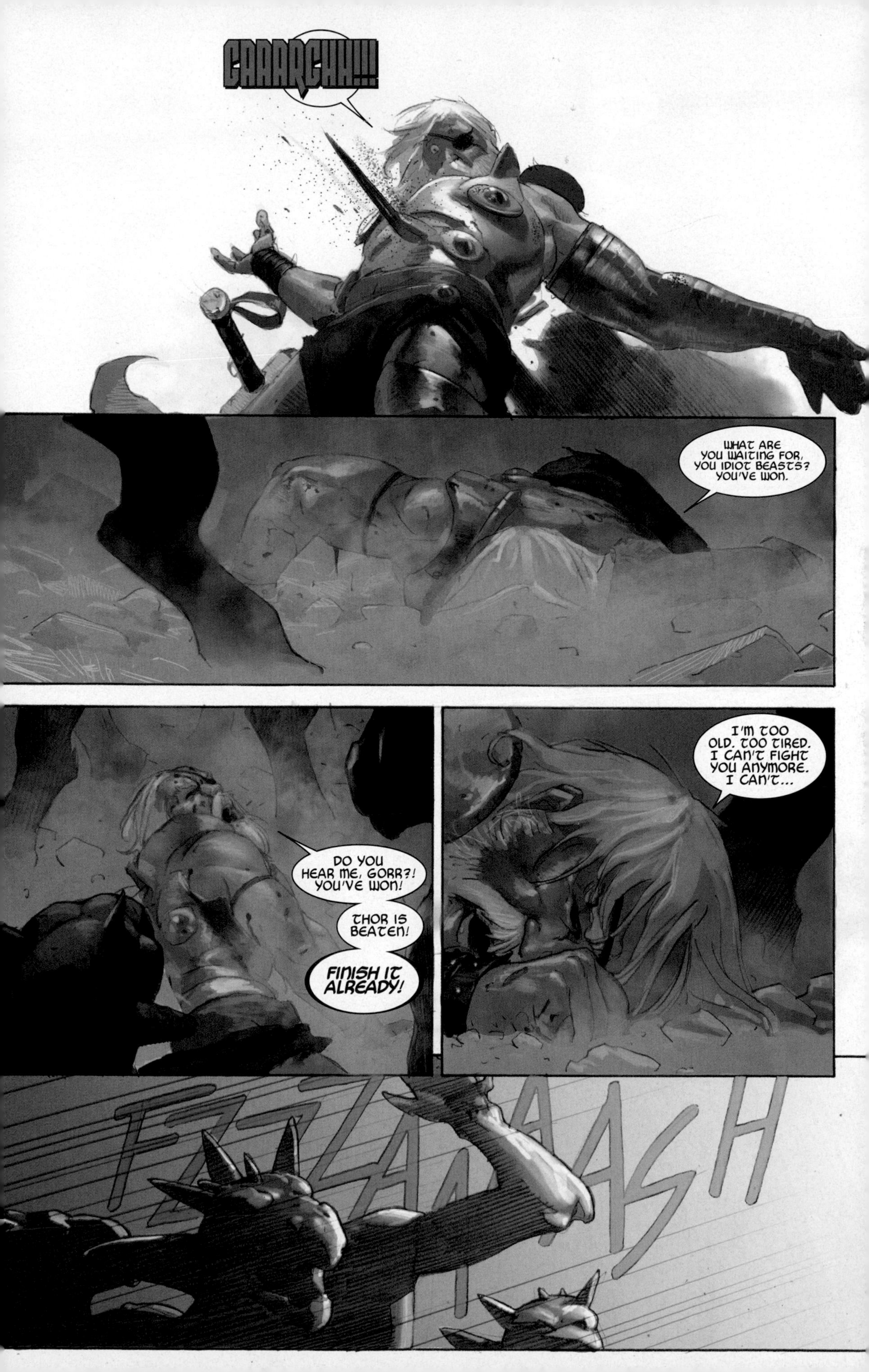
GAAARGHH!!!
WHAT ARE YOU WAITING FOR, YOU IDIOT BEASTS? YOU'VE WON.
DO YOU HEAR ME, GORR?! YOU'VE WON!
THOR IS BEATEN!
FINISH IT ALREADY!
I'M TOO OLD. TOO TIRED. I CAN'T FIGHT YOU ANYMORE. I CAN'T...
FZZZAAAASH

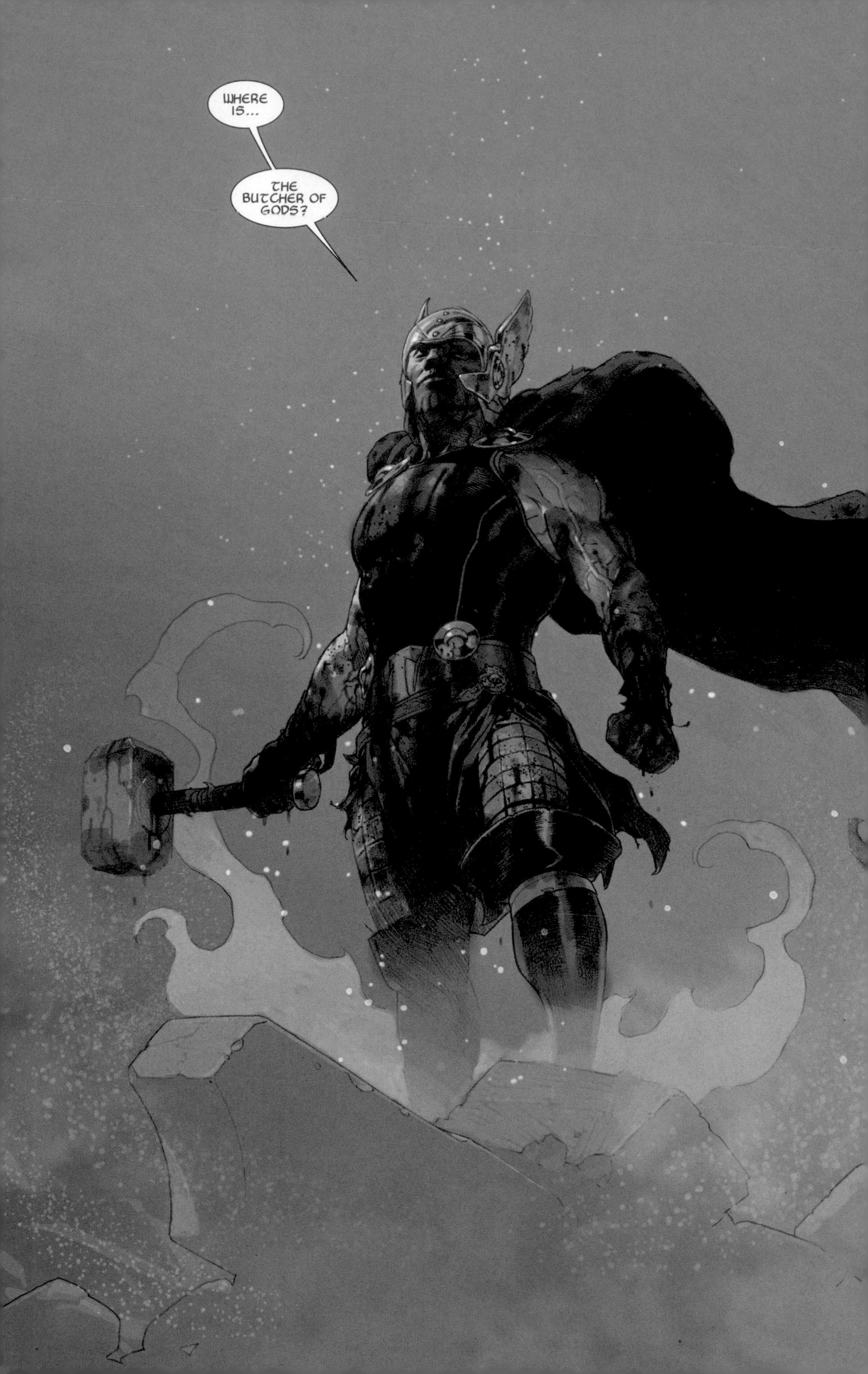
WHERE IS...
THE BUTCHER OF GODS?

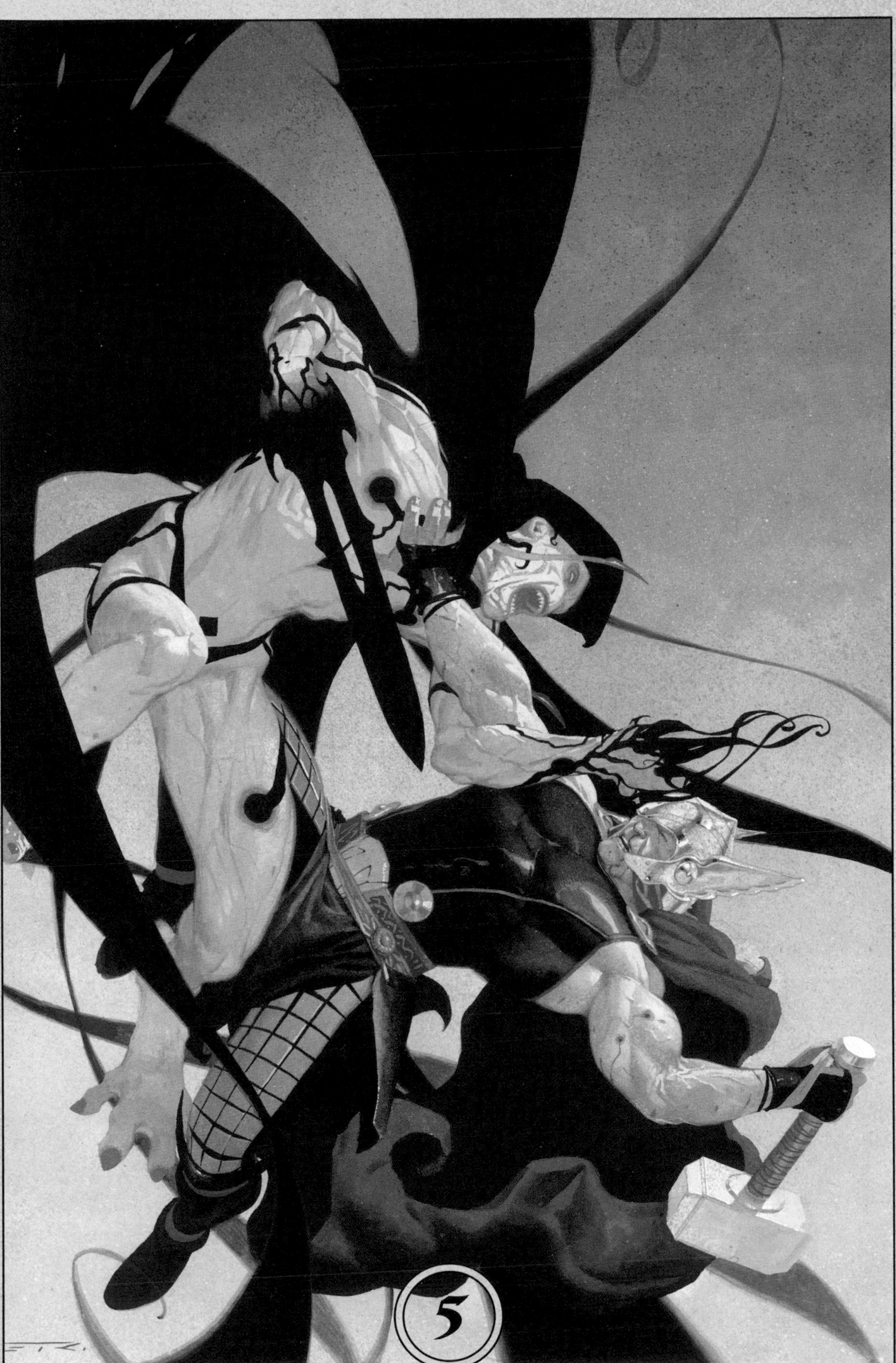
5

DREAM OF A GODLESS AGE

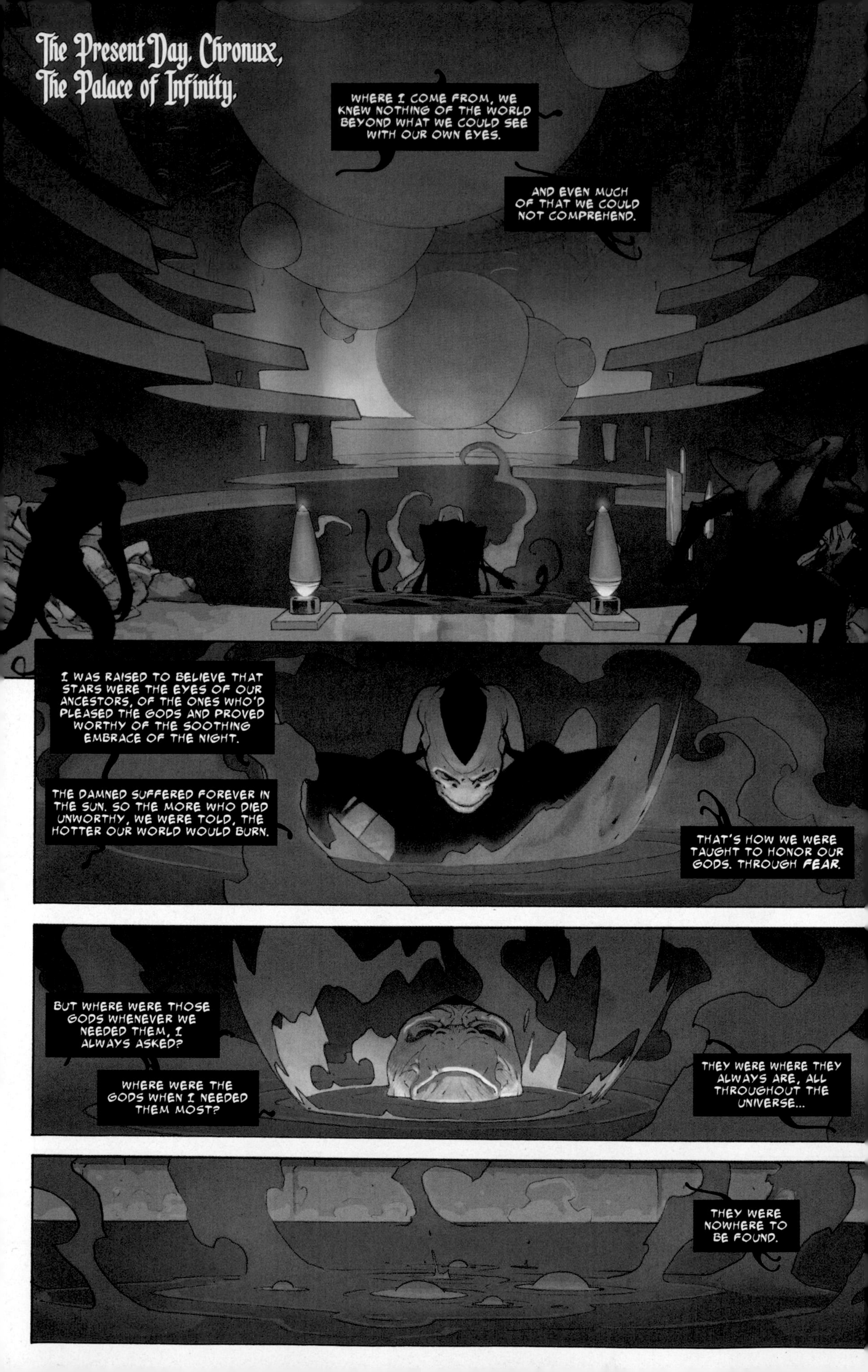
The Present Day. Chronux, The Palace of Infinity.
WHERE I COME FROM, WE KNEW NOTHING OF THE WORLD BEYOND WHAT WE COULD SEE WITH OUR OWN EYES.
AND EVEN MUCH OF THAT WE COULD NOT COMPREHEND.
I WAS RAISED TO BELIEVE THAT STARS WERE THE EYES OF OUR ANCESTORS, OF THE ONES WHO'D PLEASED THE GODS AND PROVED WORTHY OF THE SOOTHING EMBRACE OF THE NIGHT.
THE DAMNED SUFFERED FOREVER IN THE SUN. SO THE MORE WHO DIED UNWORTHY, WE WERE TOLD, THE HOTTER OUR WORLD WOULD BURN.
THAT'S HOW WE WERE TAUGHT TO HONOR OUR GODS. THROUGH FEAR.
BUT WHERE WERE THOSE GODS WHENEVER WE NEEDED THEM, I ALWAYS ASKED?
WHERE WERE THE GODS WHEN I NEEDED THEM MOST?
THEY WERE WHERE THEY ALWAYS ARE, ALL THROUGHOUT THE UNIVERSE...
THEY WERE NOWHERE TO BE FOUND.

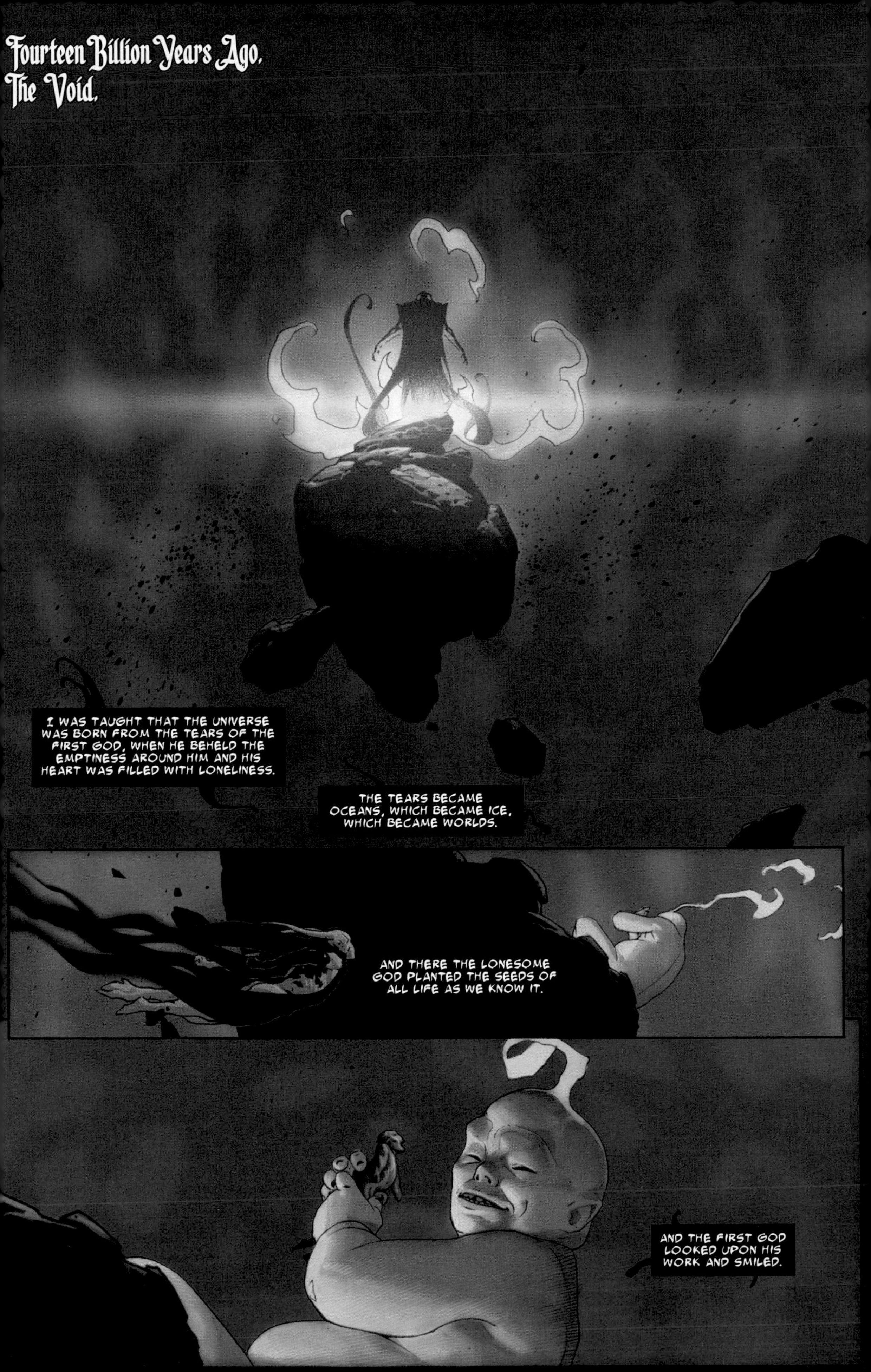
Fourteen Billion Years Ago.
The Void.
I WAS TAUGHT THAT THE UNIVERSE WAS BORN FROM THE TEARS OF THE FIRST GOD, WHEN HE BEHELD THE EMPTINESS AROUND HIM AND HIS HEART WAS FILLED WITH LONELINESS.
THE TEARS BECAME OCEANS, WHICH BECAME ICE, WHICH BECAME WORLDS.
AND THERE THE LONESOME GOD PLANTED THE SEEDS OF ALL LIFE AS WE KNOW IT.
AND THE FIRST GOD LOOKED UPON HIS WORK AND SMILED.

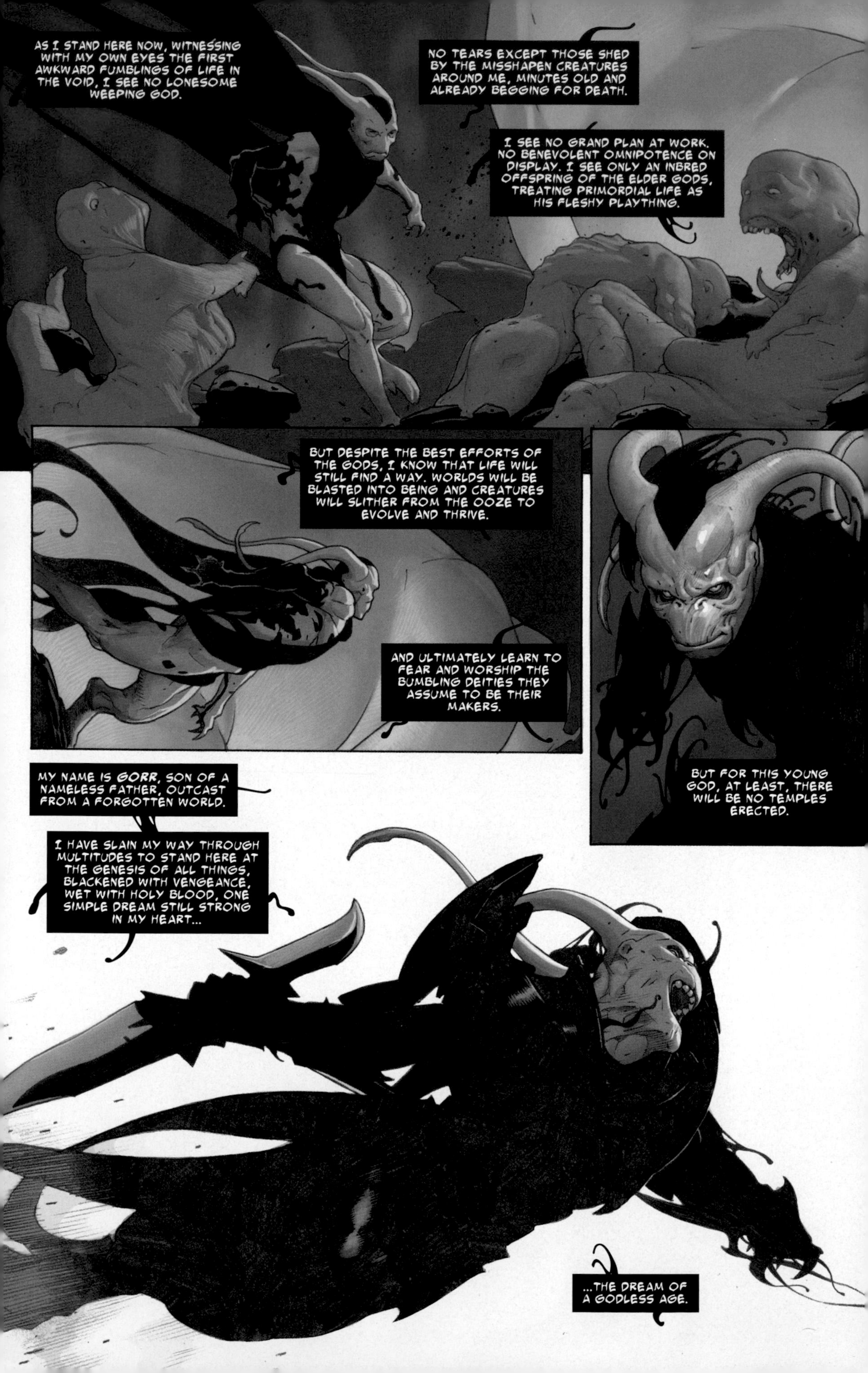
AS I STAND HERE NOW, WITNESSING WITH MY OWN EYES THE FIRST AWKWARD FUMBLINGS OF LIFE IN THE VOID, I SEE NO LONESOME WEEPING GOD.
NO TEARS EXCEPT THOSE SHED BY THE MISSHAPEN CREATURES AROUND ME, MINUTES OLD AND ALREADY BEGGING FOR DEATH.
I SEE NO GRAND PLAN AT WORK. NO BENEVOLENT OMNIPOTENCE ON DISPLAY. I SEE ONLY AN INBRED OFFSPRING OF THE ELDER GODS, TREATING PRIMORDIAL LIFE AS HIS FLESHY PLAYTHING.
BUT DESPITE THE BEST EFFORTS OF THE GODS, I KNOW THAT LIFE WILL STILL FIND A WAY. WORLDS WILL BE BLASTED INTO BEING AND CREATURES WILL SLITHER FROM THE OOZE TO EVOLVE AND THRIVE.
AND ULTIMATELY LEARN TO FEAR AND WORSHIP THE BUMBLING DEITIES THEY ASSUME TO BE THEIR MAKERS.
BUT FOR THIS YOUNG GOD, AT LEAST, THERE WILL BE NO TEMPLES ERECTED.
MY NAME IS GORR, SON OF A NAMELESS FATHER, OUTCAST FROM A FORGOTTEN WORLD.
I HAVE SLAIN MY WAY THROUGH MULTITUDES TO STAND HERE AT THE GENESIS OF ALL THINGS, BLACKENED WITH VENGEANCE, WET WITH HOLY BLOOD, ONE SIMPLE DREAM STILL STRONG IN MY HEART...
...THE DREAM OF A GODLESS AGE.

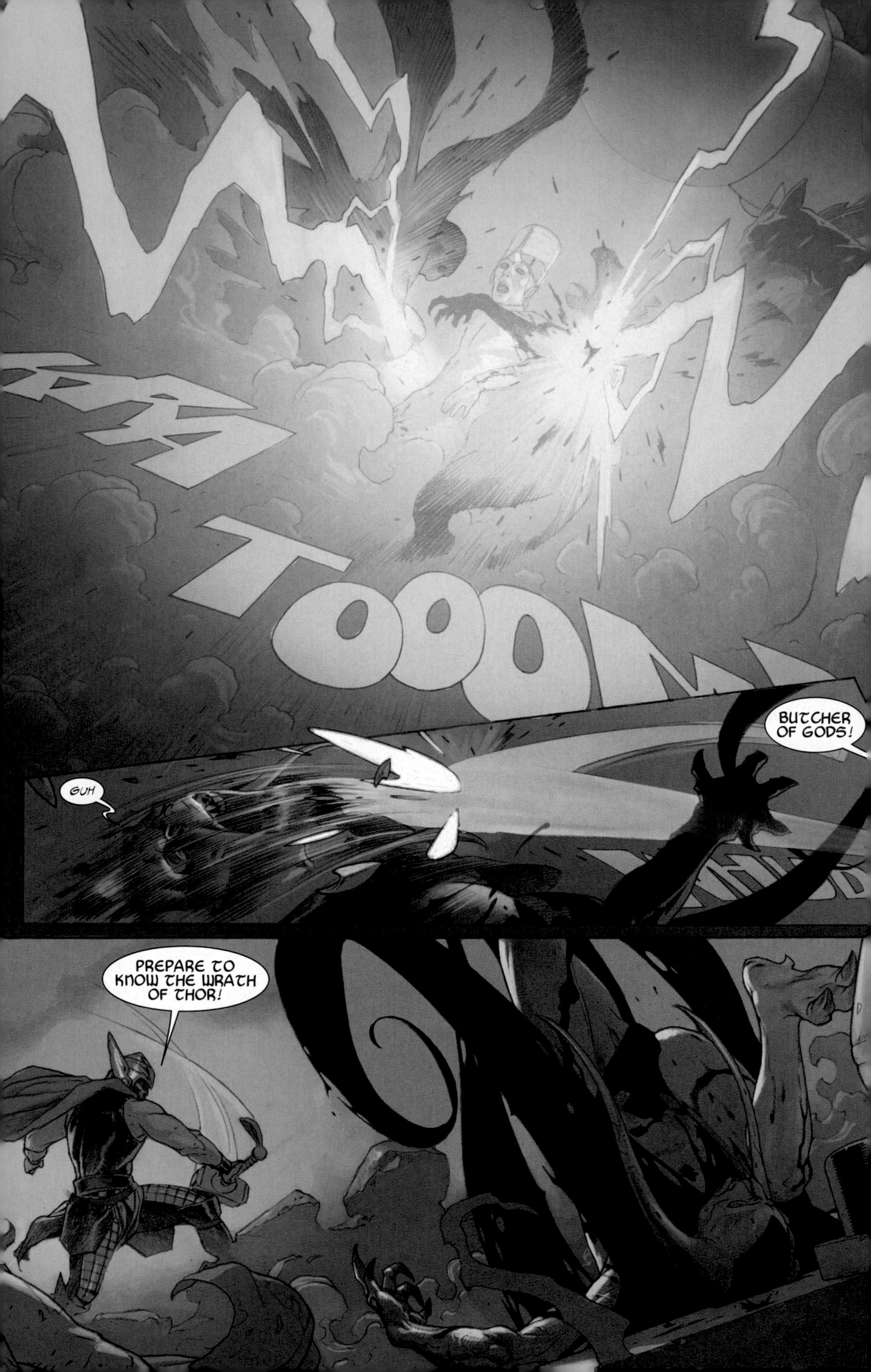
TOOOM
BUTCHER OF GODS!
GUH
PREPARE TO KNOW THE WRATH OF THOR!

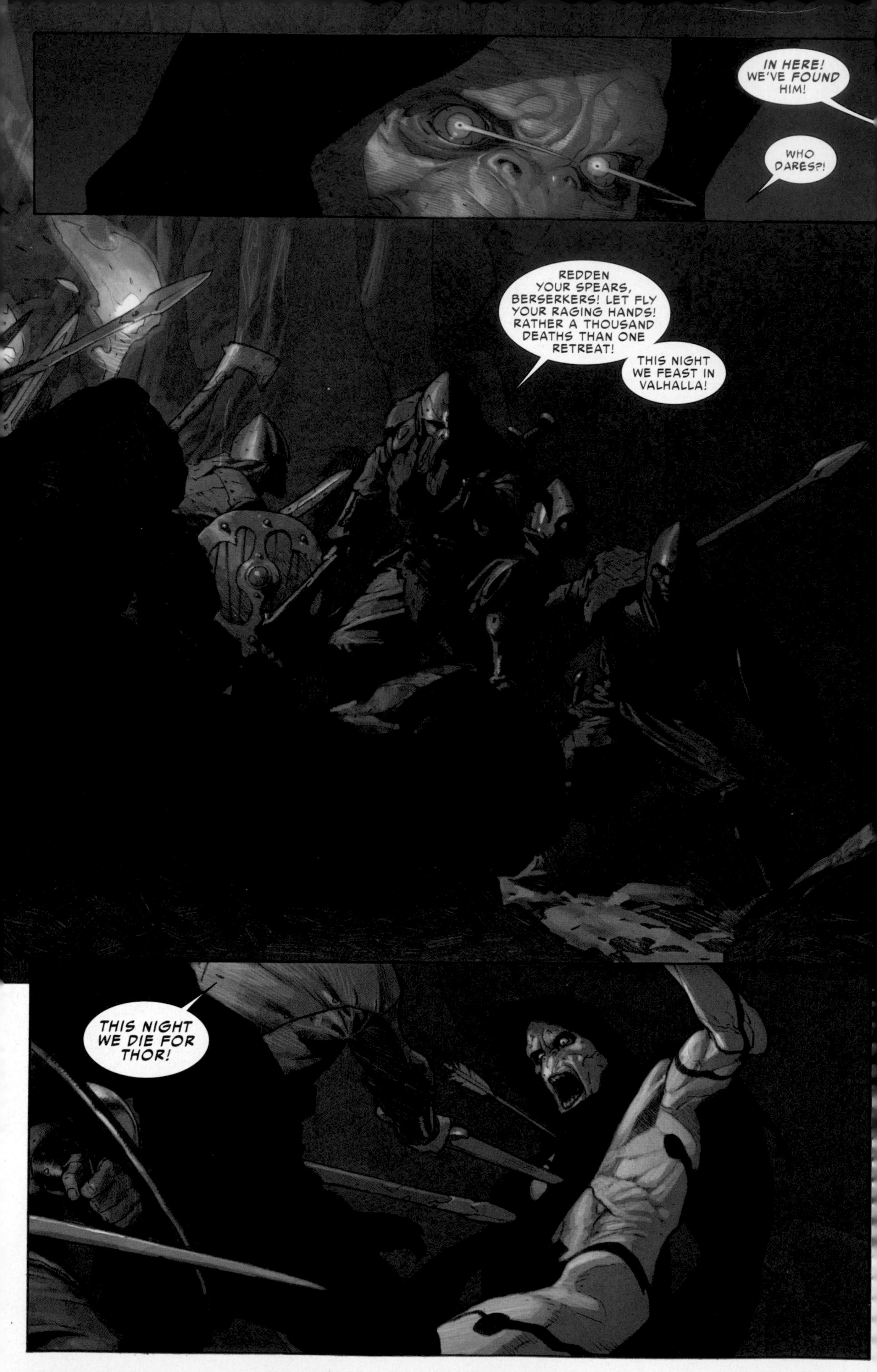
IN HERE! WE'VE FOUND HIM!
WHO DARES?!
REDDEN YOUR SPEARS, BERSERKERS! LET FLY YOUR RAGING HANDS! RATHER A THOUSAND DEATHS THAN ONE RETREAT!
THIS NIGHT WE FEAST IN VALHALLA!
THIS NIGHT WE DIE FOR THOR!

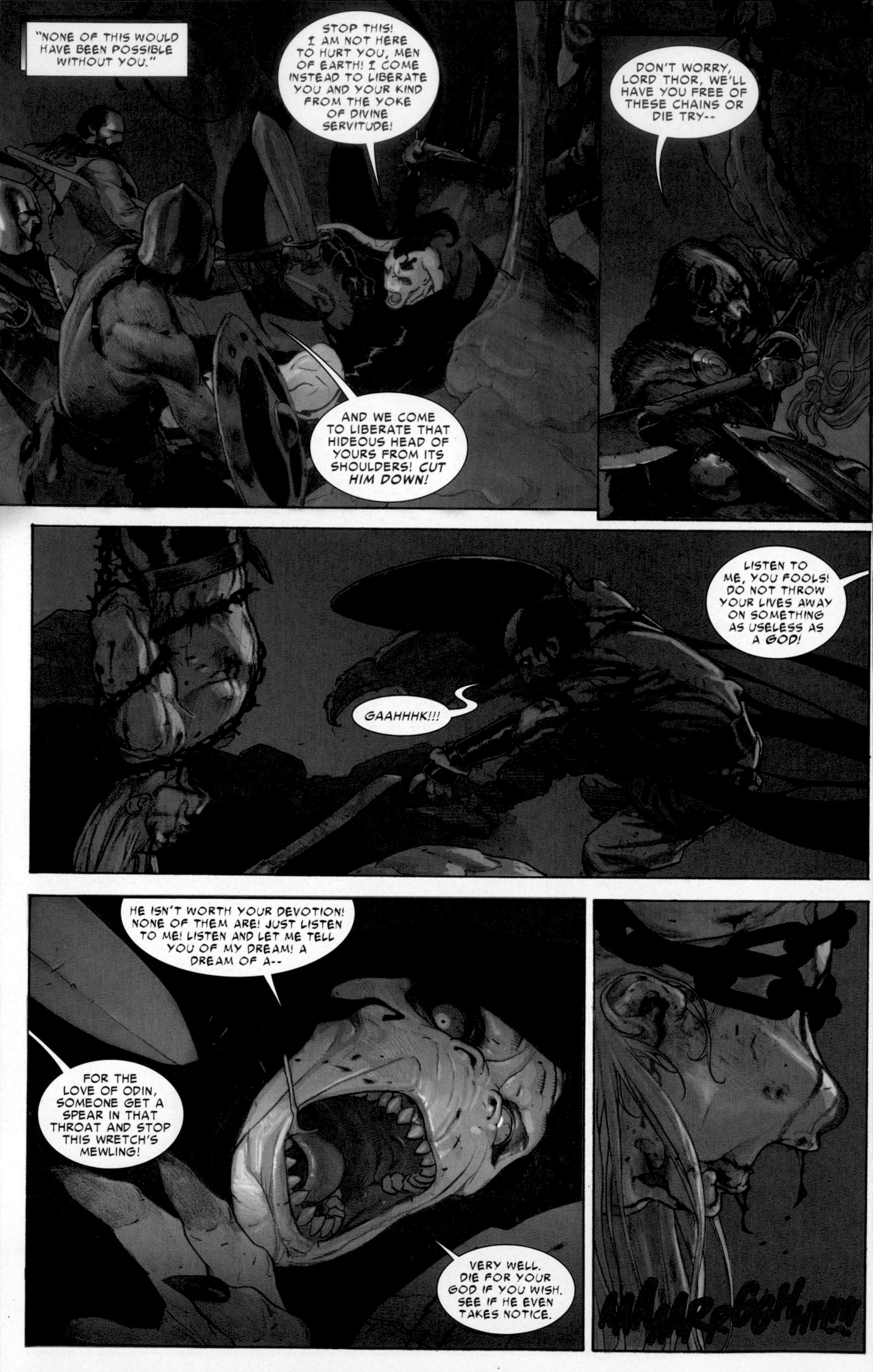
"NONE OF THIS WOULD HAVE BEEN POSSIBLE WITHOUT YOU."
STOP THIS! I AM NOT HERE TO HURT YOU, MEN OF EARTH! I COME INSTEAD TO LIBERATE YOU AND YOUR KIND FROM THE YOKE OF DIVINE SERVITUDE!
AND WE COME TO LIBERATE THAT HIDEOUS HEAD OF YOURS FROM ITS SHOULDERS! *CUT HIM DOWN!*
DON'T WORRY, LORD THOR, WE'LL HAVE YOU FREE OF THESE CHAINS OR DIE TRY--
LISTEN TO ME, YOU FOOLS! DO NOT THROW YOUR LIVES AWAY ON SOMETHING AS USELESS AS A *GOD!*
GAAHHHK!!!
HE ISN'T WORTH YOUR DEVOTION! NONE OF THEM ARE! JUST LISTEN TO ME! LISTEN AND LET ME TELL YOU OF MY DREAM! A DREAM OF A--
FOR THE LOVE OF ODIN, SOMEONE GET A SPEAR IN THAT THROAT AND STOP THIS WRETCH'S MEWLING!
VERY WELL. DIE FOR YOUR GOD IF YOU WISH. SEE IF HE EVEN TAKES NOTICE.

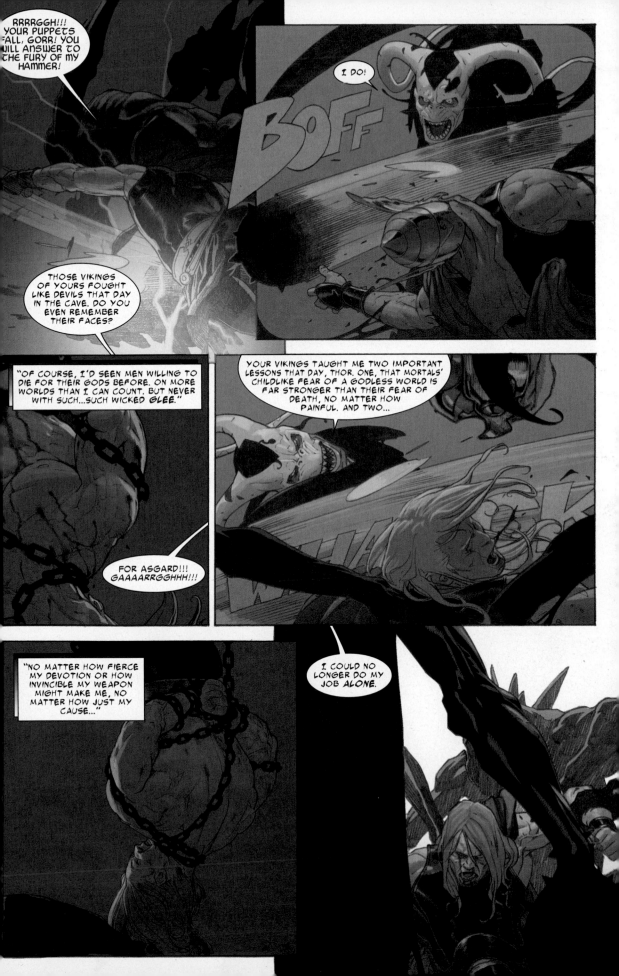

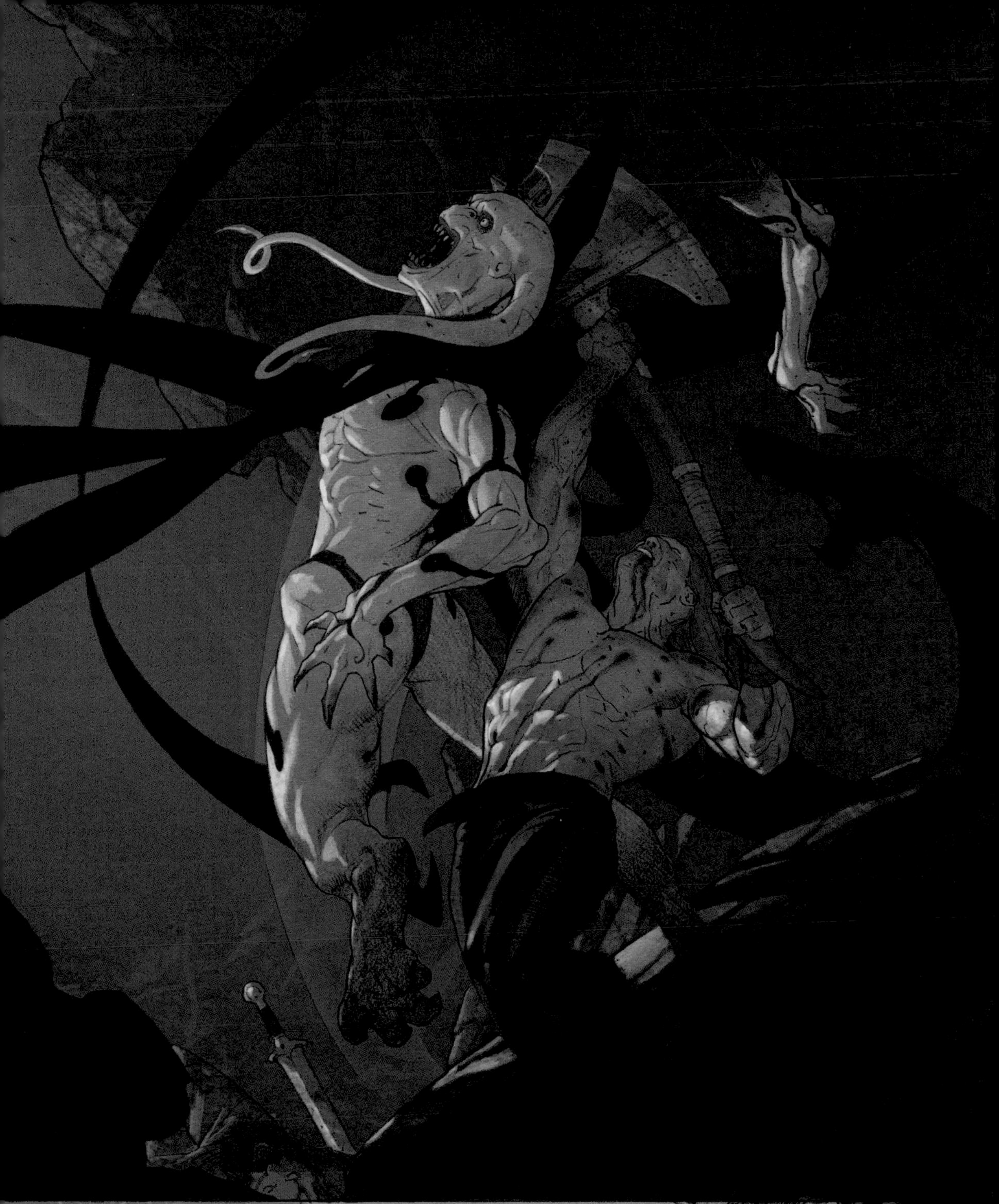

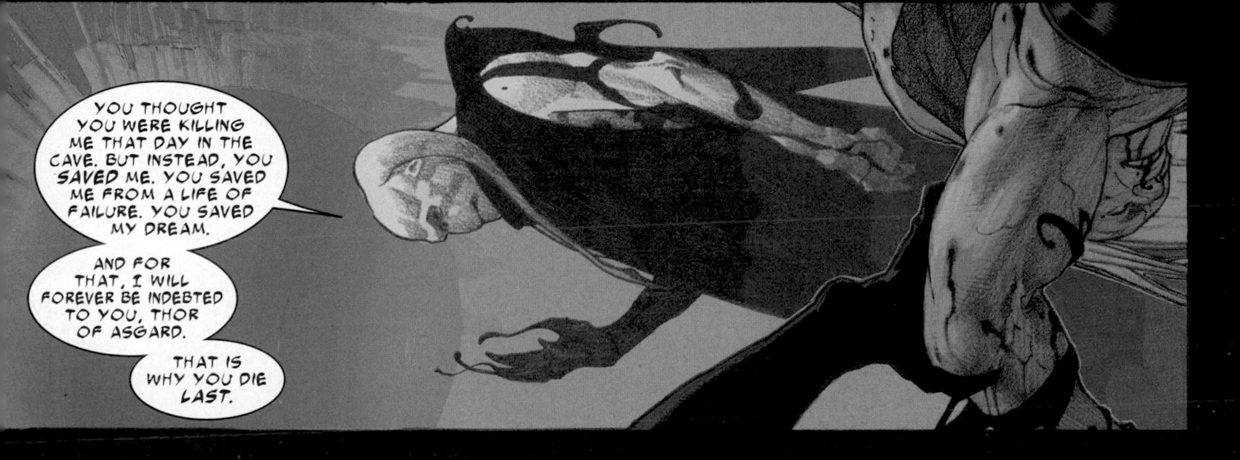
YOU THOUGHT YOU WERE KILLING ME THAT DAY IN THE CAVE. BUT INSTEAD, YOU SAVED ME. YOU SAVED ME FROM A LIFE OF FAILURE. YOU SAVED MY DREAM.
AND FOR THAT, I WILL FOREVER BE INDEBTED TO YOU, THOR OF ASGARD.
THAT IS WHY YOU DIE LAST.

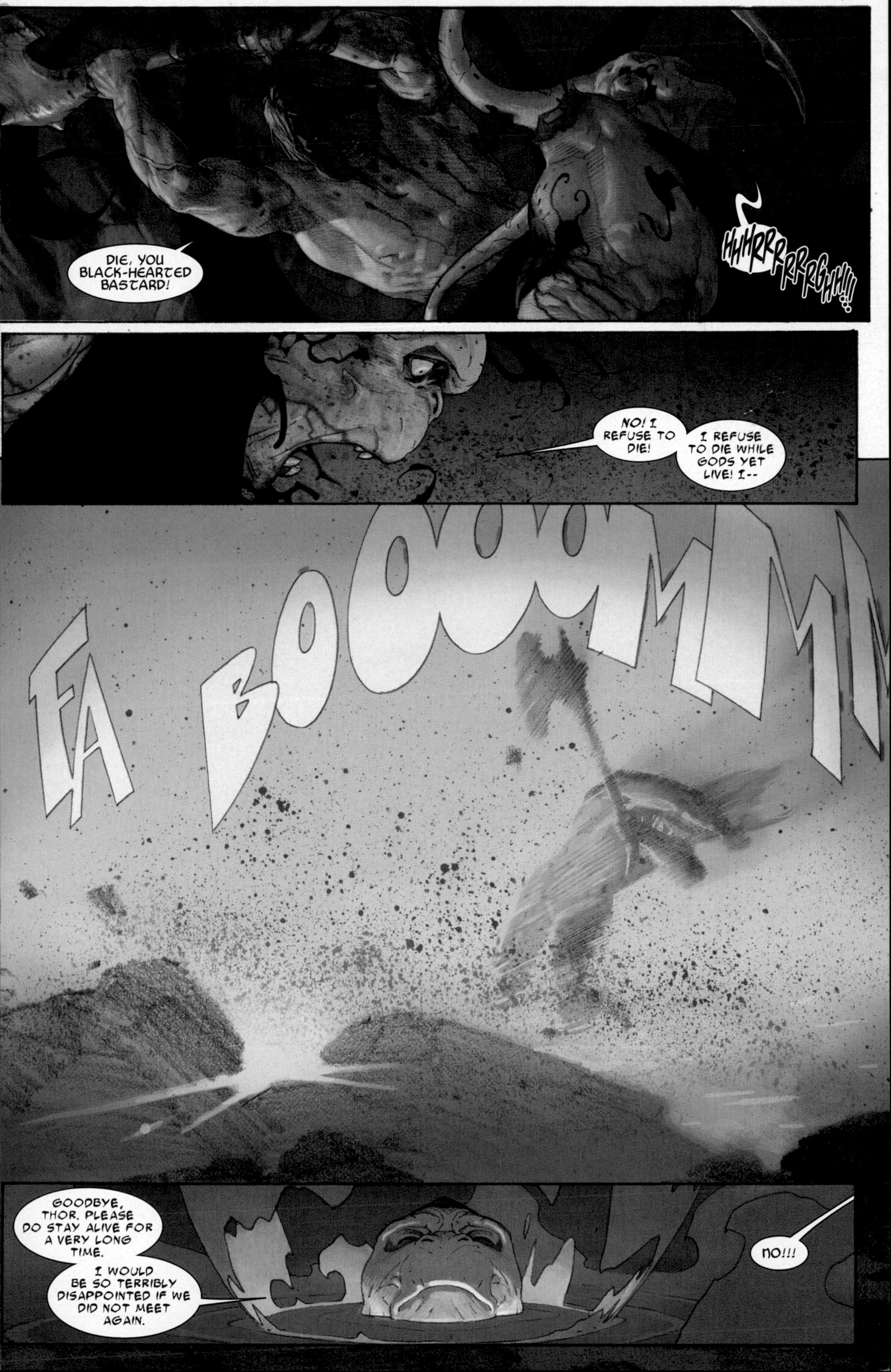
DIE, YOU BLACK-HEARTED BASTARD!
HHHRRRRRRGHH!!!
NO! I REFUSE TO DIE!
I REFUSE TO DIE WHILE GODS YET LIVE! I--
FA BOOOOMMMM
GOODBYE, THOR. PLEASE DO STAY ALIVE FOR A VERY LONG TIME.
I WOULD BE SO TERRIBLY DISAPPOINTED IF WE DID NOT MEET AGAIN.
NO!!!

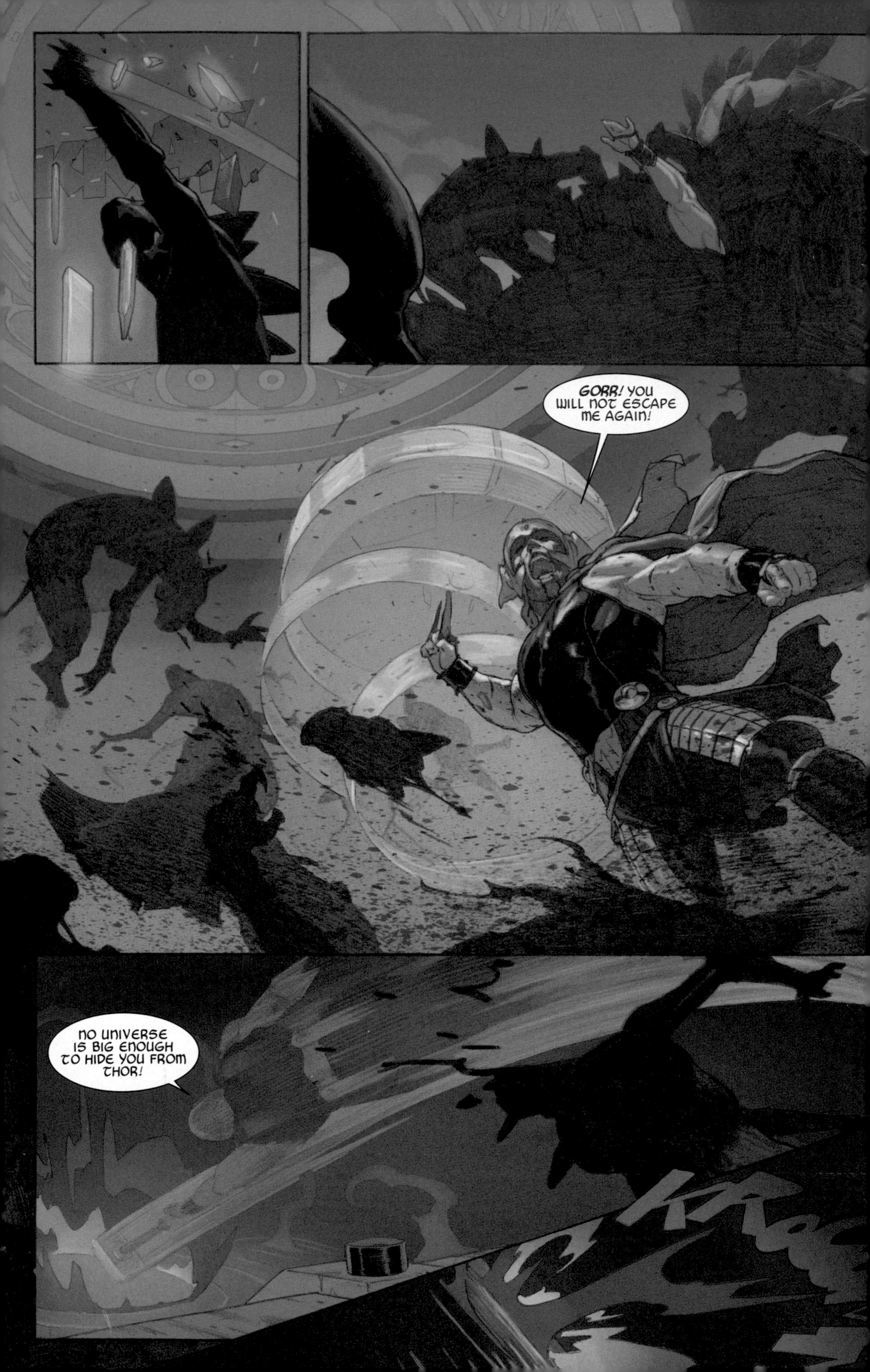
GORR! YOU WILL NOT ESCAPE ME AGAIN!
NO UNIVERSE IS BIG ENOUGH TO HIDE YOU FROM THOR!

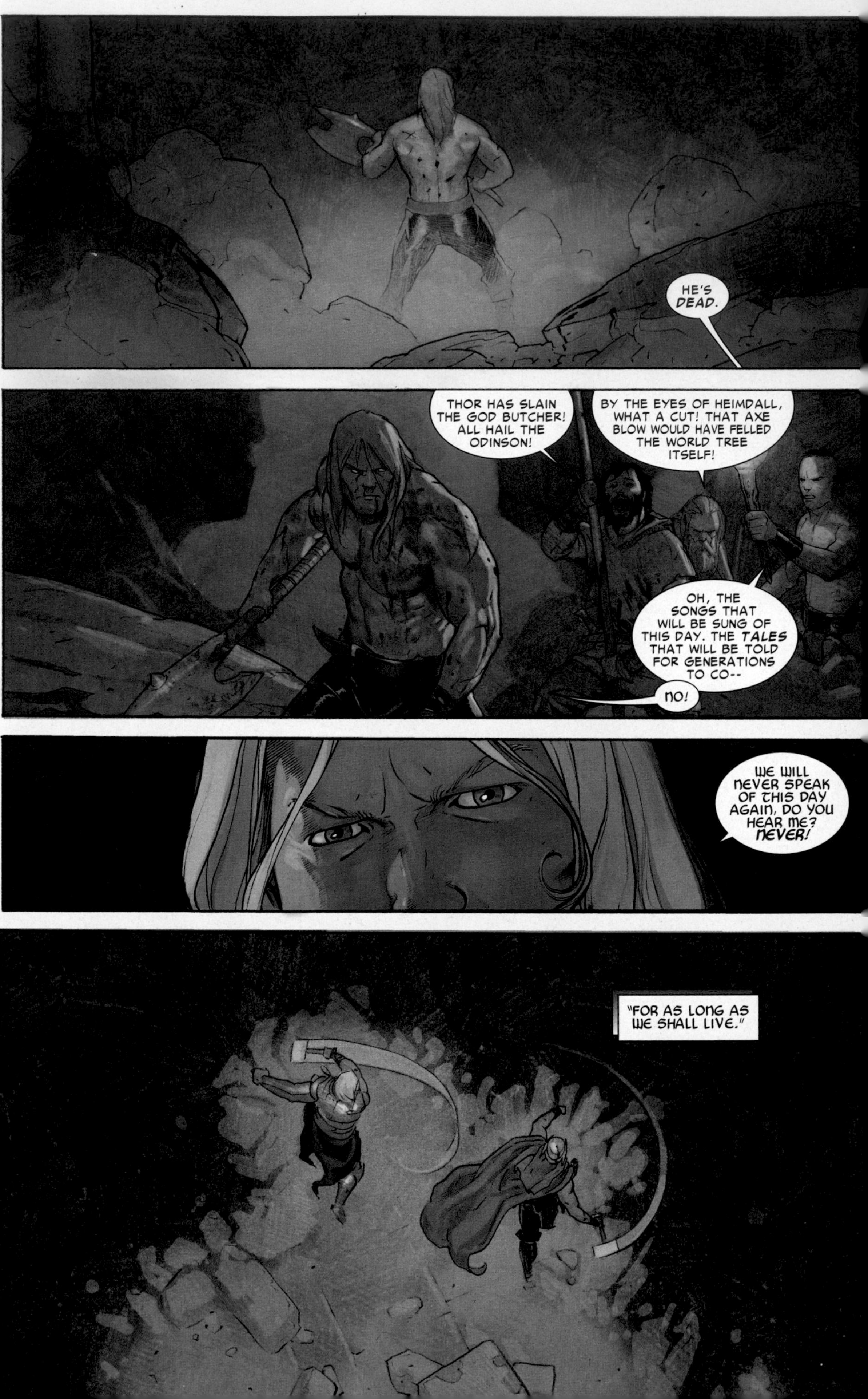
HE'S DEAD.
THOR HAS SLAIN THE GOD BUTCHER! ALL HAIL THE ODINSON!
BY THE EYES OF HEIMDALL, WHAT A CUT! THAT AXE BLOW WOULD HAVE FELLED THE WORLD TREE ITSELF!
OH, THE SONGS THAT WILL BE SUNG OF THIS DAY. THE TALES THAT WILL BE TOLD FOR GENERATIONS TO CO--
NO!
WE WILL NEVER SPEAK OF THIS DAY AGAIN, DO YOU HEAR ME? NEVER!
"FOR AS LONG AS WE SHALL LIVE."

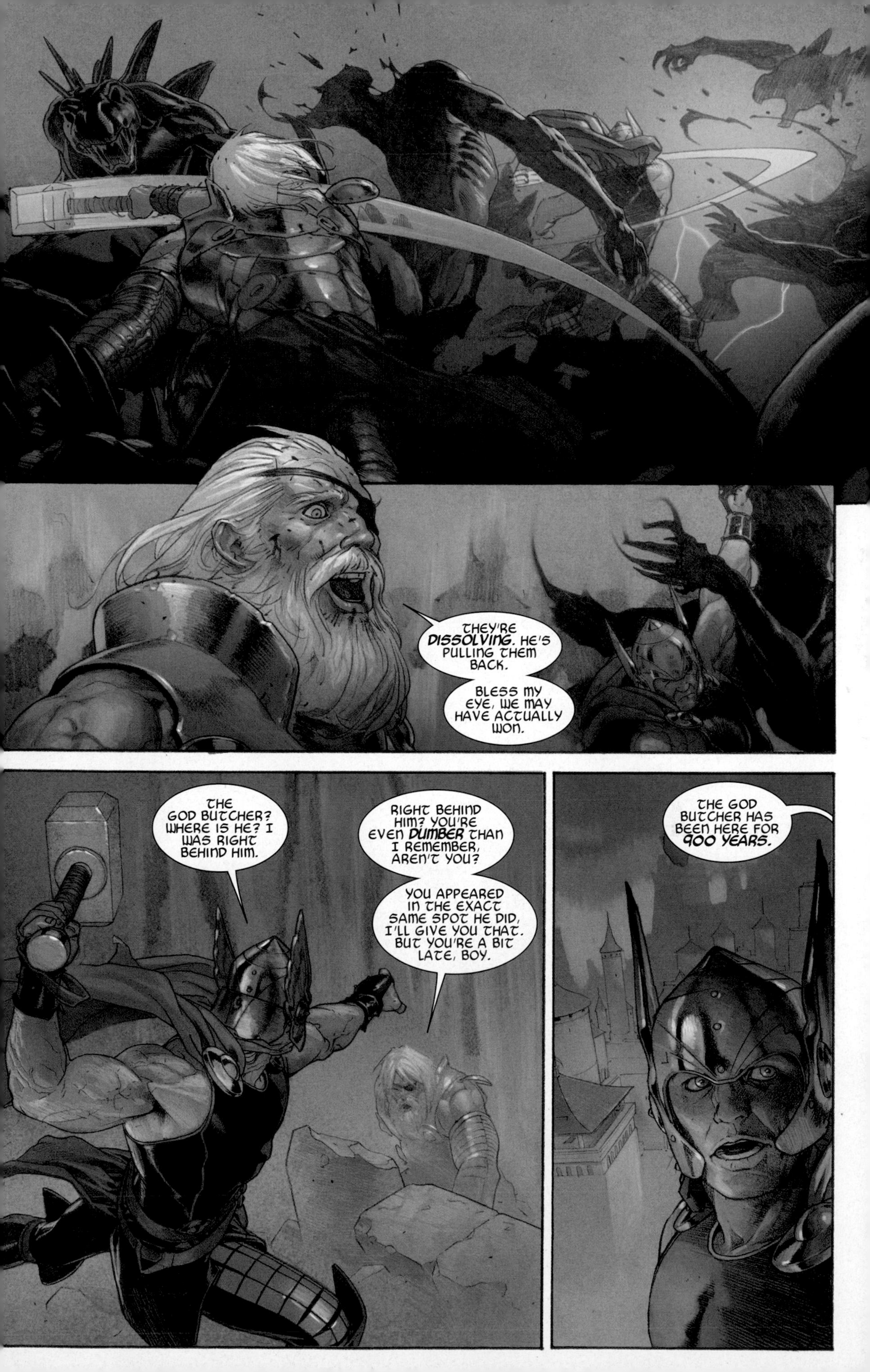
THEY'RE DISSOLVING. HE'S PULLING THEM BACK.
BLESS MY EYE, WE MAY HAVE ACTUALLY WON.
THE GOD BUTCHER? WHERE IS HE? I WAS RIGHT BEHIND HIM.
RIGHT BEHIND HIM? YOU'RE EVEN DUMBER THAN I REMEMBER, AREN'T YOU?
YOU APPEARED IN THE EXACT SAME SPOT HE DID, I'LL GIVE YOU THAT. BUT YOU'RE A BIT LATE, BOY.
THE GOD BUTCHER HAS BEEN HERE FOR 900 YEARS.

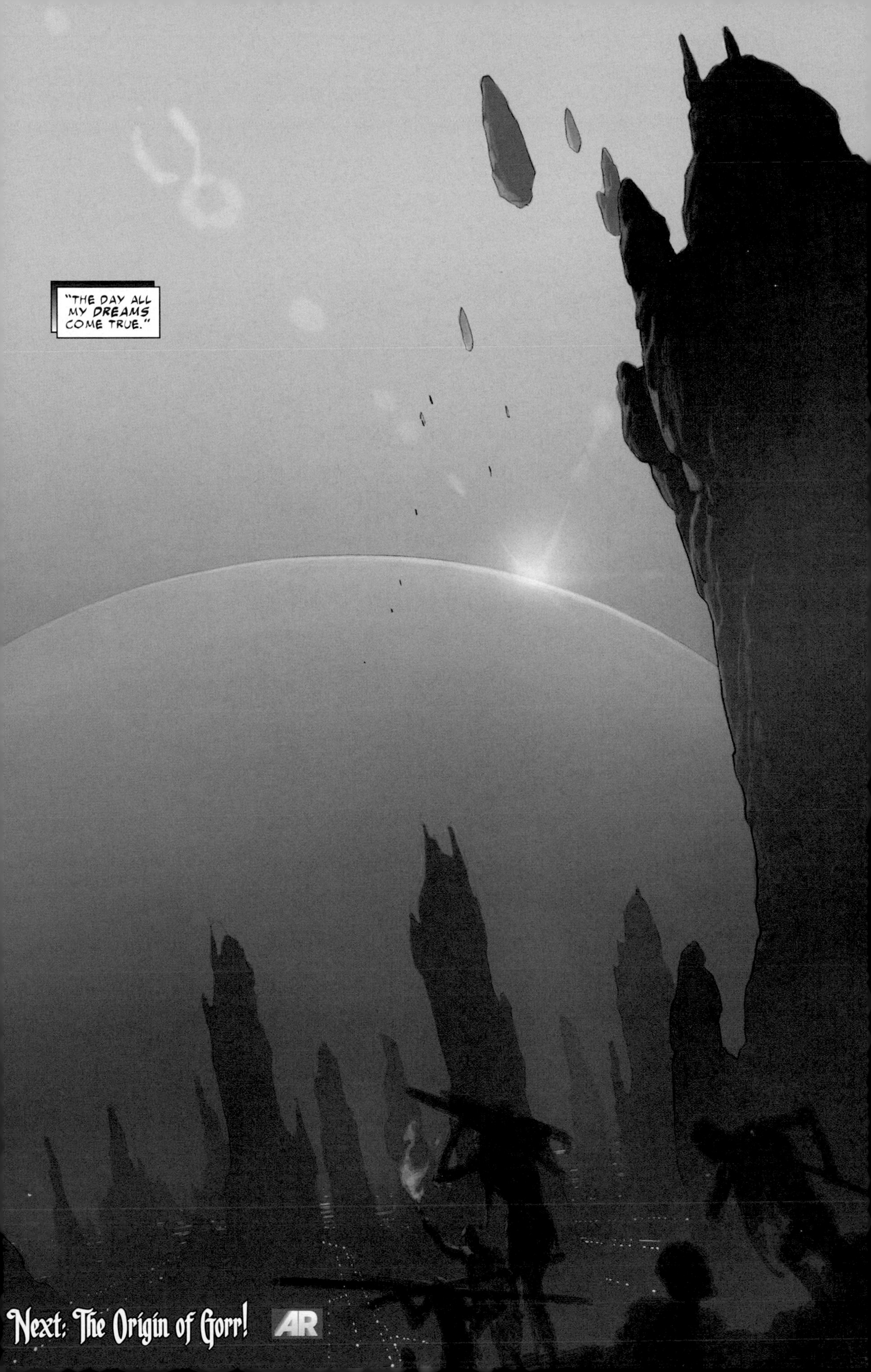
"THE DAY ALL MY DREAMS COME TRUE."
Next: The Origin of Gorr!

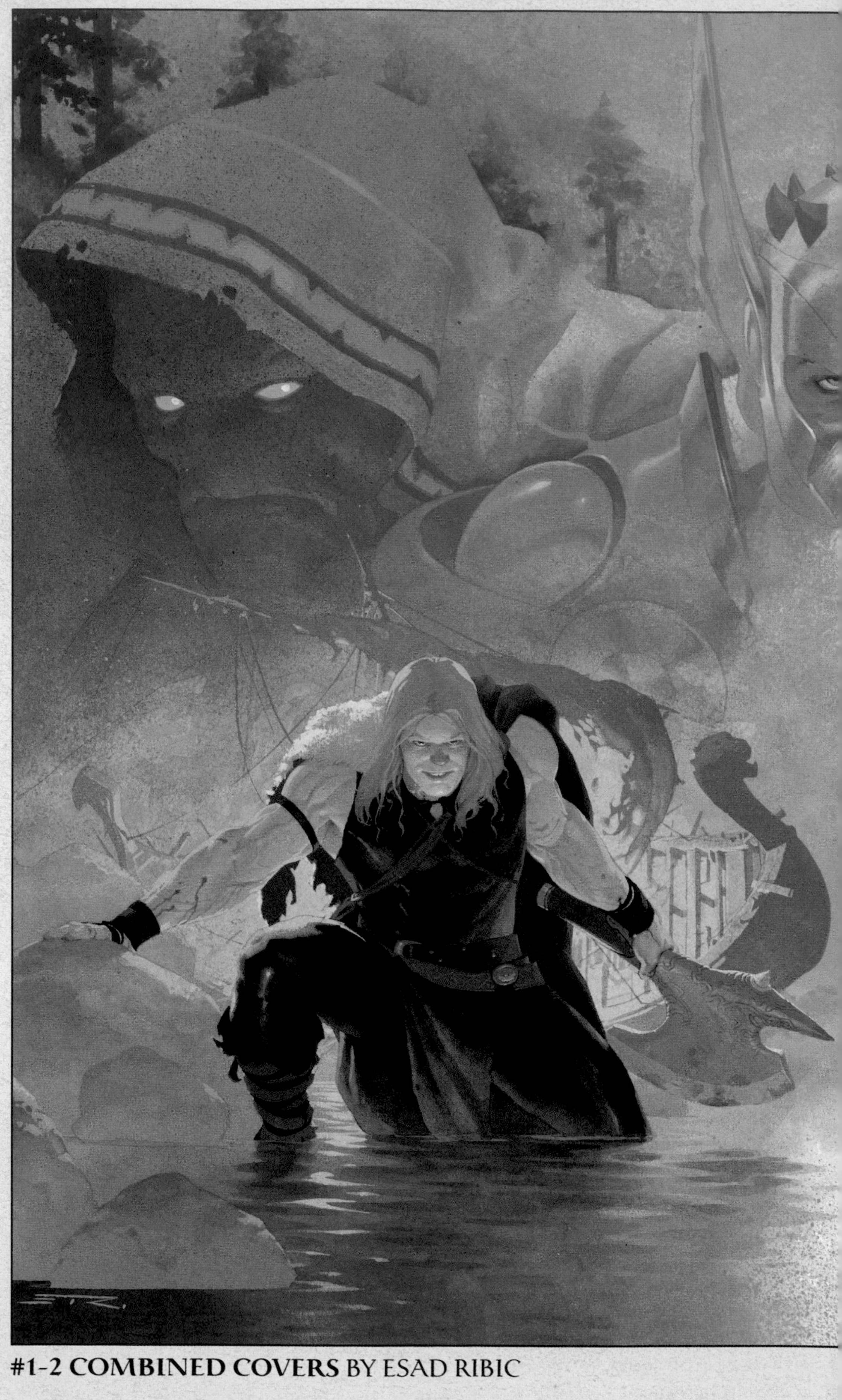

#1-2 COMBINED COVERS BY ESAD RIBIC

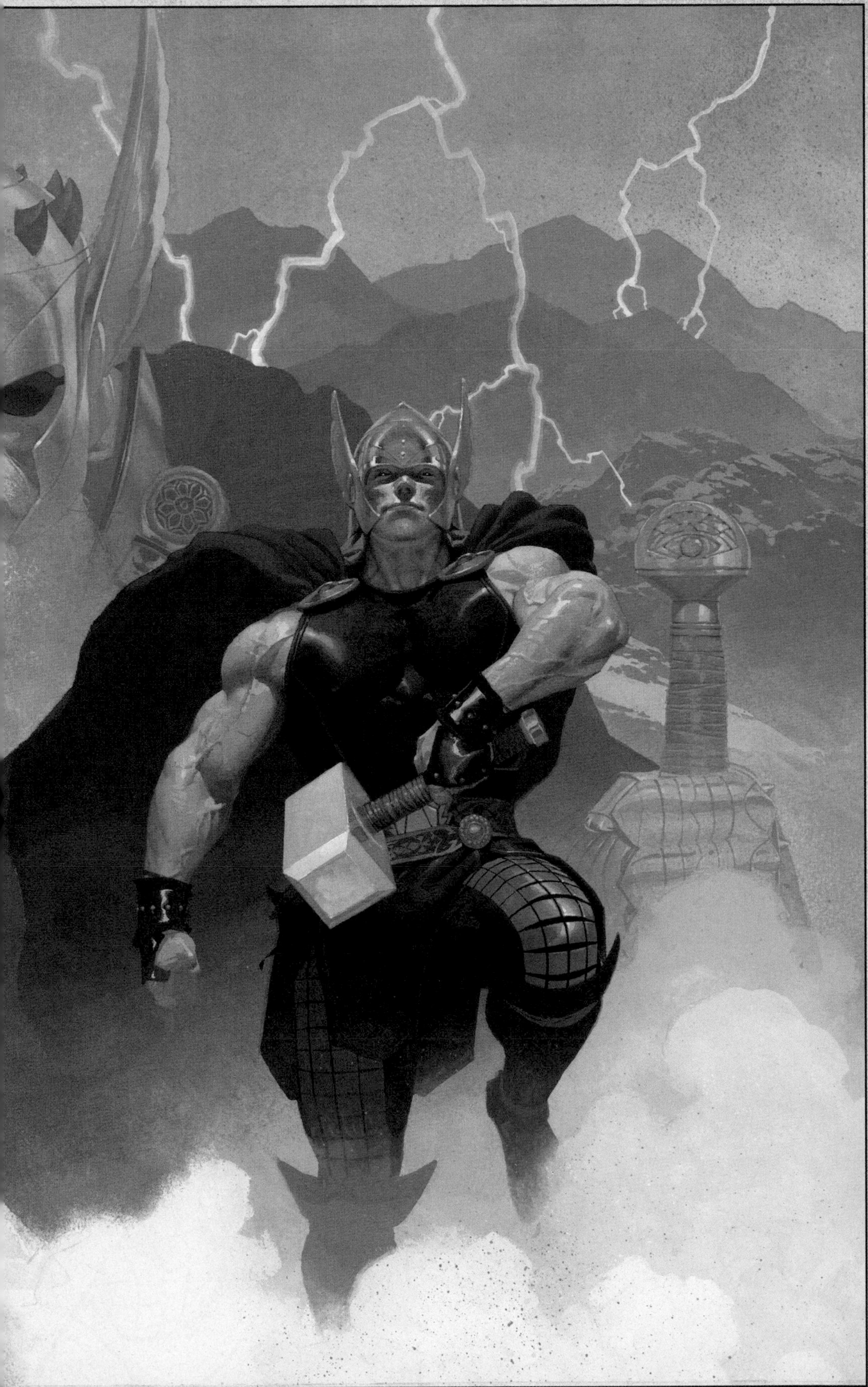

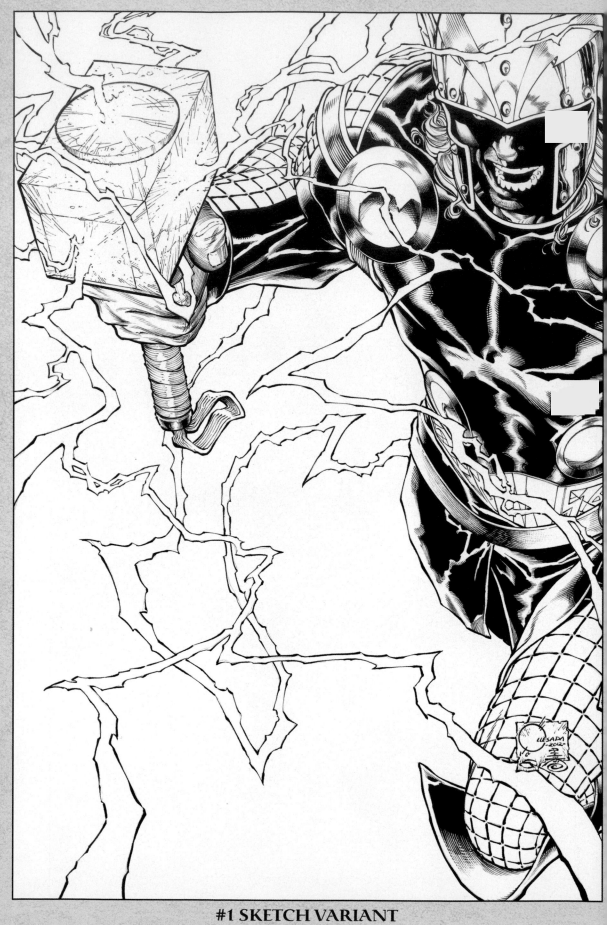

#1 SKETCH VARIANT
BY JOE QUESADA & DANNY MIKI

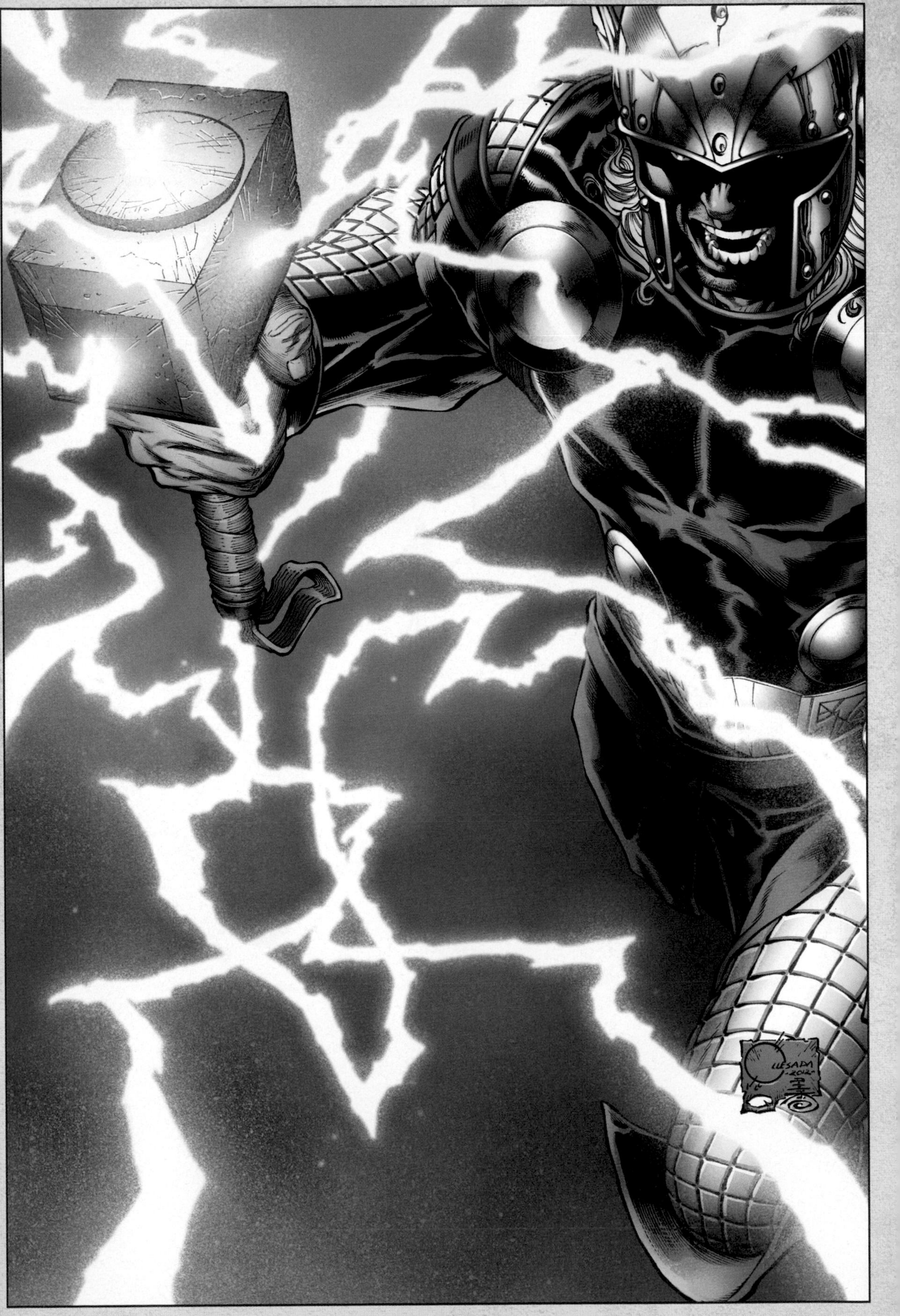

#1 VARIANT
BY JOE QUESADA, DANNY MIKI & RICHARD ISANOVE

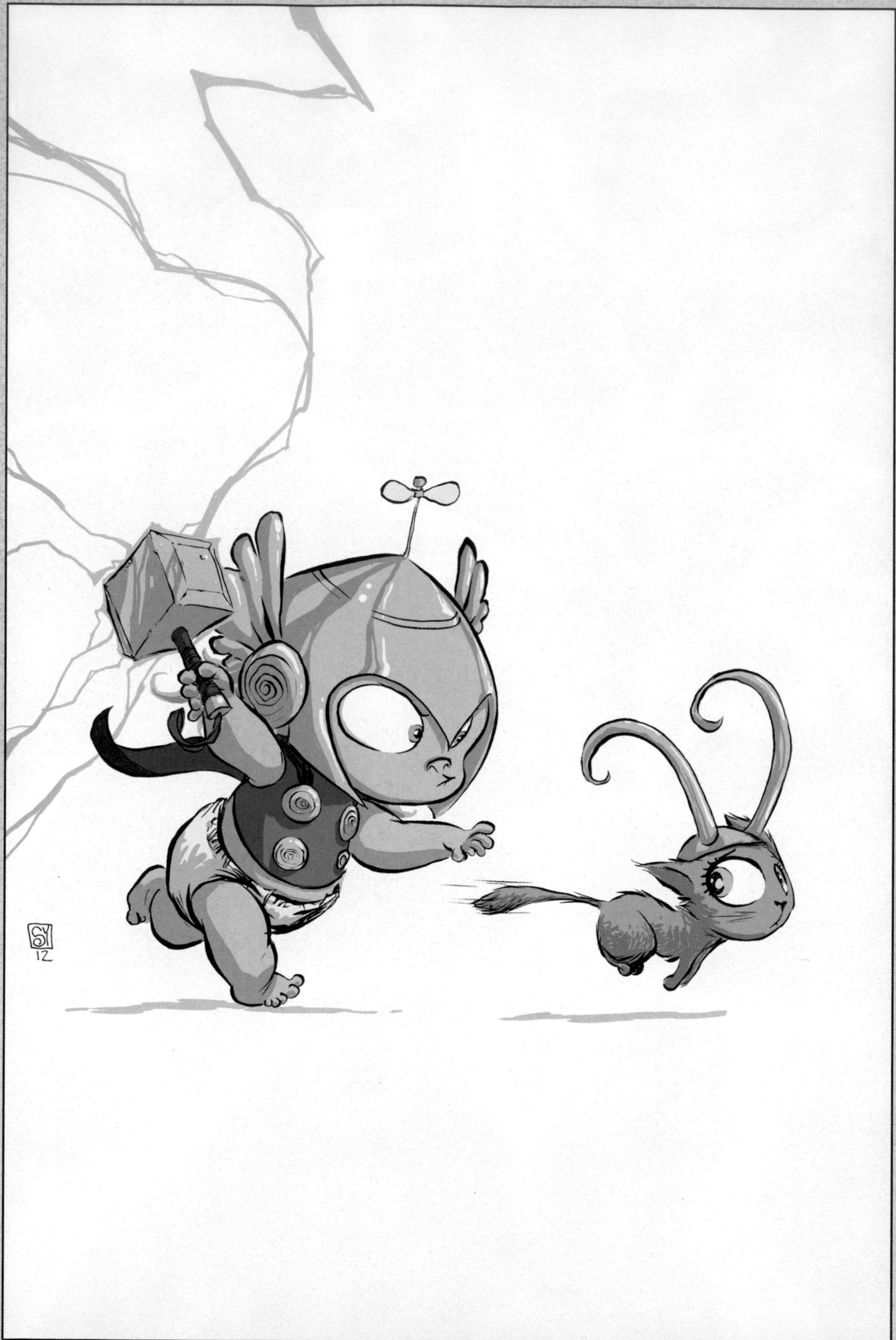

#1 VARIANT
BY SKOTTIE YOUNG

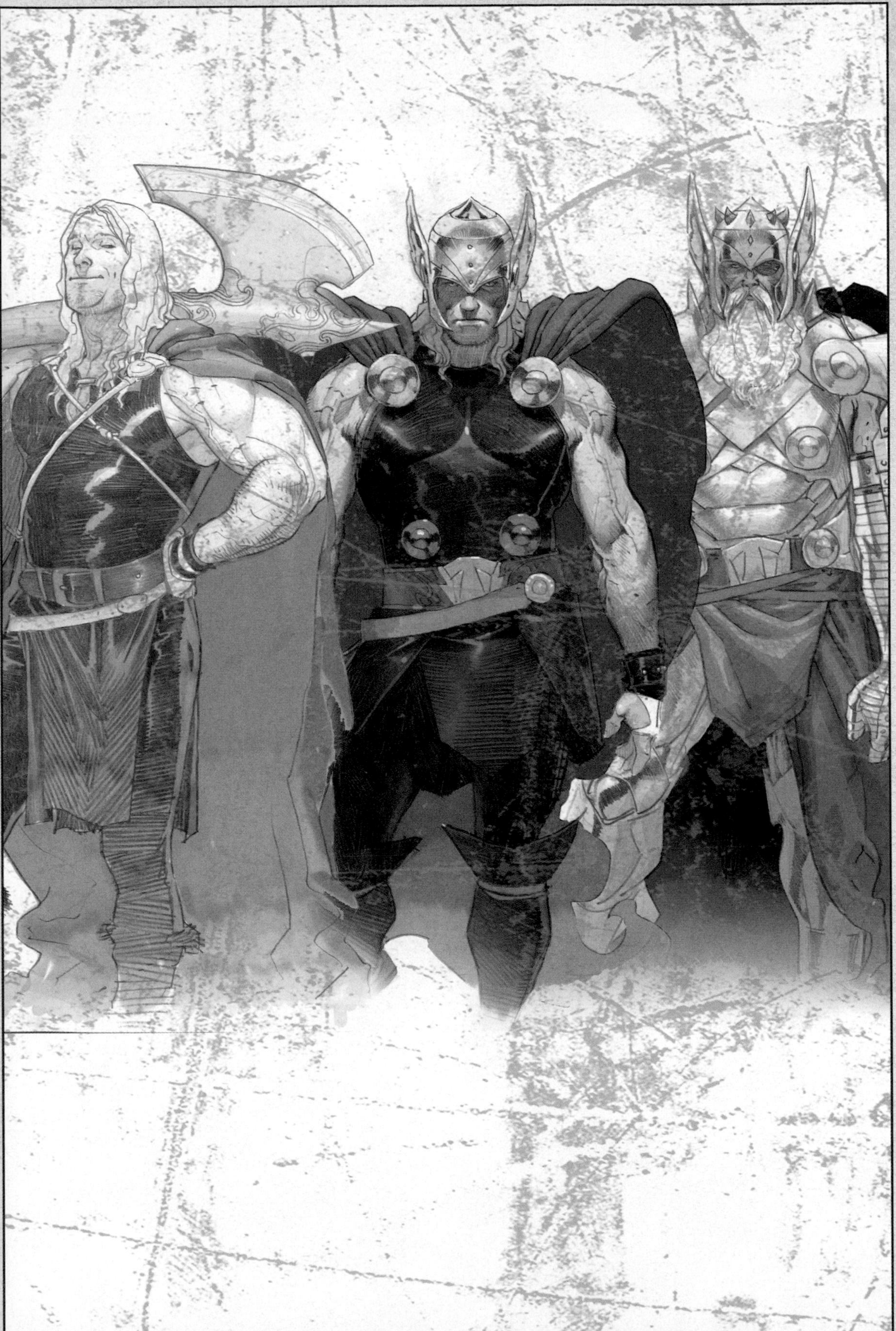

#1 DESIGN VARIANT
BY ESAD RIBIC

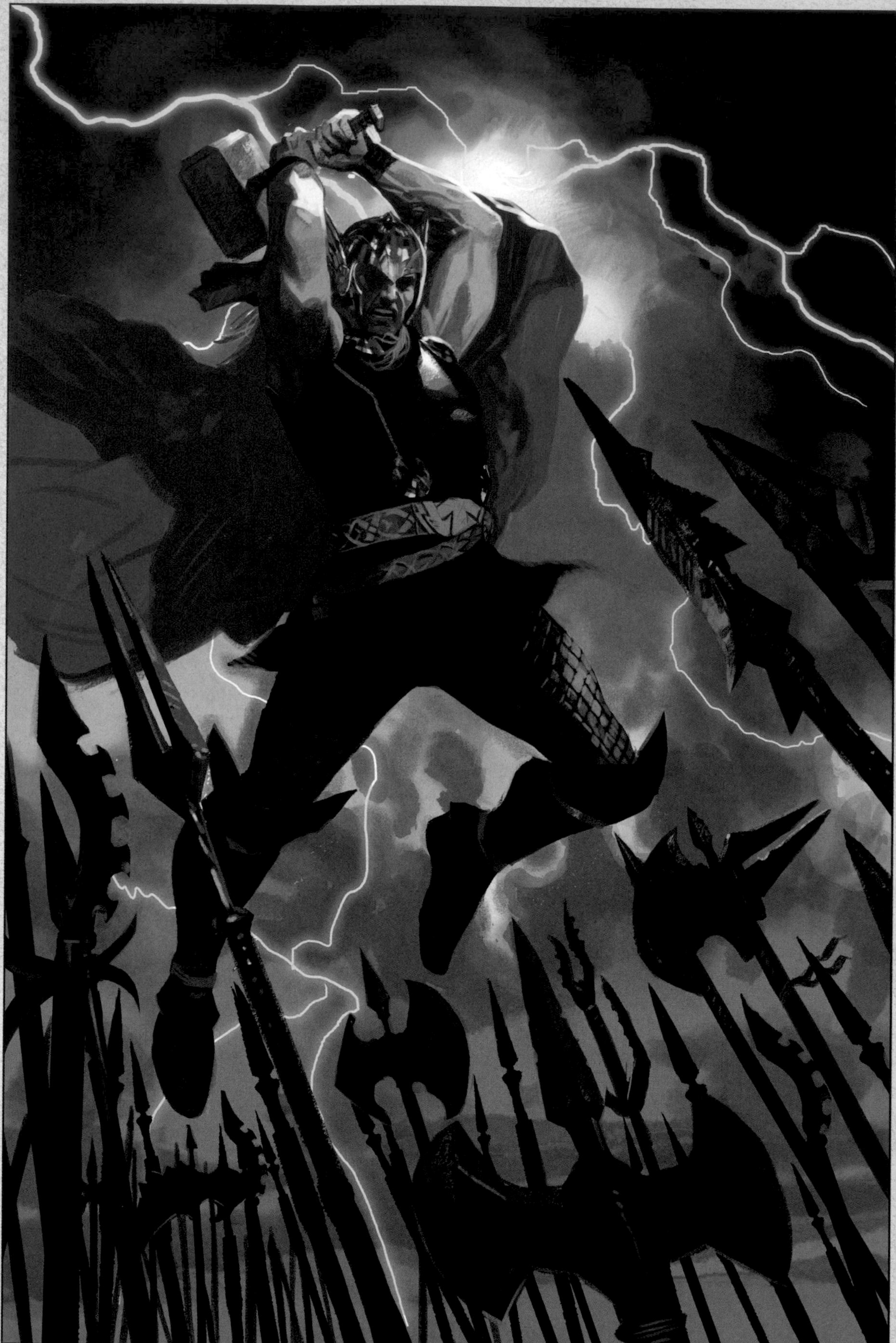

#1 VARIANT
BY DANIEL ACUÑA

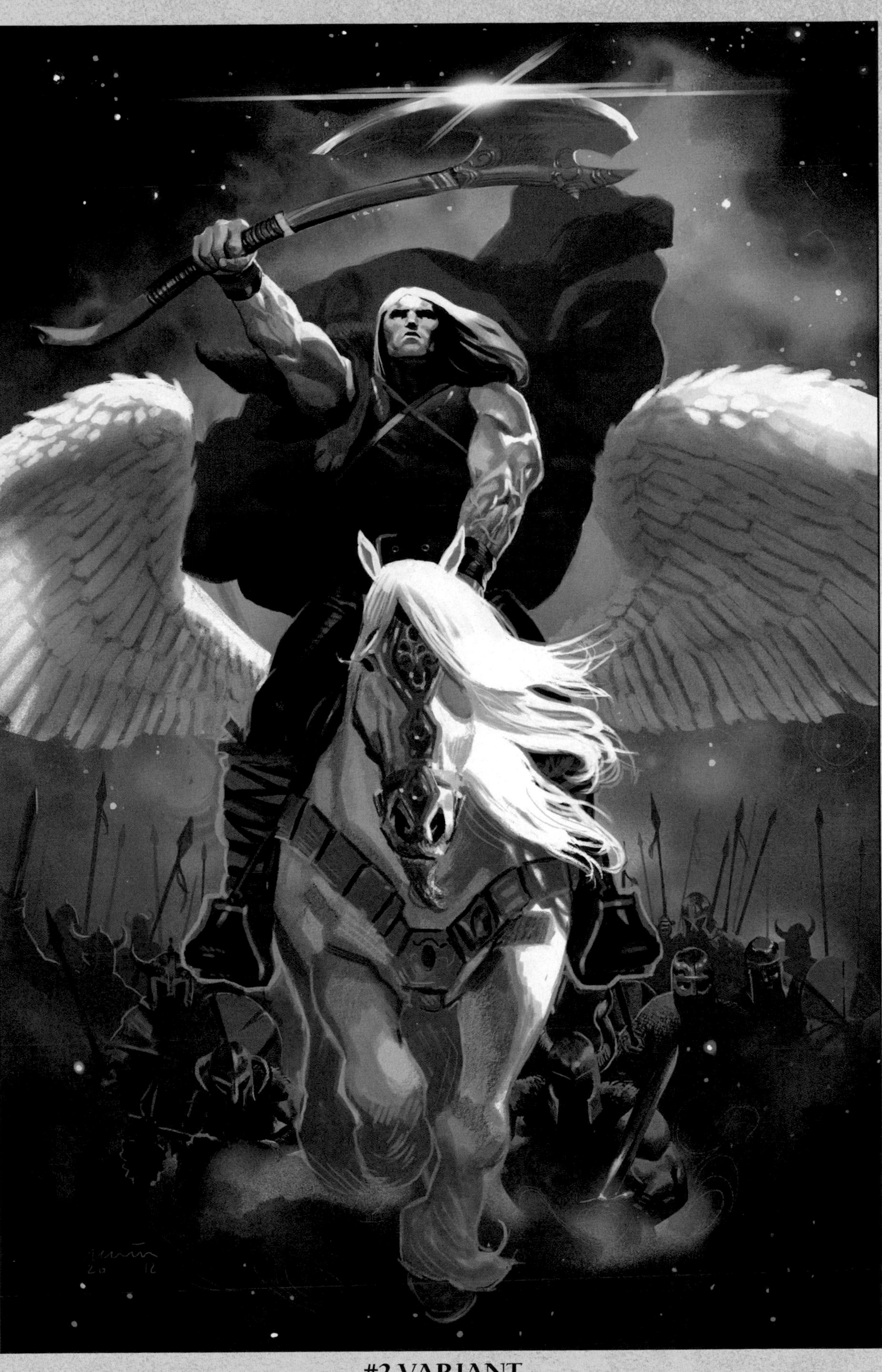

#2 VARIANT
BY DANIEL ACUÑA

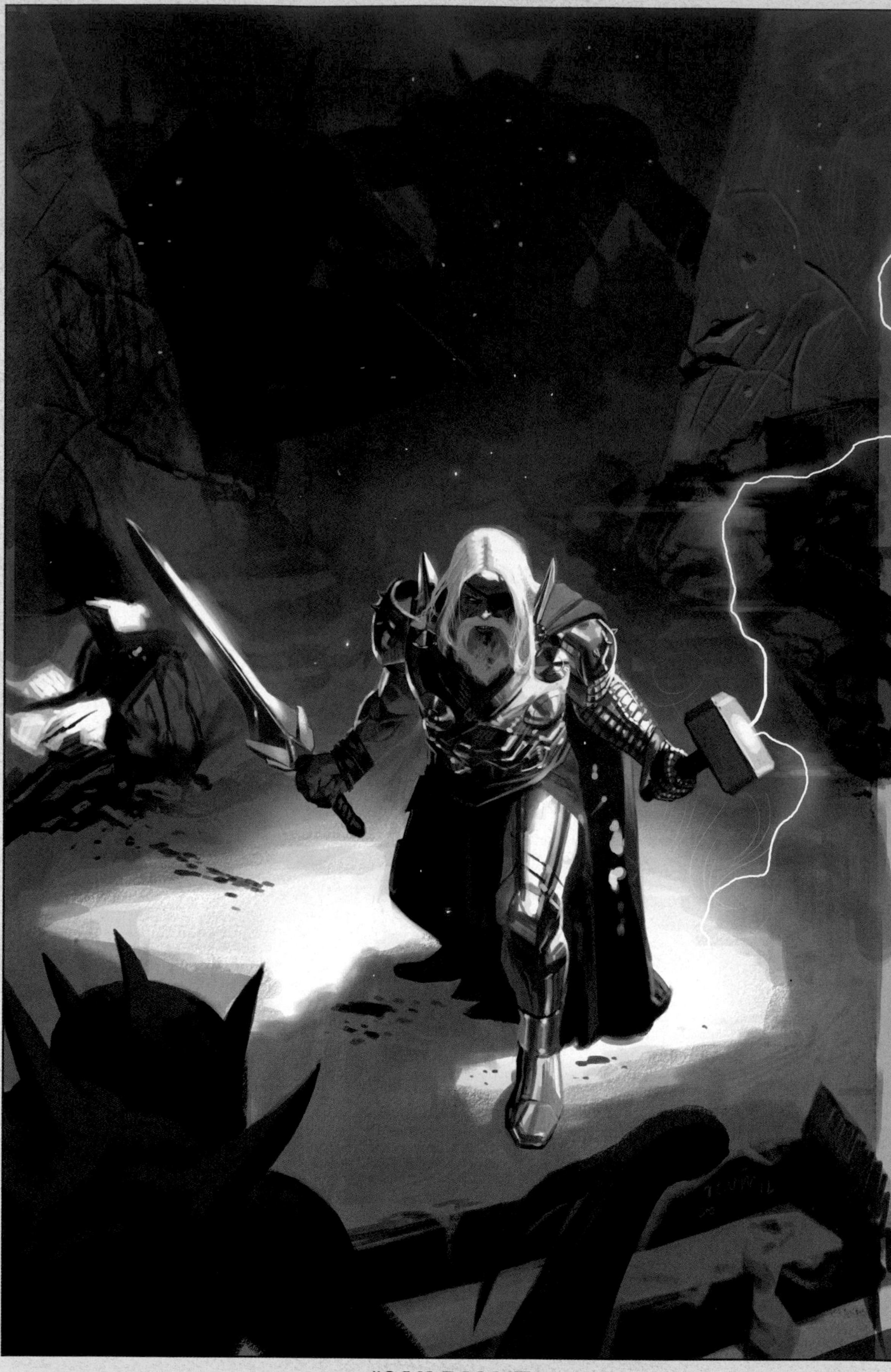

#3 VARIANT
BY DANIEL ACUÑA

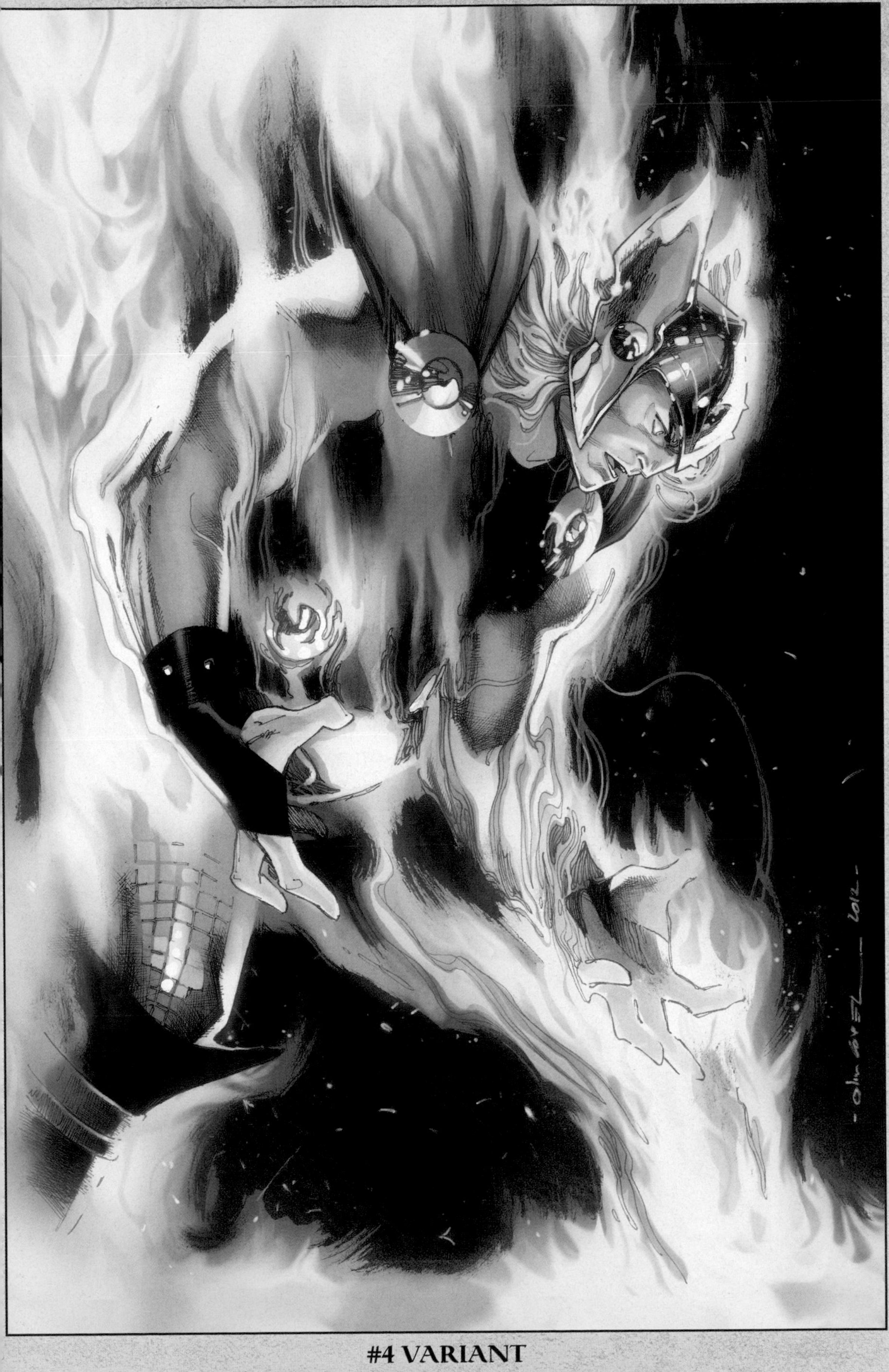

#4 VARIANT
BY OLIVIER COIPEL & LAURA MARTIN

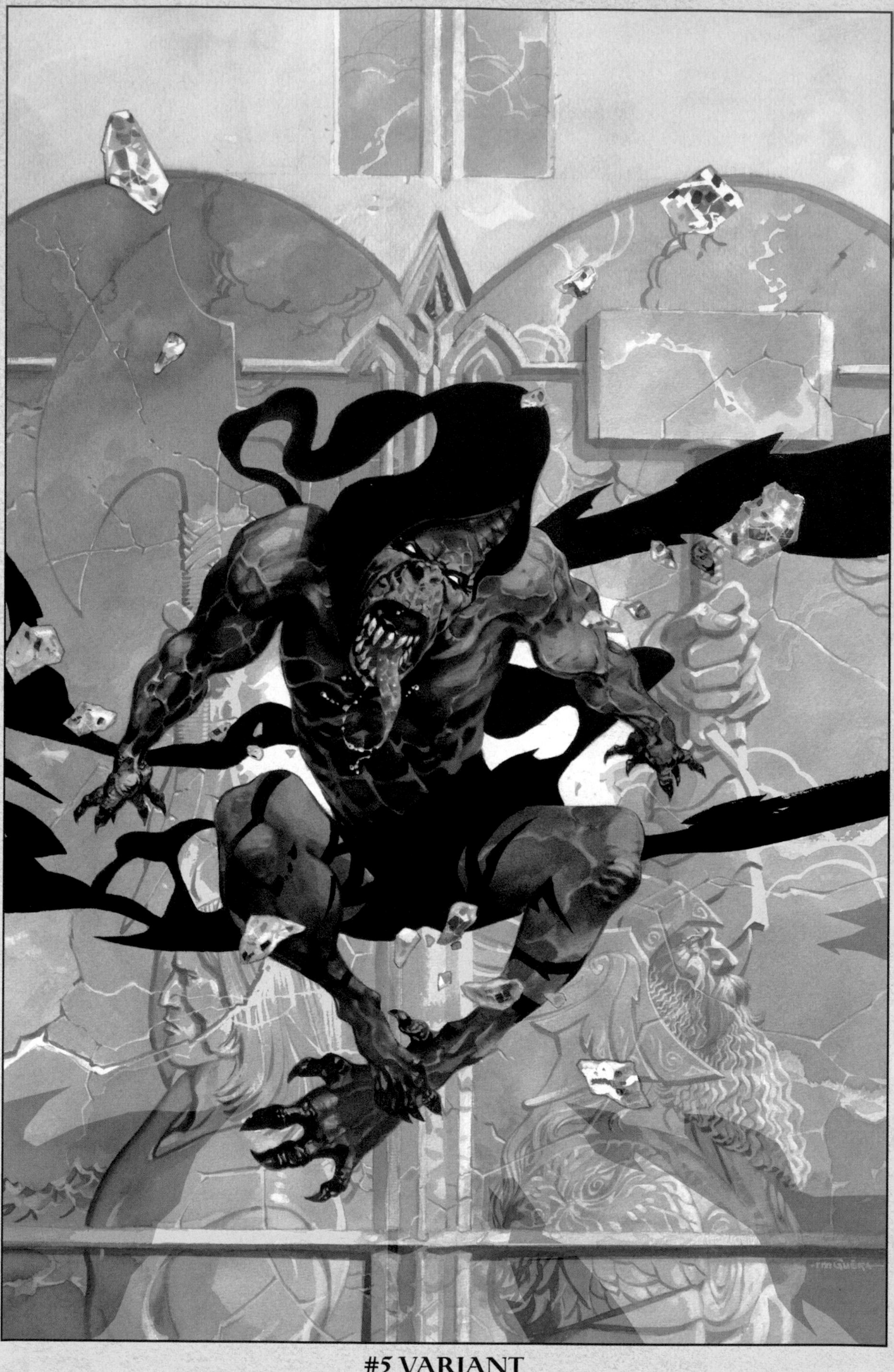

#5 VARIANT
BY R.M. GUÊRA

ESAD RIBIC SKETCHBOOK

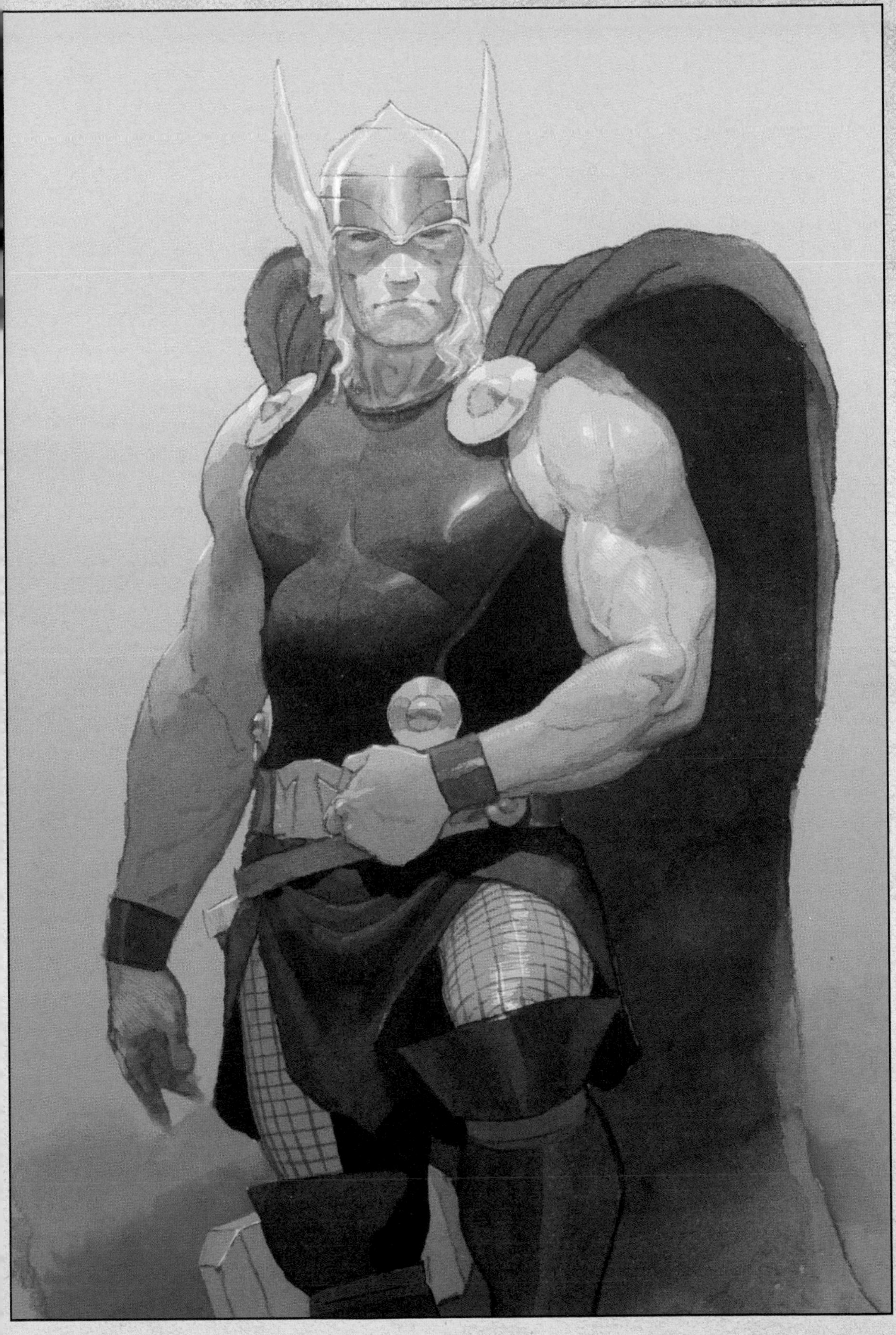

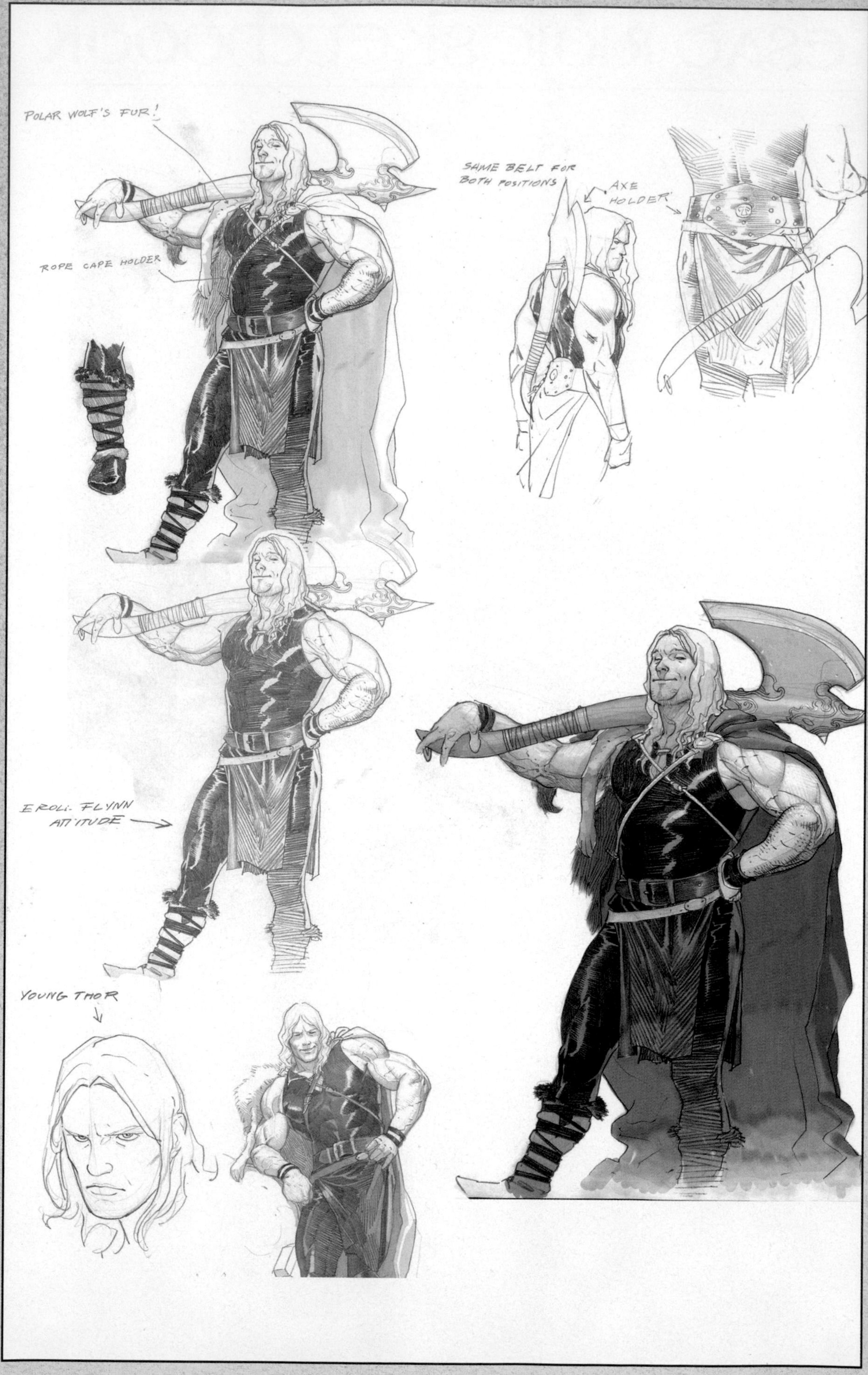
POLAR WOLF'S FUR!
ROPE CAPE HOLDER
SAME BELT FOR BOTH POSITIONS
AXE HOLDER
EROLL FLYNN ATTITUDE
YOUNG THOR

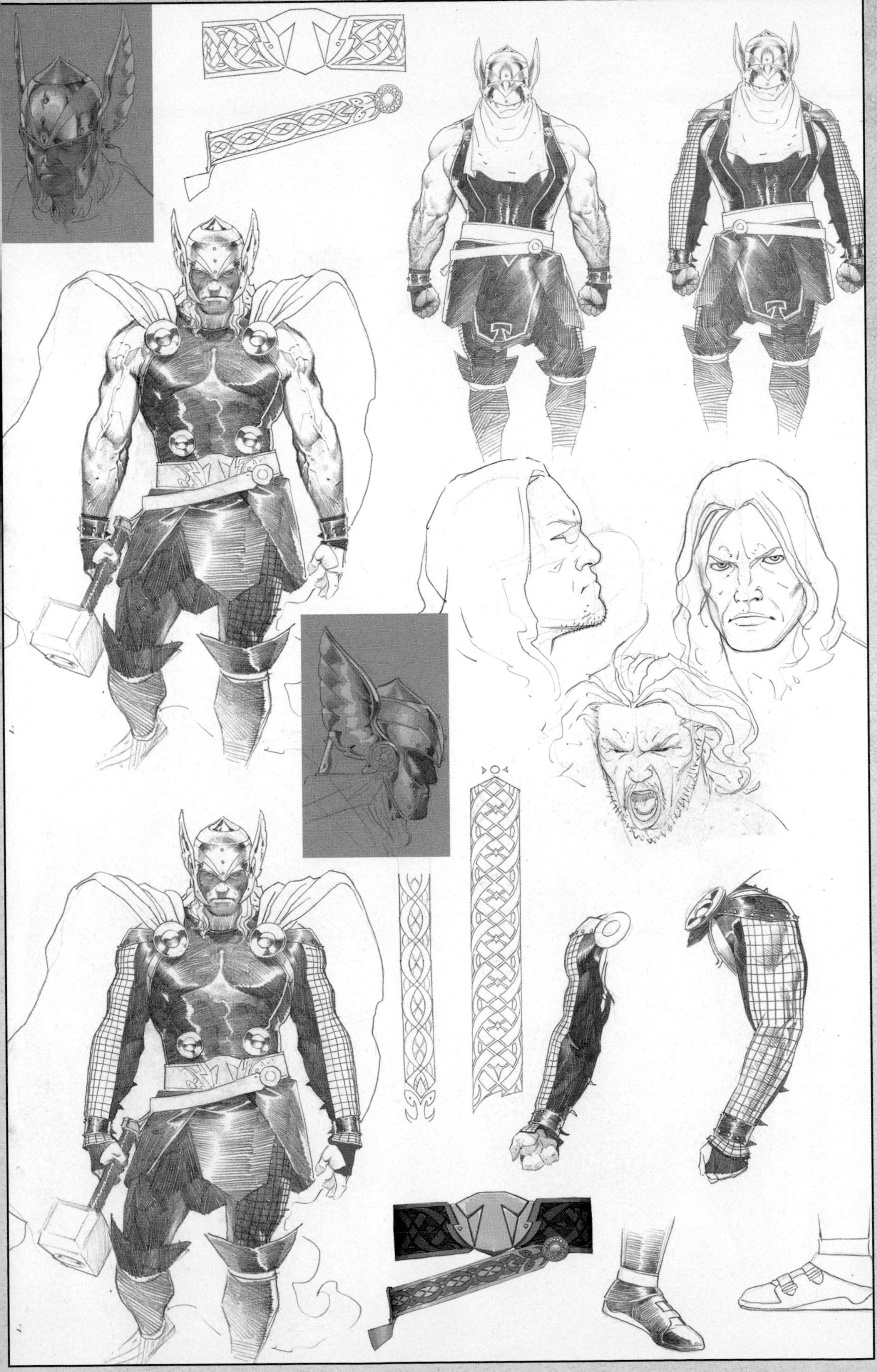

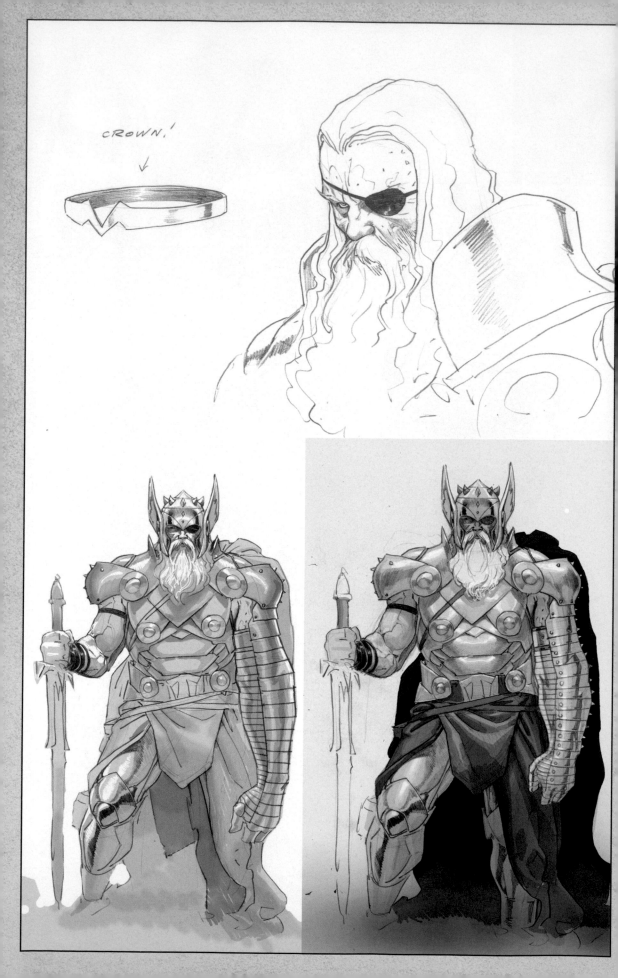

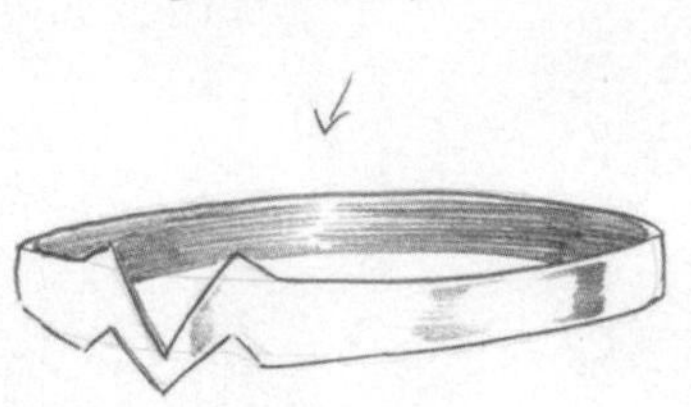
CROWN!

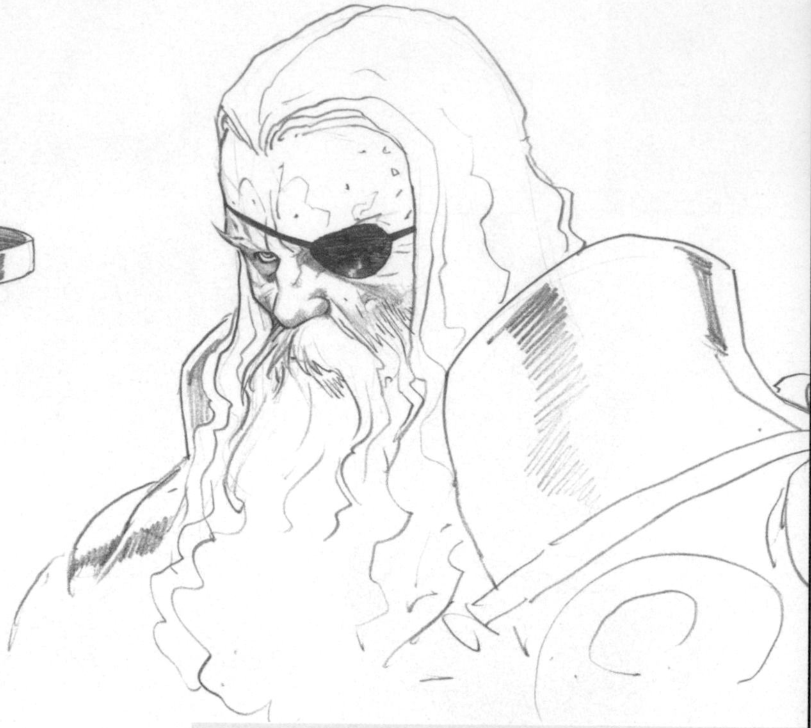

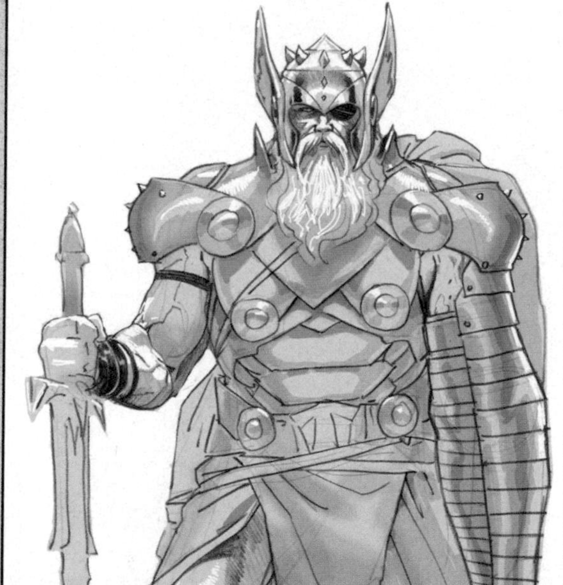

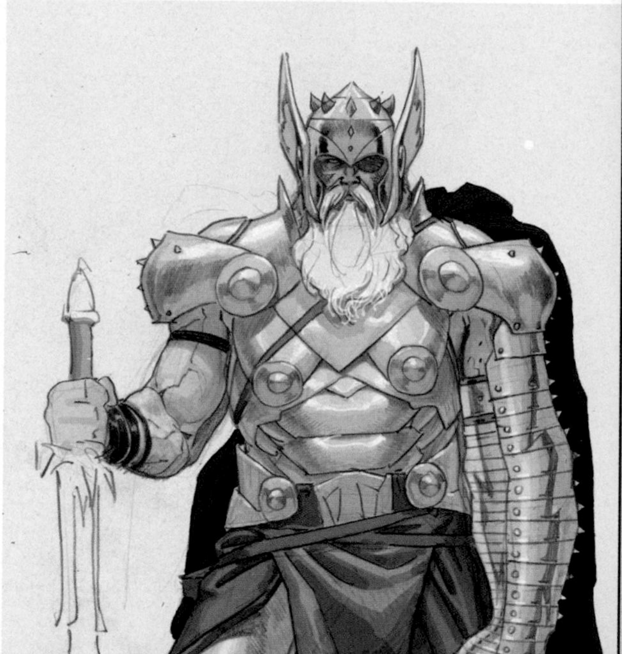

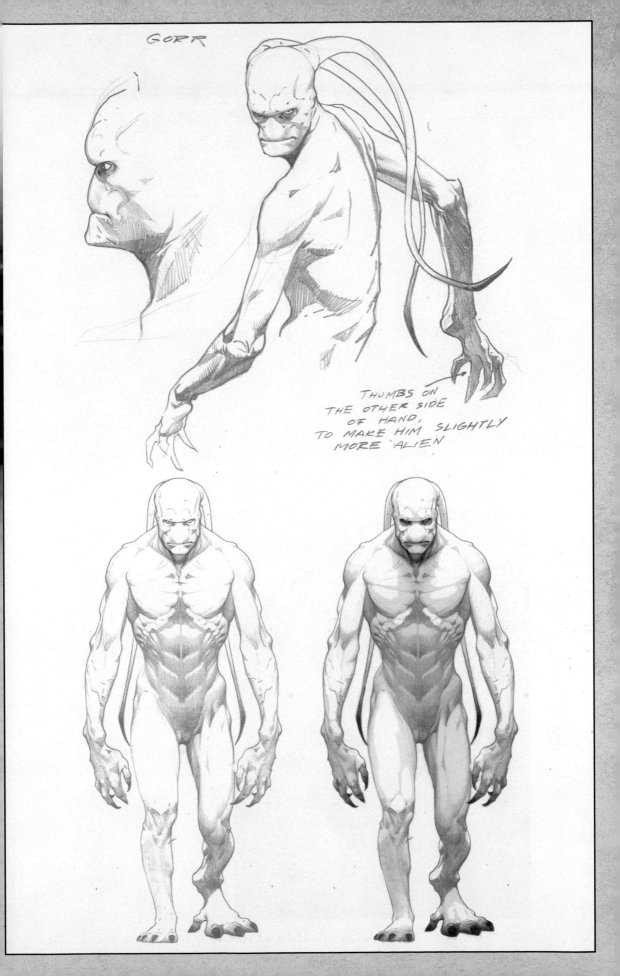

GORR

THUMBS ON
THE OTHER SIDE
OF HAND,
TO MAKE HIM SLIGHTLY
MORE 'ALIEN'

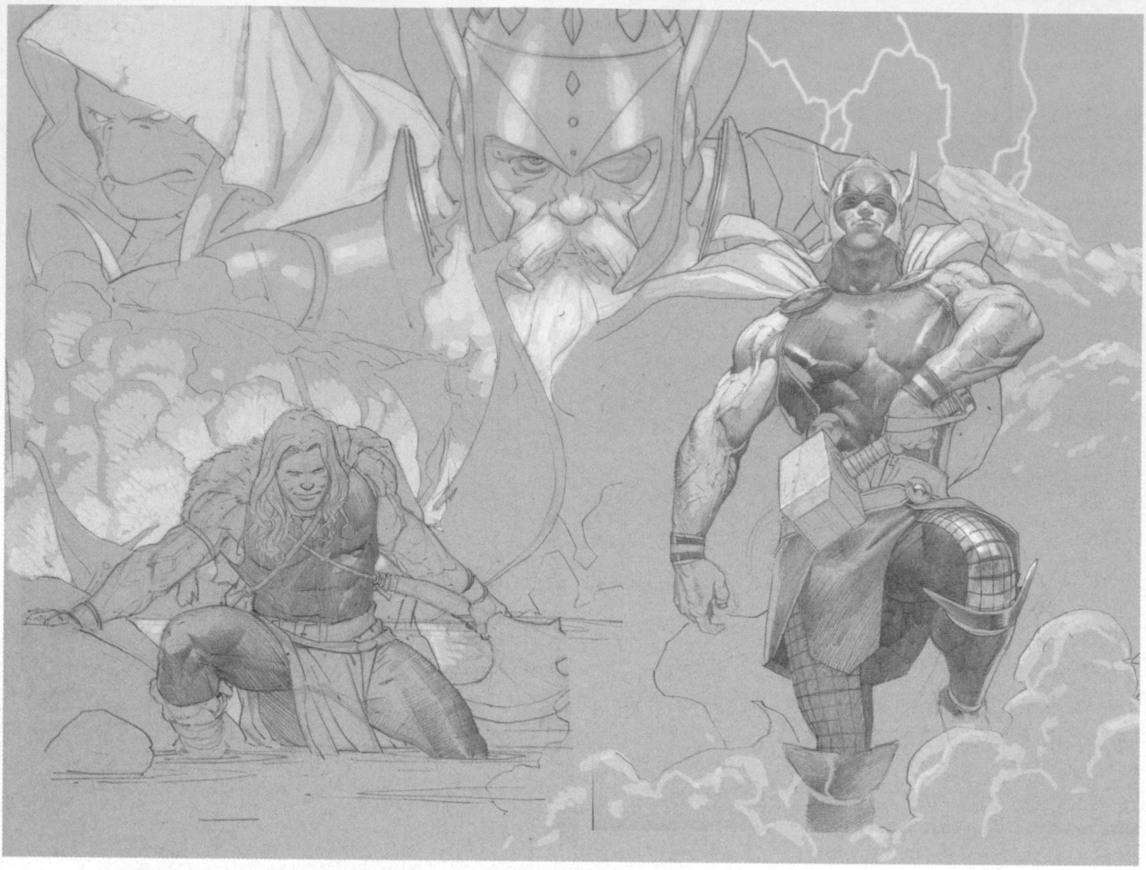

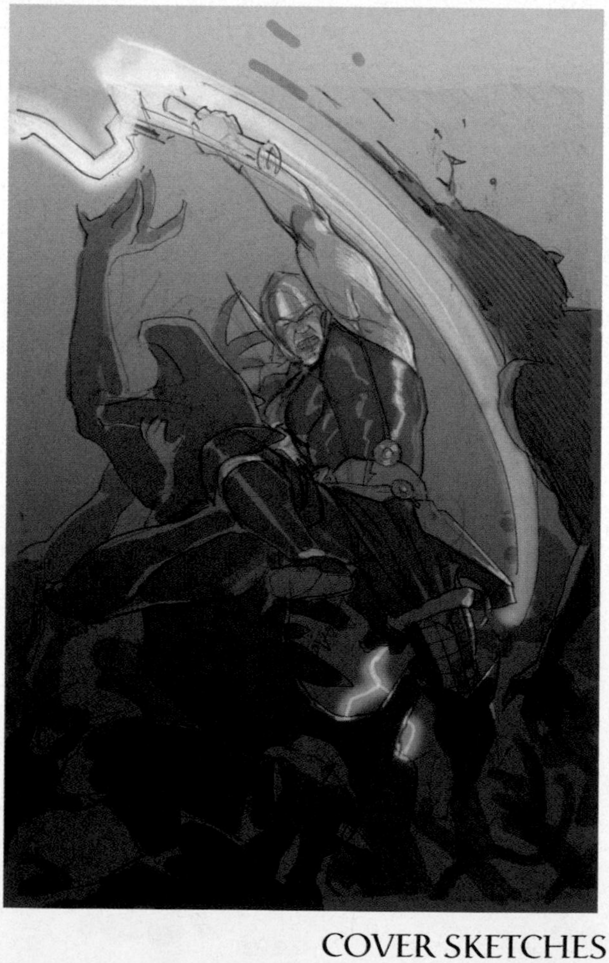

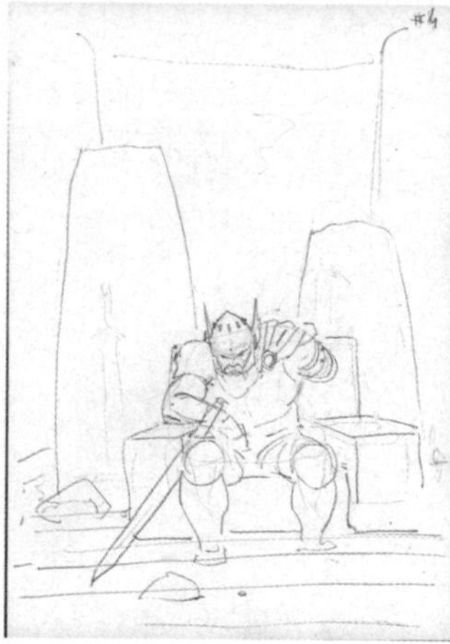
#4

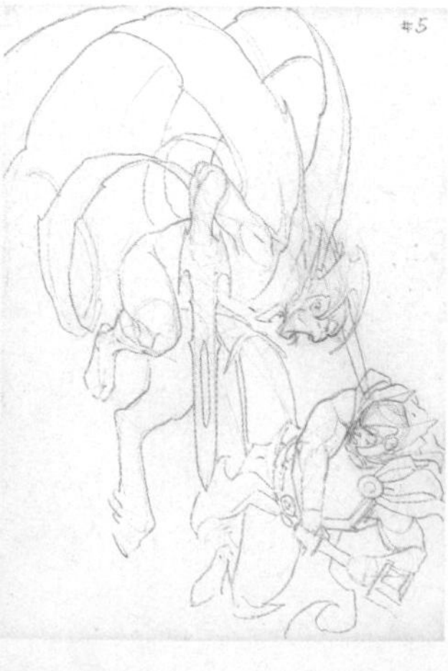
#5

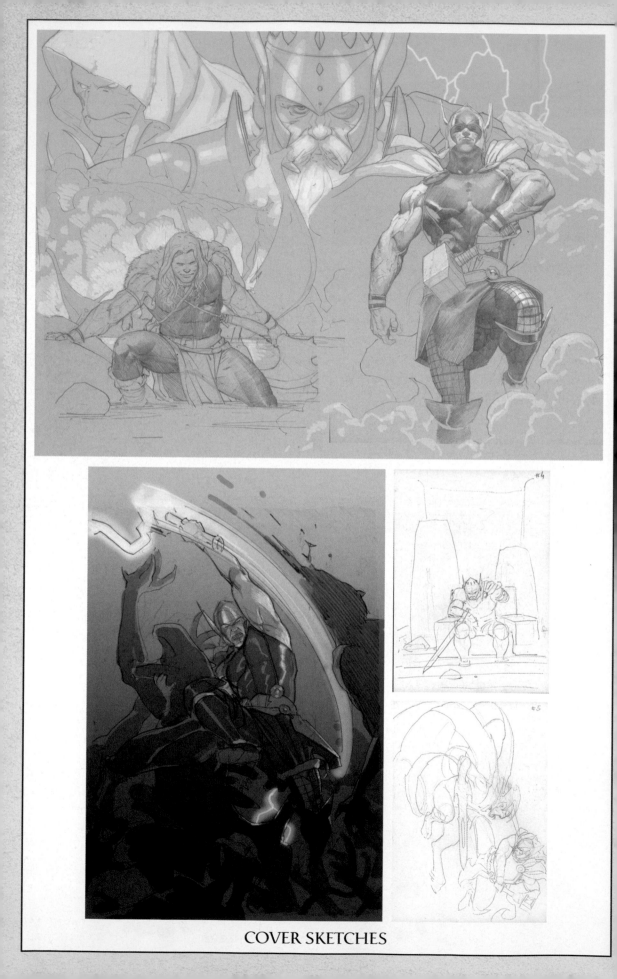

COVER SKETCHES

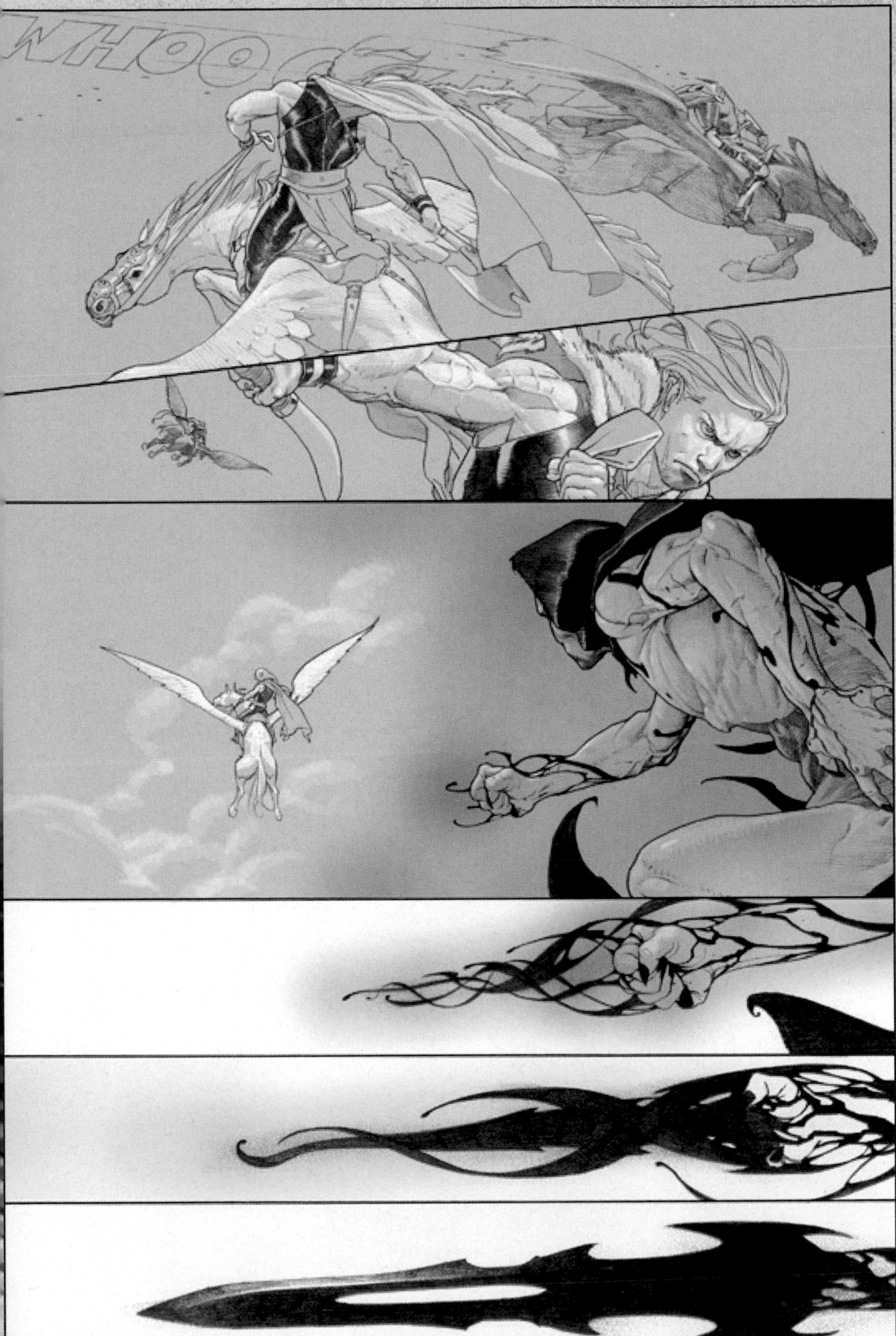

#2, PAGE 9 PENCILS

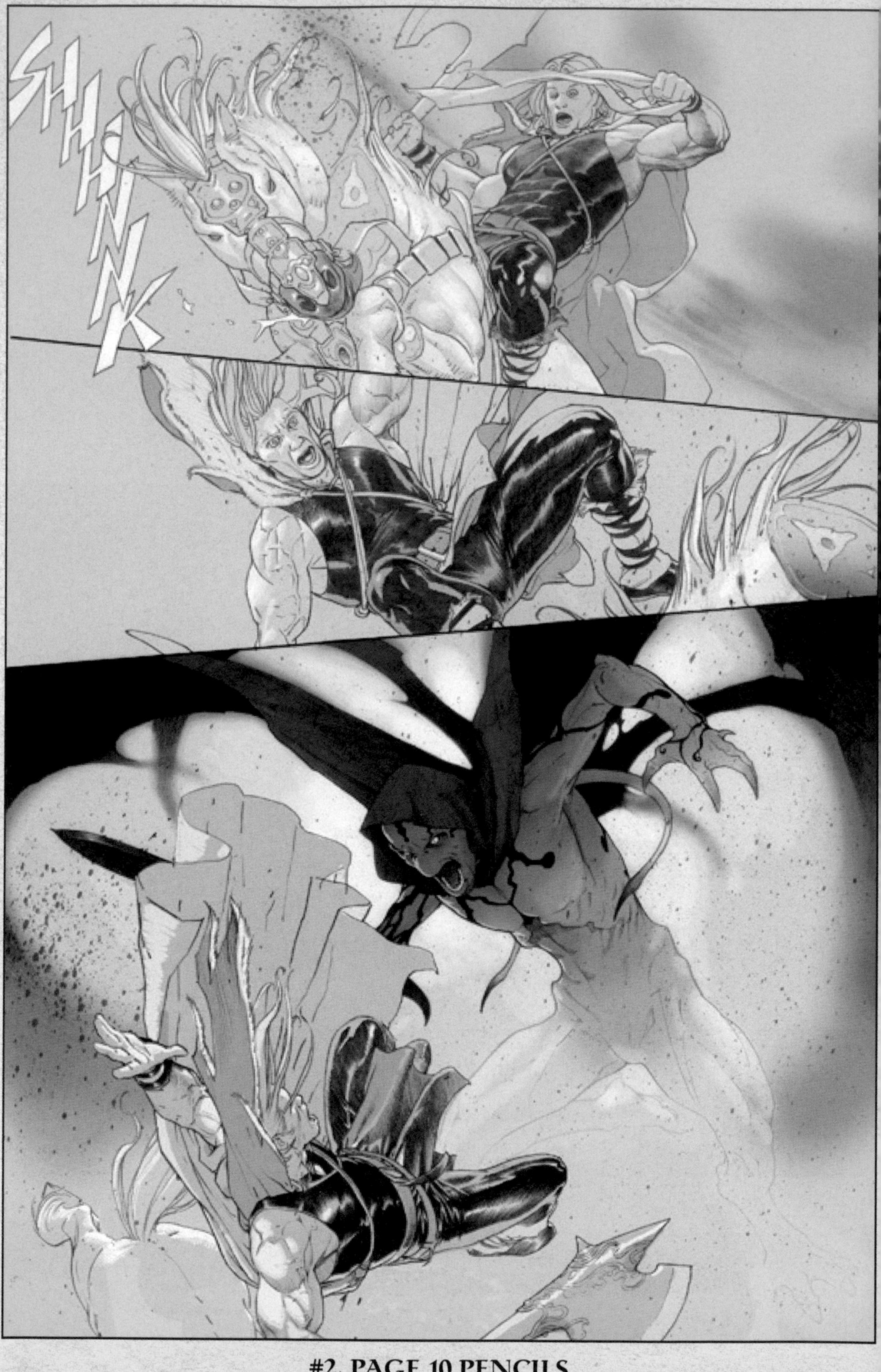
SHHHNNK

#2, PAGE 10 PENCILS

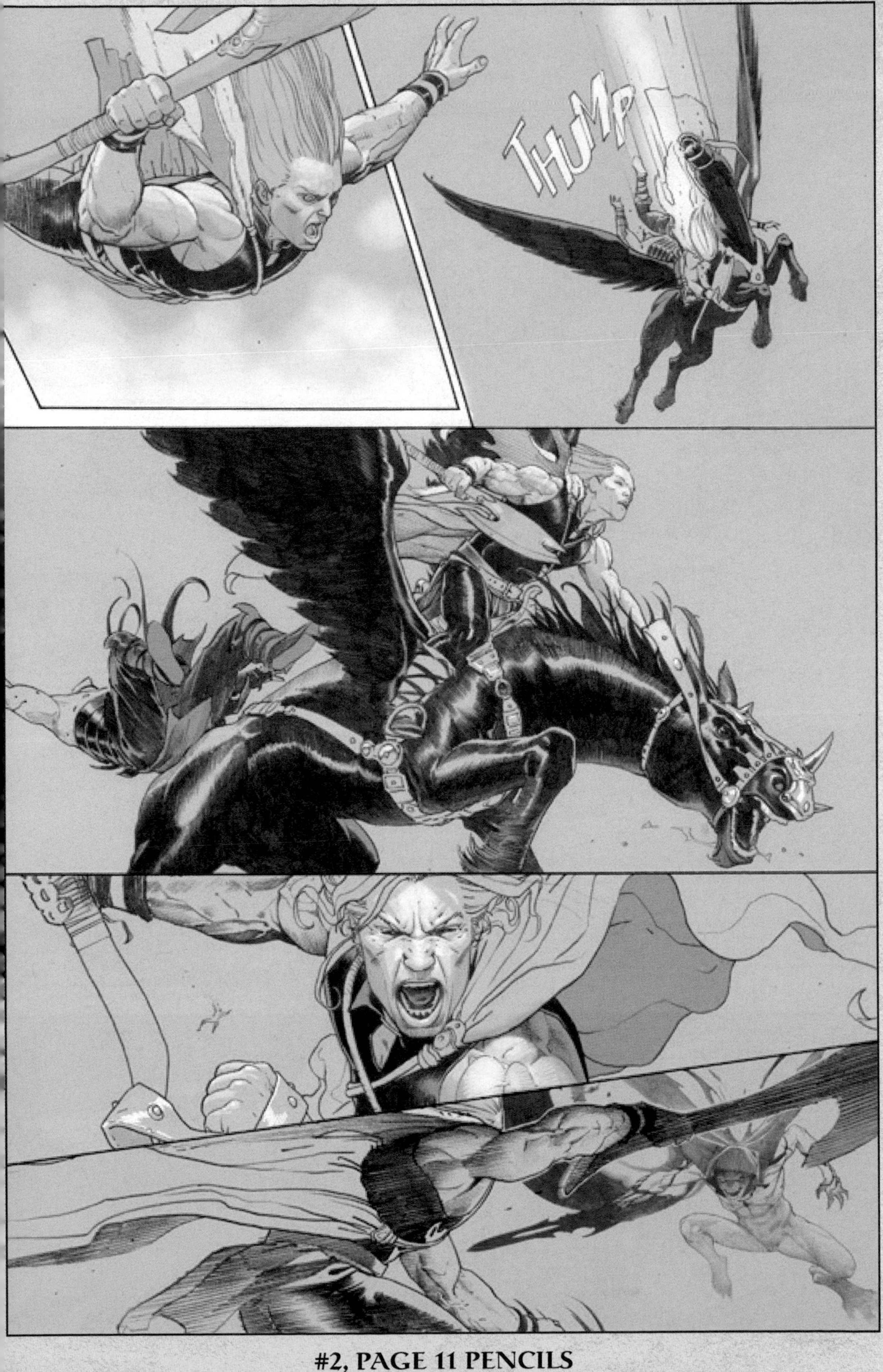
THUMP

#2, PAGE 11 PENCILS

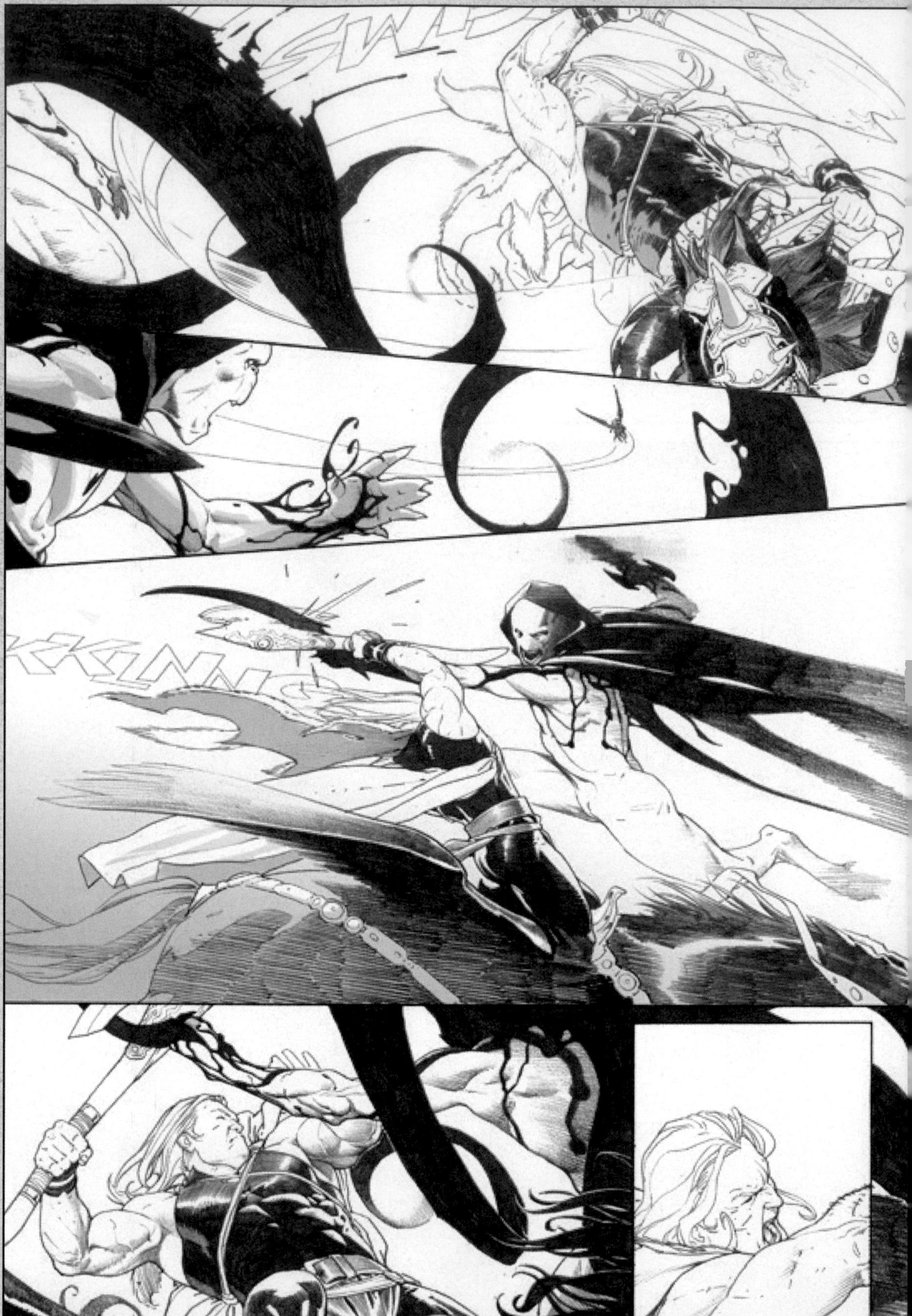

#2, PAGE 12 PENCILS

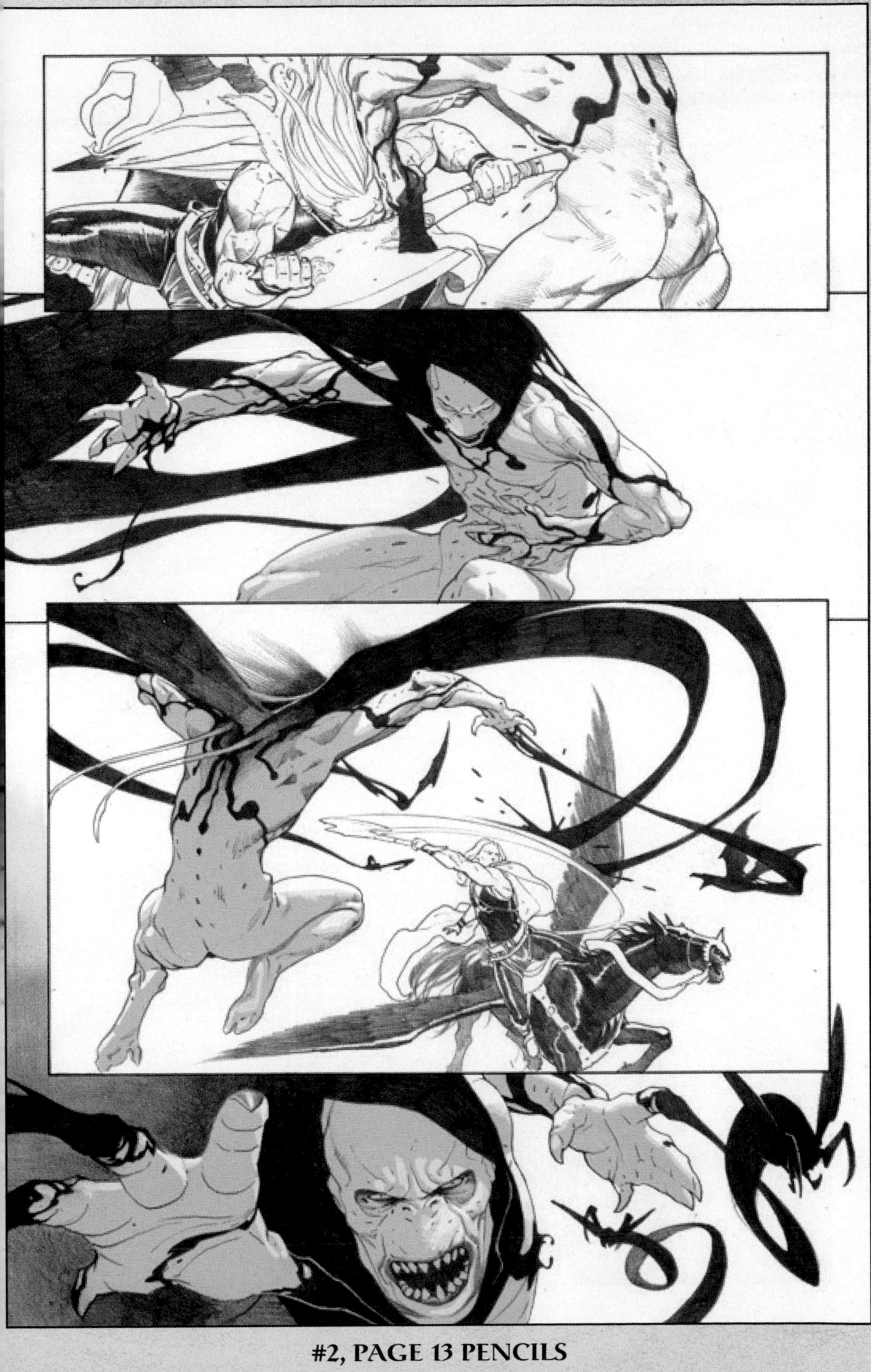

#2, PAGE 13 PENCILS

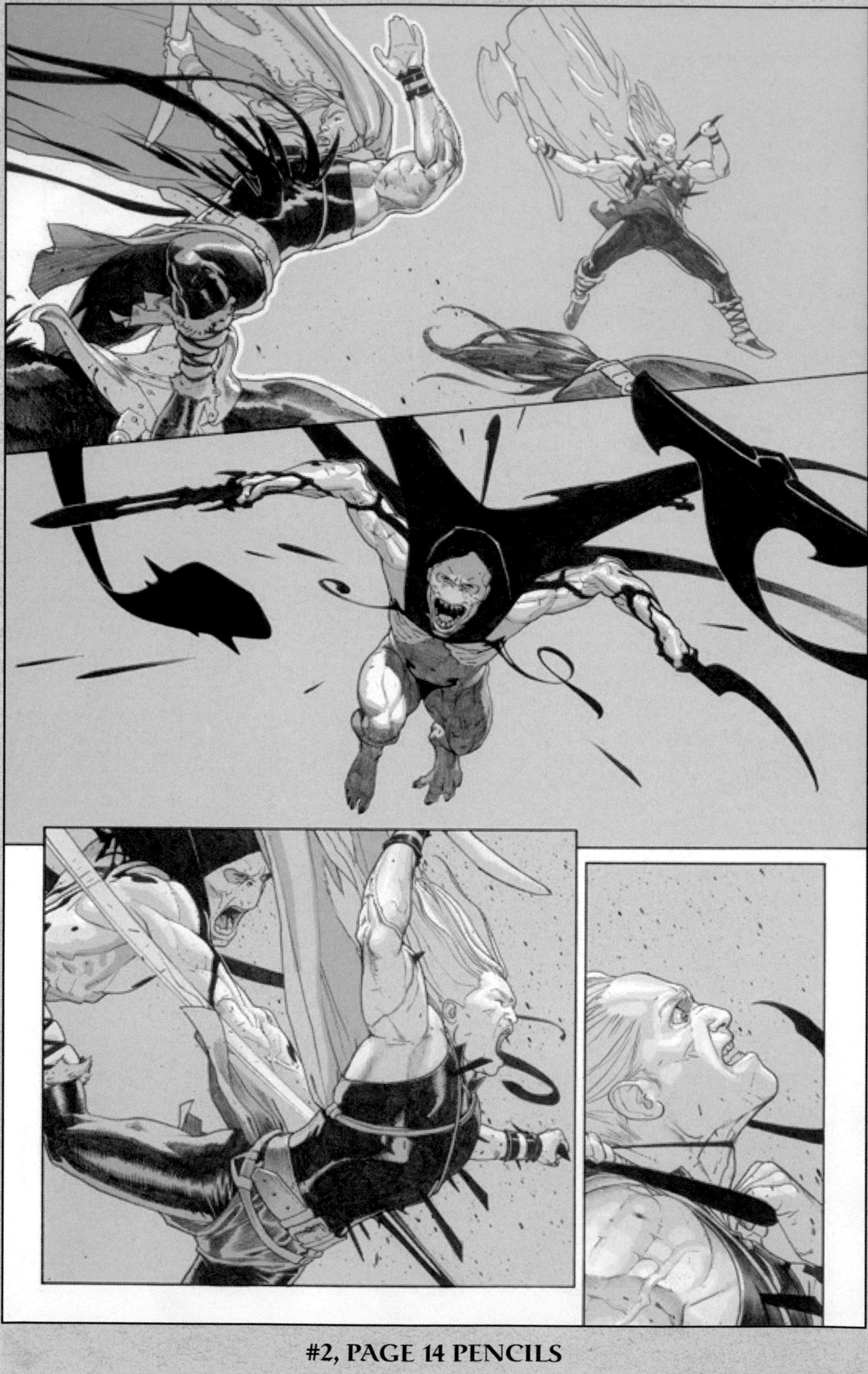

#2, PAGE 14 PENCILS

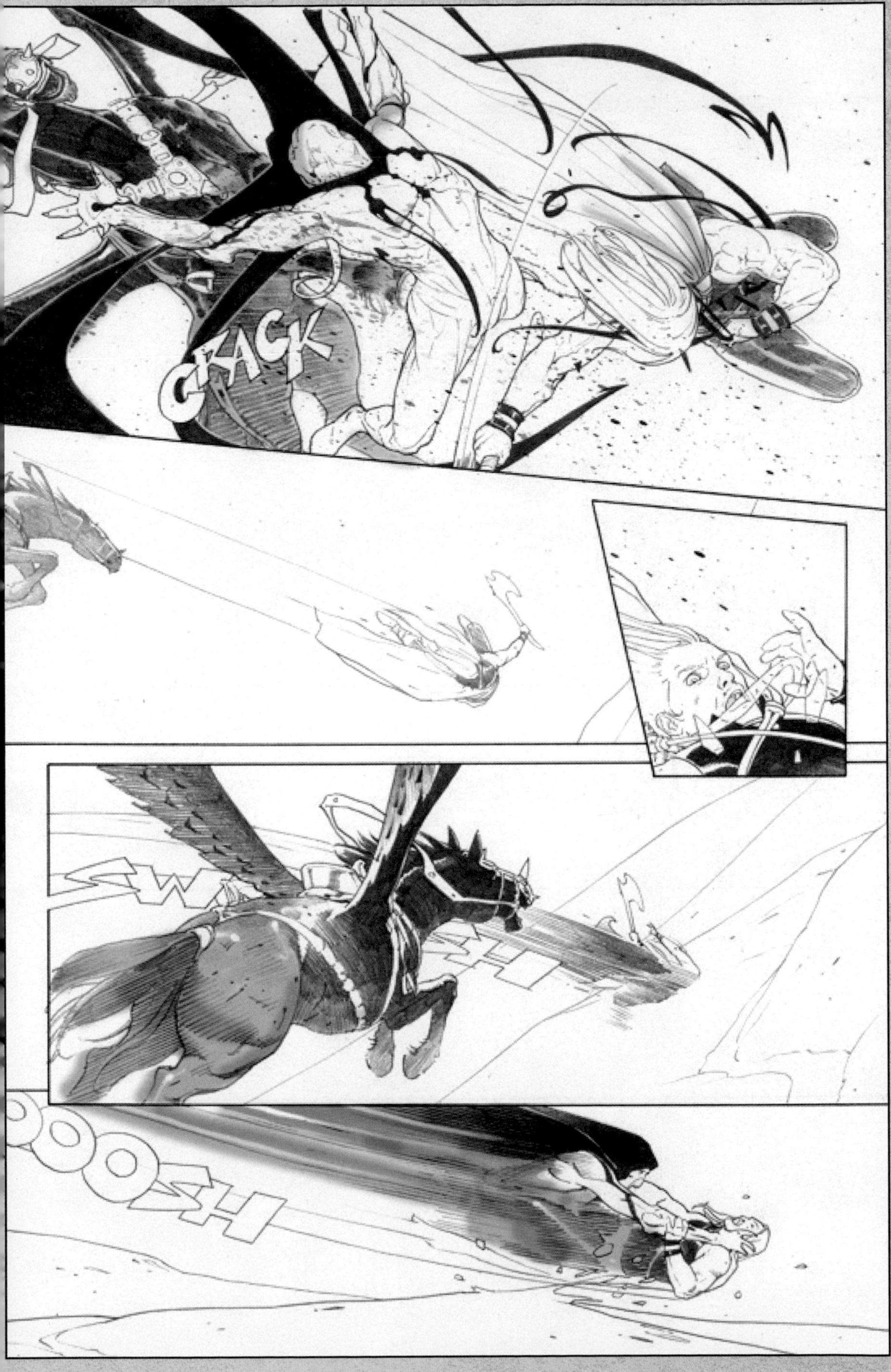
CRACK

#2, PAGE 15 PENCILS

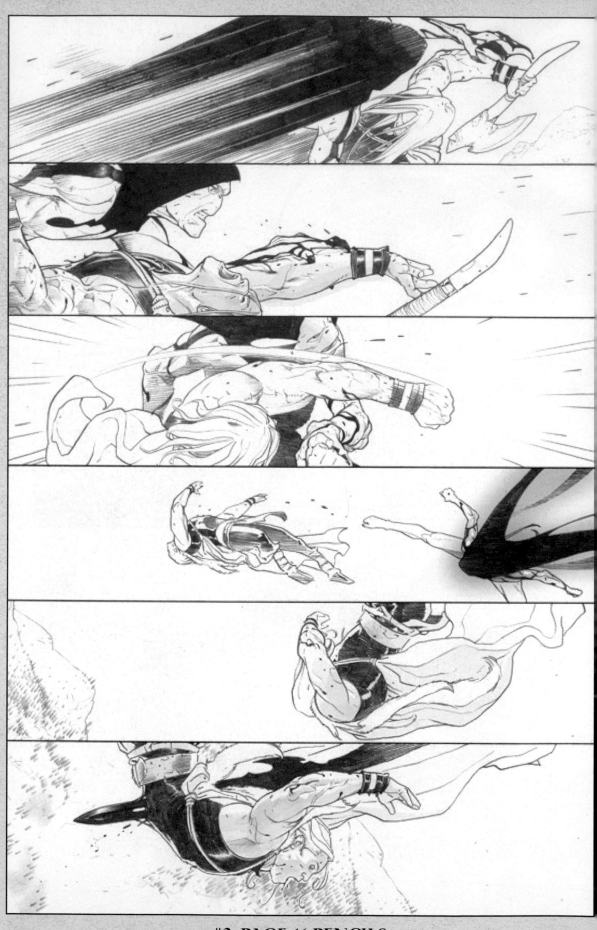

#2, PAGE 16 PENCILS

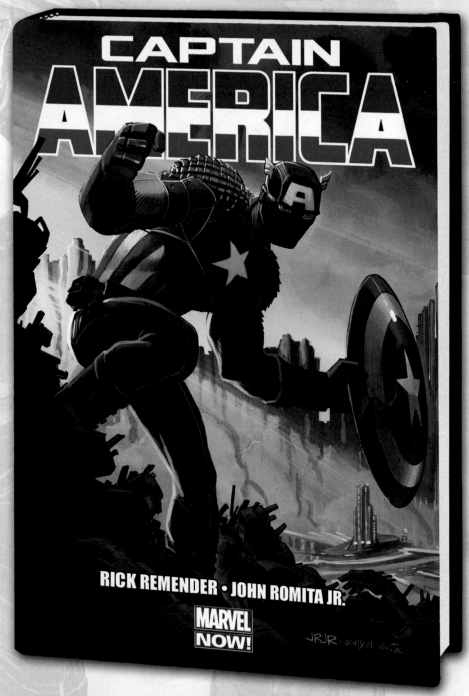

TO ACCESS THE FREE *MARVEL AUGMENTED REALITY APP* THAT ENHANCES AND CHANGES THE WAY YOU EXPERIENCE COMICS:

1. Download the app for free via marvel.com/ARapp
2. Launch the app on your camera-enabled Apple iOS® or Android™ device*
3. Hold your mobile device's camera over any cover or panel with the AR graphic
4. Sit back and see the future of comics in action!

*Available on most camera-enabled Apple iOS® and Android™ devices. Content subject to change and availability.

THOR GOD OF THUNDER AR INDEX

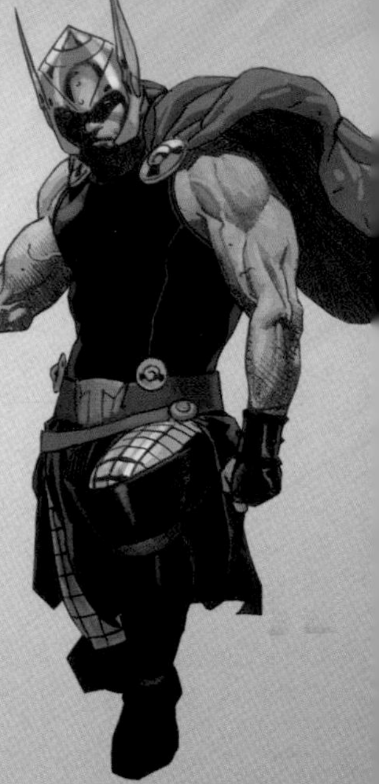